French Milk

Lucy Knisley

A Touchstone Book
Published by Simon & Schuster
New York London Toronto Sydney

Touchstone
A Division of Simon & Schuster, Inc
1230 Avenue of the Americas
New York, NY 10020

First Touchstone trade paperback edition October 2008

TOUCHSTONE and colophon are registered trademarks of Simon & Schuster, Inc.

For information about special discounts for bulk purchases, please contact
Simon & Schuster Special Sales at 1-800-456-6798 or business@simonandschuster.com.

Manufactured in the United States of America

1 3 5 7 9 10 8 6 4 2

Library of Congress Cataloging-in-Publication Data is available.

ISBN-13: 978-1-4165-7534-4
ISBN-10: 1-4165-7534-0

A previous version of this work was originally published by Epigraph Publishing in 2007.

DURING JANUARY OF 2007, MY MOTHER AND I
LIVED IN A SMALL RENTAL APARTMENT
IN PARIS IN ORDER TO CELEBRATE
MY MOTHER'S TURNING FIFTY
(AND MY TURNING TWENTY-TWO).

THE FOLLOWING IS THE DRAWN JOURNAL
THAT I KEPT IN THE COURSE OF THE TRIP.

THE TITLE IS PARTLY IN REFERENCE
TO MY LOVE FOR THE FRESH WHOLE MILK
THAT I FOUND SO DIFFERENT FROM
AMERICAN PROCESSED DAIRY.

THIS ALSO DEALS WITH THE VALUABLE AND
SIGNIFICANT INFLUENCE THAT WE
TAKE IN FROM OUR MOTHERS, AS WELL AS
MY OWN STRUGGLE TOWARD ADULTHOOD
AT AN AGE WHEN WE SO DESPERATELY
CLING TO OUR ADOLESCENCE.

WITH THANKS TO MY MOTHER,
FOR HOLDING THE MAP

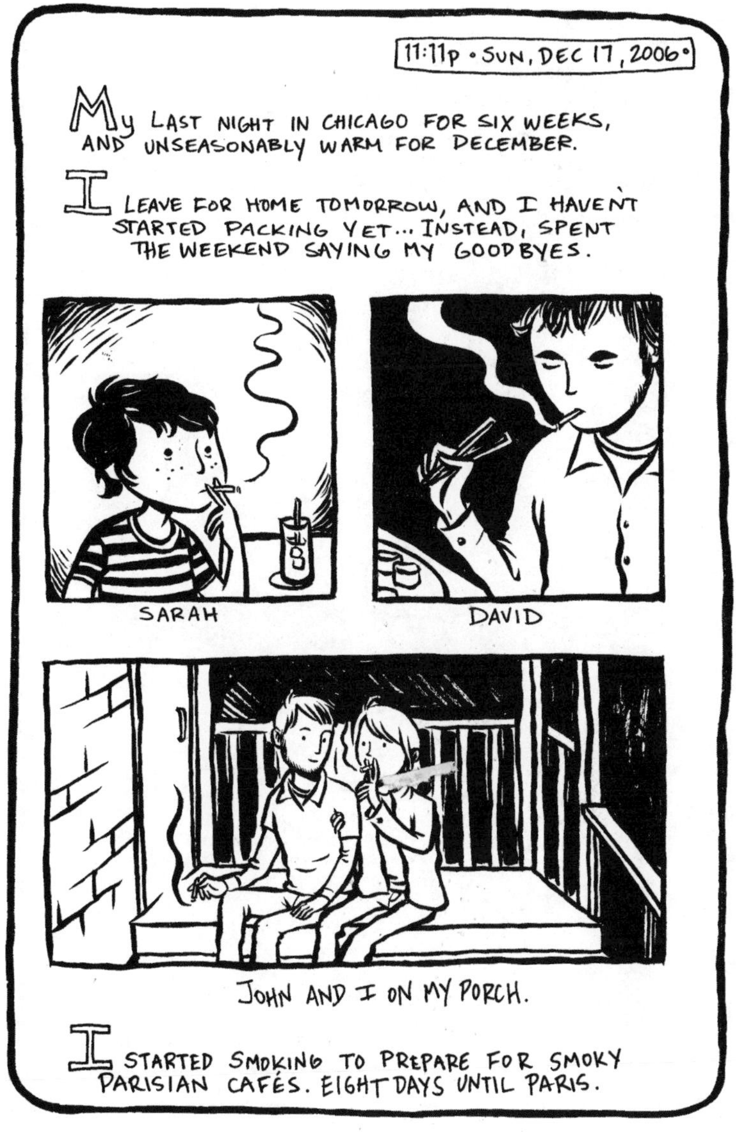
11:11p • SUN, DEC 17, 2006 •
MY LAST NIGHT IN CHICAGO FOR SIX WEEKS, AND UNSEASONABLY WARM FOR DECEMBER.
I LEAVE FOR HOME TOMORROW, AND I HAVEN'T STARTED PACKING YET... INSTEAD, SPENT THE WEEKEND SAYING MY GOODBYES.
SARAH
DAVID
JOHN AND I ON MY PORCH.
I STARTED SMOKING TO PREPARE FOR SMOKY PARISIAN CAFÉS. EIGHT DAYS UNTIL PARIS.

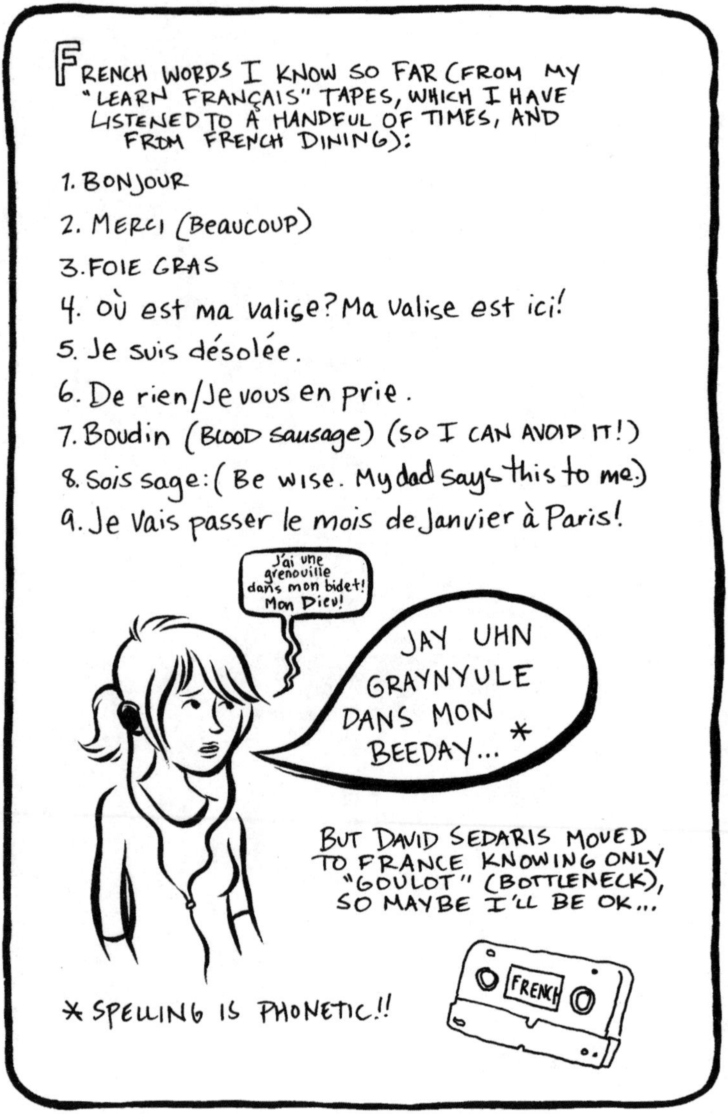
FRENCH WORDS I KNOW SO FAR (FROM MY "LEARN FRANÇAIS" TAPES, WHICH I HAVE LISTENED TO A HANDFUL OF TIMES, AND FROM FRENCH DINING):
1. BONJOUR
2. MERCI (BEAUCOUP)
3. FOIE GRAS
4. Où est ma valise? Ma valise est ici!
5. Je suis désolée.
6. De rien/Je vous en prie.
7. Boudin (BLOOD sausage) (SO I CAN AVOID IT!)
8. Sois sage: (Be wise. My dad says this to me.)
9. Je vais passer le mois de Janvier à Paris!
J'ai une grenouille dans mon bidet! Mon Dieu!
JAY UHN GRAYNYULE DANS MON BEEDAY... *
BUT DAVID SEDARIS MOVED TO FRANCE KNOWING ONLY "GOULOT" (BOTTLENECK), SO MAYBE I'LL BE OK...
FRENCH
* SPELLING IS PHONETIC!!

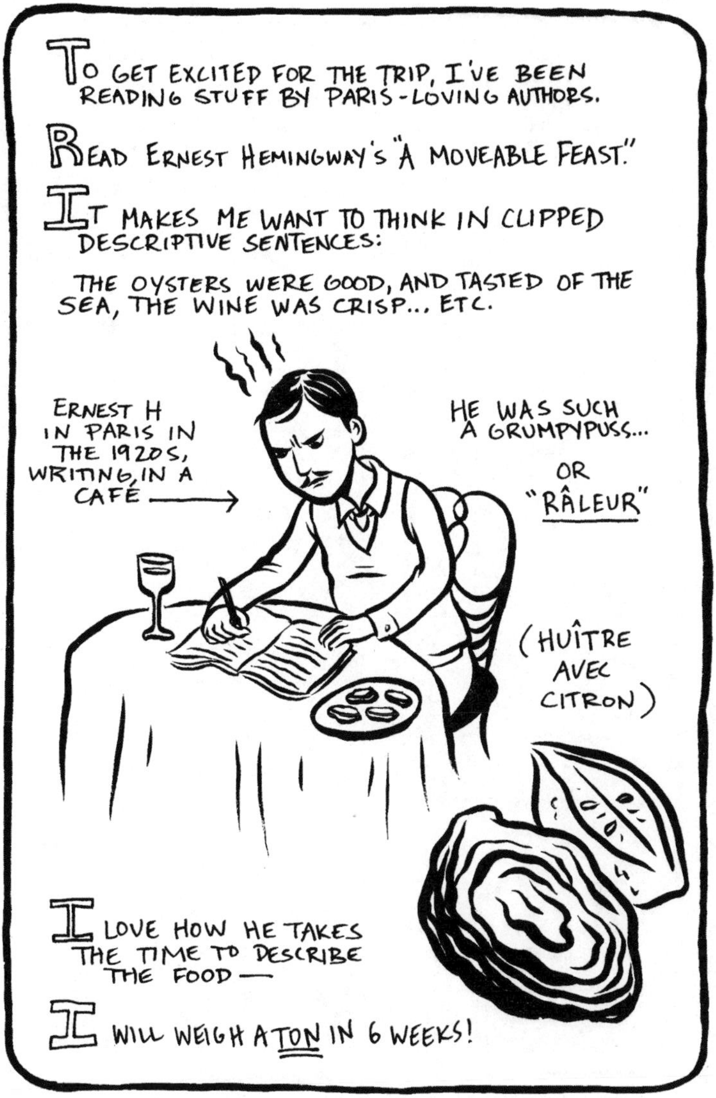
TO GET EXCITED FOR THE TRIP, I'VE BEEN READING STUFF BY PARIS-LOVING AUTHORS.
READ ERNEST HEMINGWAY'S "A MOVEABLE FEAST."
IT MAKES ME WANT TO THINK IN CLIPPED DESCRIPTIVE SENTENCES:
THE OYSTERS WERE GOOD, AND TASTED OF THE SEA, THE WINE WAS CRISP... ETC.
ERNEST H IN PARIS IN THE 1920S, WRITING IN A CAFÉ
HE WAS SUCH A GRUMPYPUSS...
OR "RÂLEUR"
(HUÎTRE AVEC CITRON)
I LOVE HOW HE TAKES THE TIME TO DESCRIBE THE FOOD—
I WILL WEIGH A TON IN 6 WEEKS!

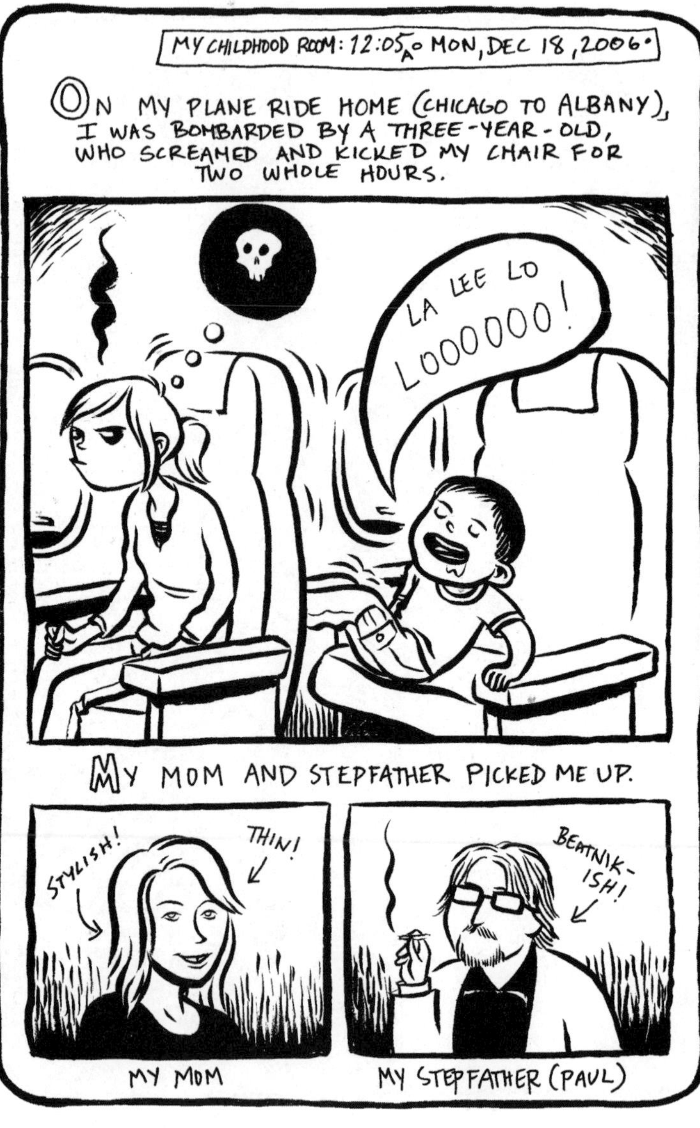

MY CHILDHOOD ROOM: 12:05 A.M. MON, DEC 18, 2006.
ON MY PLANE RIDE HOME (CHICAGO TO ALBANY), I WAS BOMBARDED BY A THREE-YEAR-OLD, WHO SCREAMED AND KICKED MY CHAIR FOR TWO WHOLE HOURS.
LA LEE LO LOOOOOO!
MY MOM AND STEPFATHER PICKED ME UP.
STYLISH!
THIN!
MY MOM
BEATNIK-ISH!
MY STEPFATHER (PAUL)

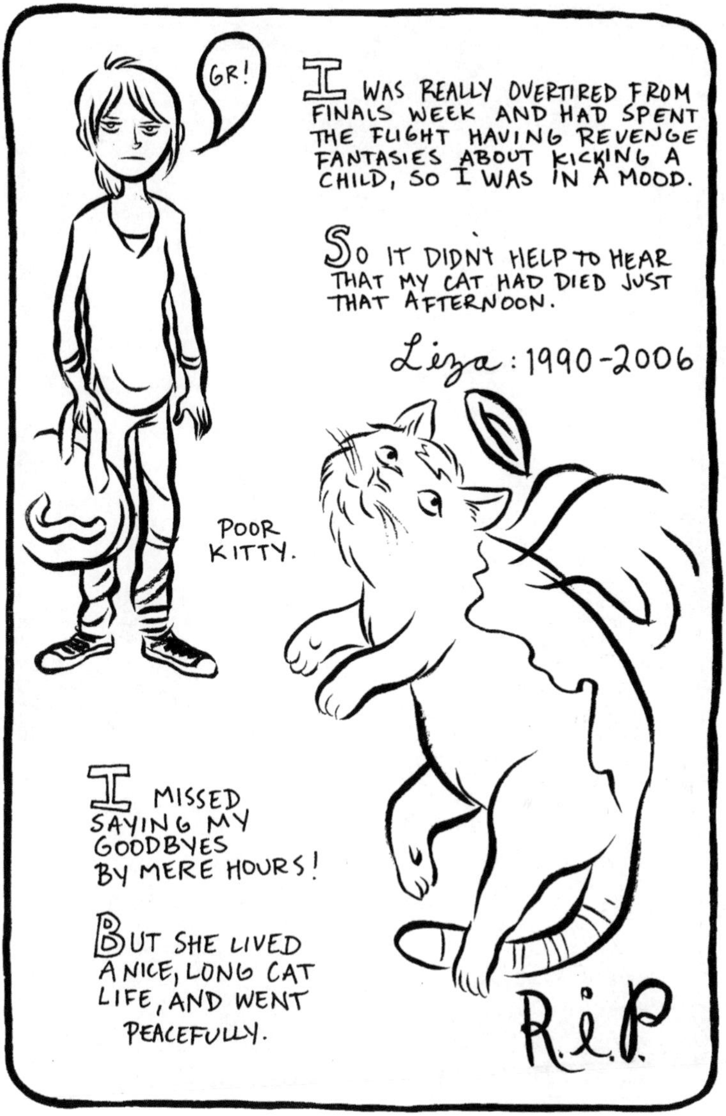

GR!
I WAS REALLY OVERTIRED FROM FINALS WEEK AND HAD SPENT THE FLIGHT HAVING REVENGE FANTASIES ABOUT KICKING A CHILD, SO I WAS IN A MOOD.
SO IT DIDN'T HELP TO HEAR THAT MY CAT HAD DIED JUST THAT AFTERNOON.
Liza: 1990-2006
POOR KITTY.
I MISSED SAYING MY GOODBYES BY MERE HOURS!
BUT SHE LIVED A NICE, LONG CAT LIFE, AND WENT PEACEFULLY.
R.I.P.

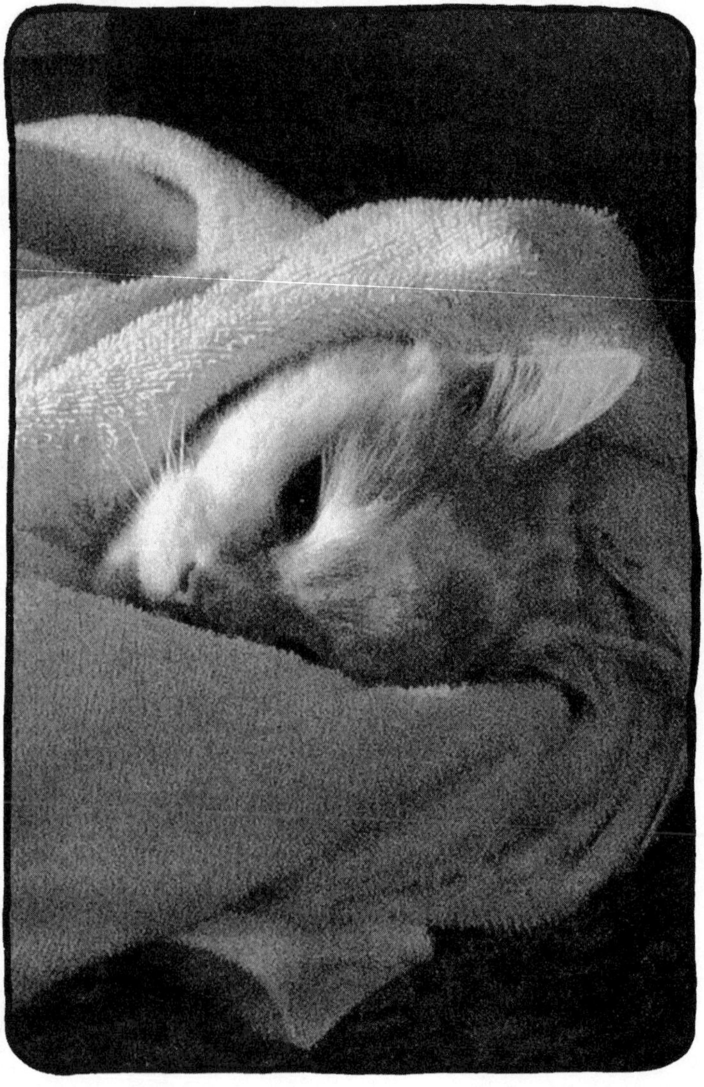

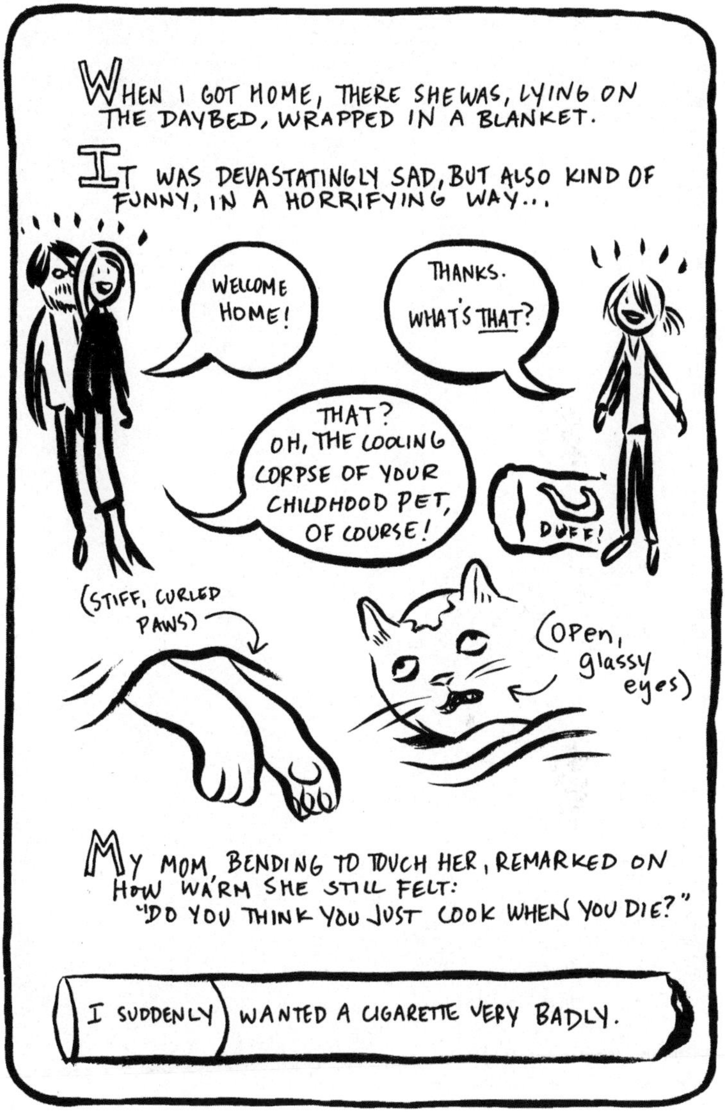
WHEN I GOT HOME, THERE SHE WAS, LYING ON THE DAYBED, WRAPPED IN A BLANKET.
IT WAS DEVASTATINGLY SAD, BUT ALSO KIND OF FUNNY, IN A HORRIFYING WAY...
WELCOME HOME!
THANKS. WHAT'S THAT?
THAT? OH, THE COOLING CORPSE OF YOUR CHILDHOOD PET, OF COURSE!
DUFF!
(STIFF, CURLED PAWS)
(Open, glassy eyes)
MY MOM, BENDING TO TOUCH HER, REMARKED ON HOW WARM SHE STILL FELT:
"DO YOU THINK YOU JUST COOK WHEN YOU DIE?"
I SUDDENLY WANTED A CIGARETTE VERY BADLY.

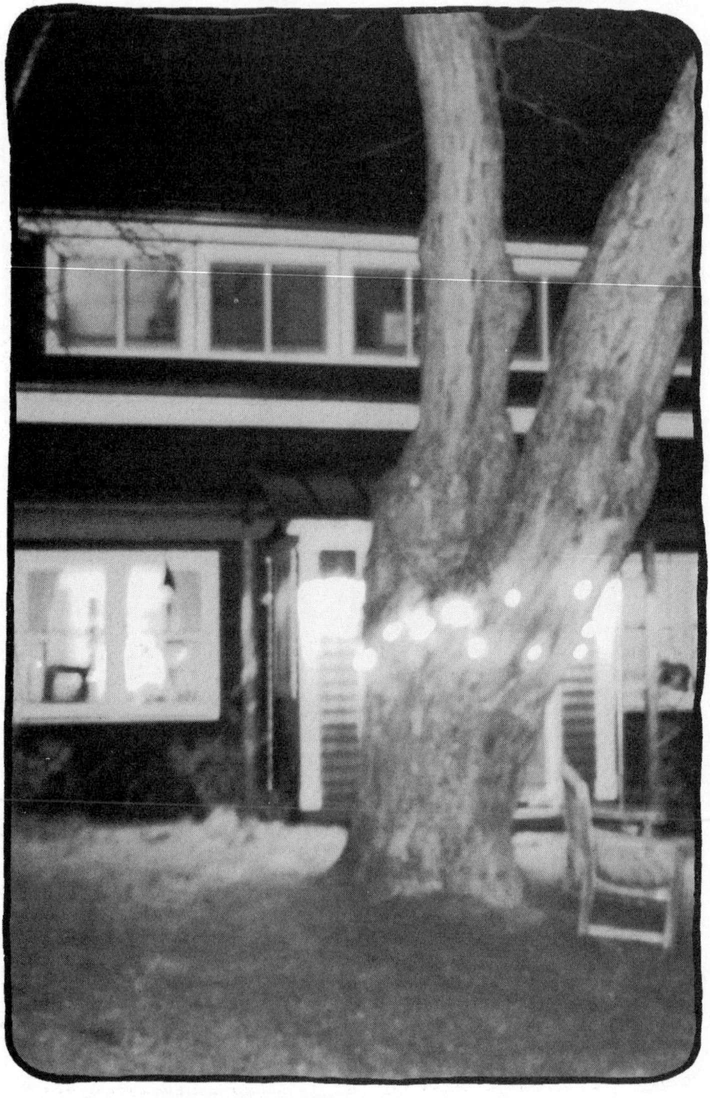

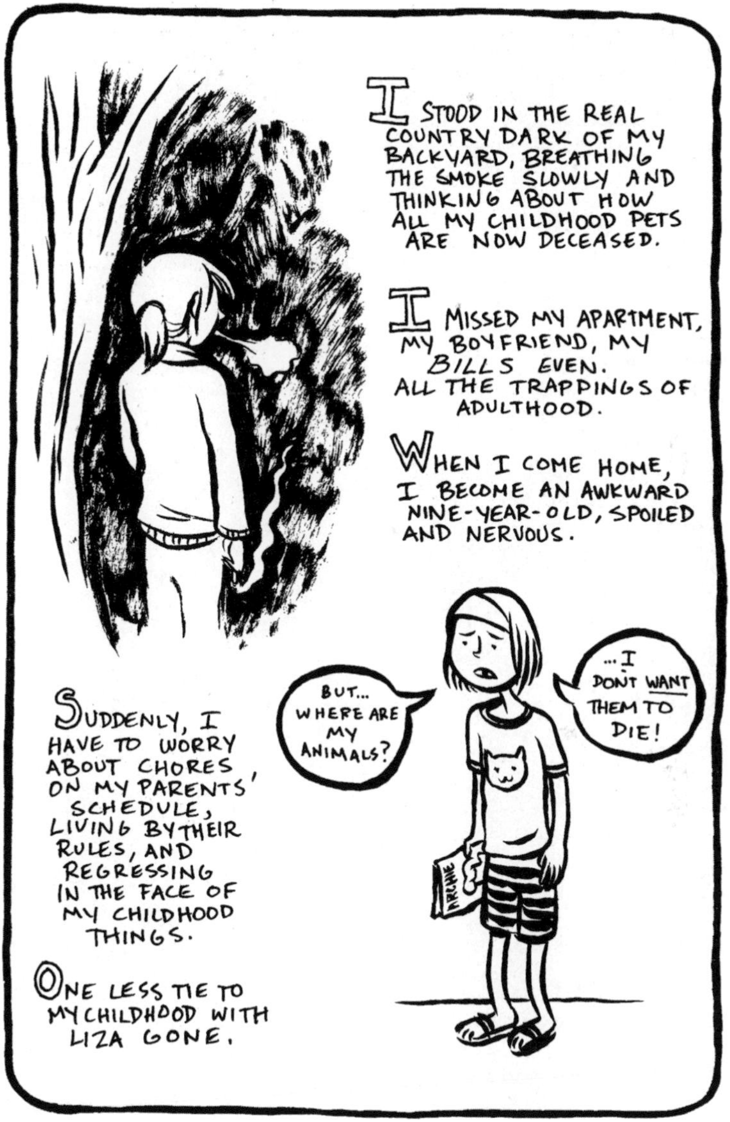
I STOOD IN THE REAL COUNTRY DARK OF MY BACKYARD, BREATHING THE SMOKE SLOWLY AND THINKING ABOUT HOW ALL MY CHILDHOOD PETS ARE NOW DECEASED.
I MISSED MY APARTMENT, MY BOYFRIEND, MY BILLS EVEN. ALL THE TRAPPINGS OF ADULTHOOD.
WHEN I COME HOME, I BECOME AN AWKWARD NINE-YEAR-OLD, SPOILED AND NERVOUS.
SUDDENLY, I HAVE TO WORRY ABOUT CHORES ON MY PARENTS' SCHEDULE, LIVING BY THEIR RULES, AND REGRESSING IN THE FACE OF MY CHILDHOOD THINGS.
BUT... WHERE ARE MY ANIMALS?
...I DON'T WANT THEM TO DIE!
ARCHIE
ONE LESS TIE TO MY CHILDHOOD WITH LIZA GONE.

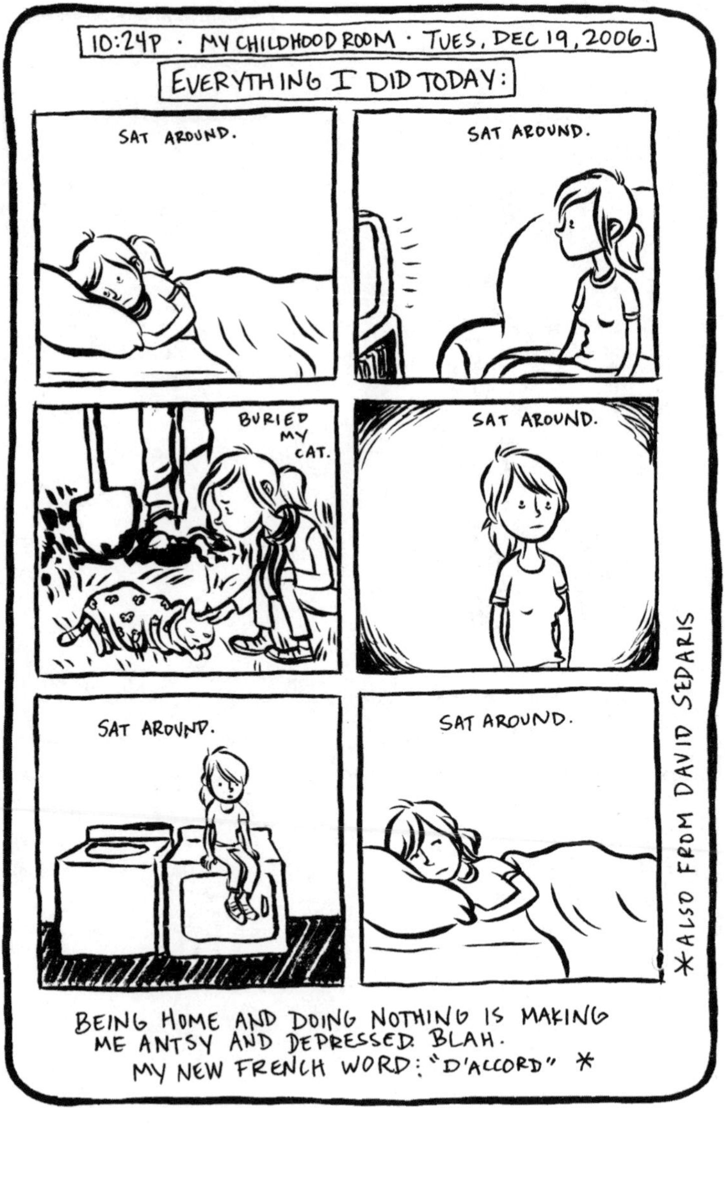
10:24P · MY CHILDHOOD ROOM · TUES, DEC 19, 2006.
EVERYTHING I DID TODAY:
SAT AROUND.
SAT AROUND.
BURIED MY CAT.
SAT AROUND.
SAT AROUND.
SAT AROUND.
*ALSO FROM DAVID SEDARIS
BEING HOME AND DOING NOTHING IS MAKING ME ANTSY AND DEPRESSED. BLAH.
MY NEW FRENCH WORD: "D'ACCORD" *

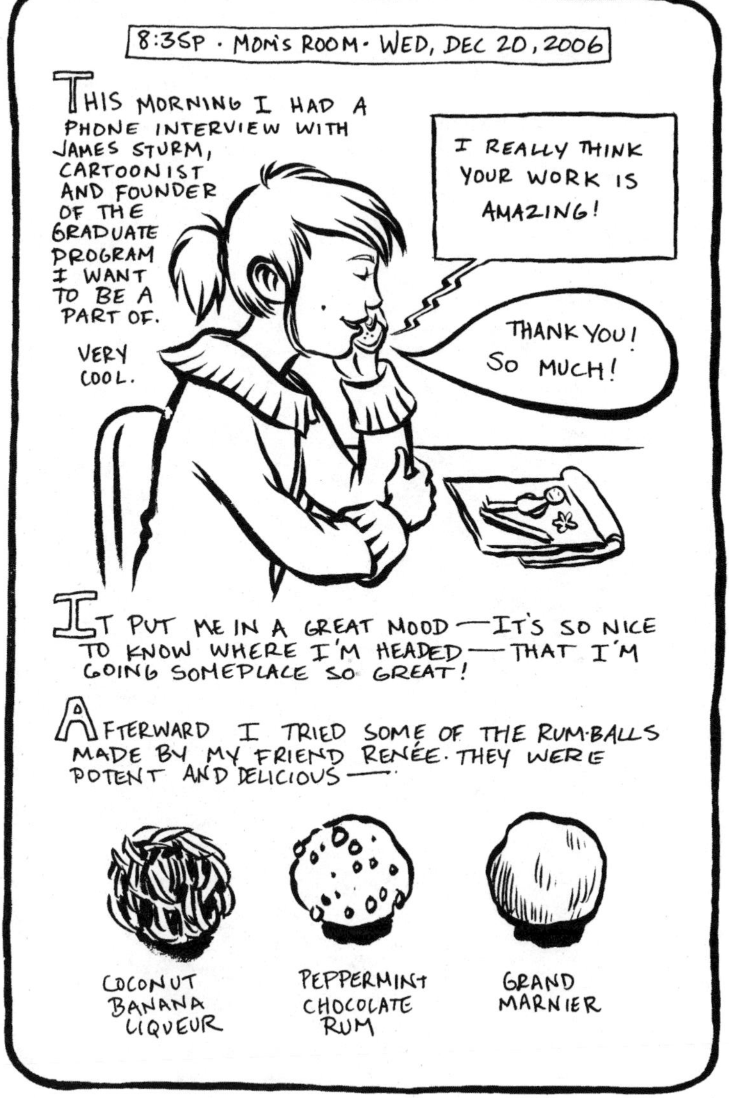
8:35P · MOM'S ROOM · WED, DEC 20, 2006
THIS MORNING I HAD A PHONE INTERVIEW WITH JAMES STURM, CARTOONIST AND FOUNDER OF THE GRADUATE PROGRAM I WANT TO BE A PART OF.
VERY COOL.
I REALLY THINK YOUR WORK IS AMAZING!
THANK YOU! SO MUCH!
IT PUT ME IN A GREAT MOOD—IT'S SO NICE TO KNOW WHERE I'M HEADED—THAT I'M GOING SOMEPLACE SO GREAT!
AFTERWARD I TRIED SOME OF THE RUM·BALLS MADE BY MY FRIEND RENÉE. THEY WERE POTENT AND DELICIOUS—.
COCONUT BANANA LIQUEUR
PEPPERMINT CHOCOLATE RUM
GRAND MARNIER

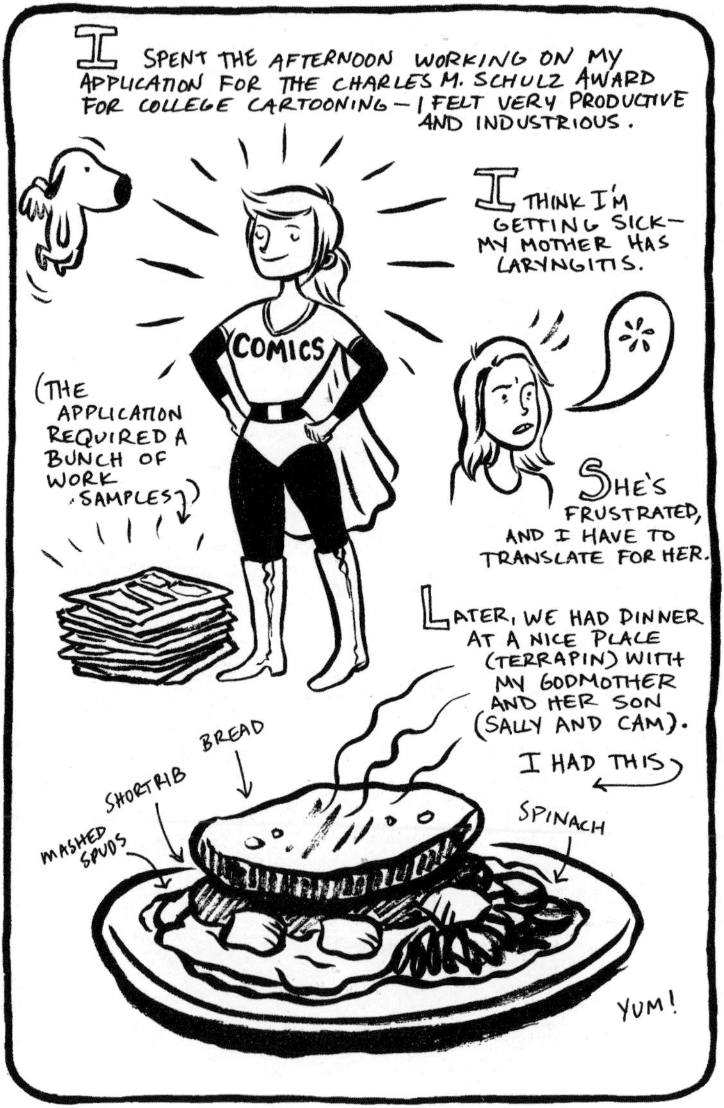
I SPENT THE AFTERNOON WORKING ON MY APPLICATION FOR THE CHARLES M. SCHULZ AWARD FOR COLLEGE CARTOONING — I FELT VERY PRODUCTIVE AND INDUSTRIOUS.
COMICS
(THE APPLICATION REQUIRED A BUNCH OF WORK SAMPLES)
I THINK I'M GETTING SICK— MY MOTHER HAS LARYNGITIS.
SHE'S FRUSTRATED, AND I HAVE TO TRANSLATE FOR HER.
LATER, WE HAD DINNER AT A NICE PLACE (TERRAPIN) WITH MY GODMOTHER AND HER SON (SALLY AND CAM).
I HAD THIS
BREAD
SHORTRIB
MASHED SPUDS
SPINACH
YUM!

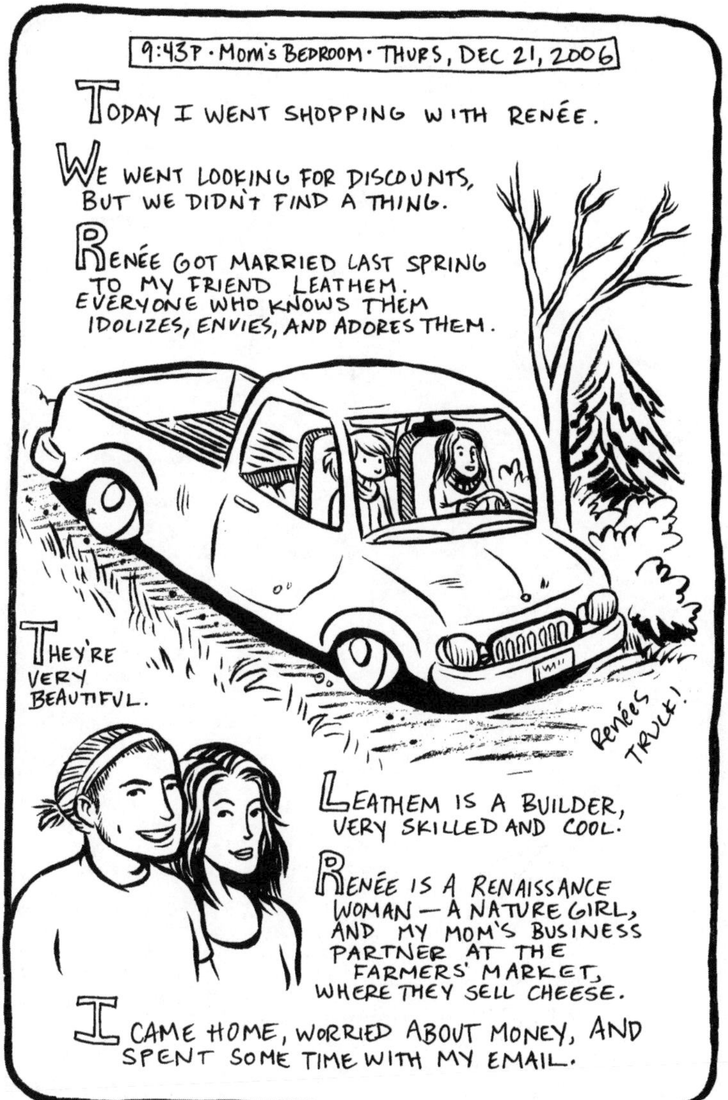
9:43P · MOM'S BEDROOM · THURS, DEC 21, 2006
TODAY I WENT SHOPPING WITH RENÉE.
WE WENT LOOKING FOR DISCOUNTS, BUT WE DIDN'T FIND A THING.
RENÉE GOT MARRIED LAST SPRING TO MY FRIEND LEATHEM. EVERYONE WHO KNOWS THEM IDOLIZES, ENVIES, AND ADORES THEM.
THEY'RE VERY BEAUTIFUL.
Renée's TRUCK!
LEATHEM IS A BUILDER, VERY SKILLED AND COOL.
RENÉE IS A RENAISSANCE WOMAN — A NATURE GIRL, AND MY MOM'S BUSINESS PARTNER AT THE FARMERS' MARKET, WHERE THEY SELL CHEESE.
I CAME HOME, WORRIED ABOUT MONEY, AND SPENT SOME TIME WITH MY EMAIL.

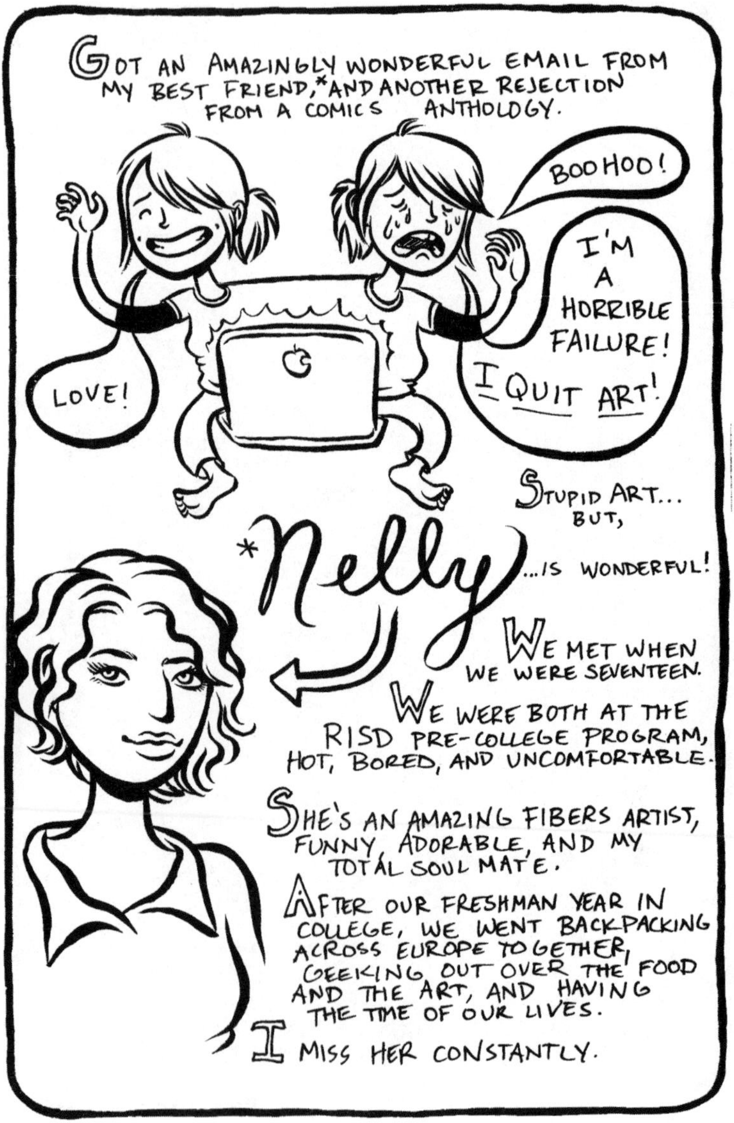
GOT AN AMAZINGLY WONDERFUL EMAIL FROM MY BEST FRIEND,* AND ANOTHER REJECTION FROM A COMICS ANTHOLOGY.
BOO HOO!
I'M A HORRIBLE FAILURE! I QUIT ART!
LOVE!
STUPID ART... BUT,
*Nelly ...IS WONDERFUL!
WE MET WHEN WE WERE SEVENTEEN.
WE WERE BOTH AT THE RISD PRE-COLLEGE PROGRAM, HOT, BORED, AND UNCOMFORTABLE.
SHE'S AN AMAZING FIBERS ARTIST, FUNNY, ADORABLE, AND MY TOTAL SOUL MATE.
AFTER OUR FRESHMAN YEAR IN COLLEGE, WE WENT BACKPACKING ACROSS EUROPE TOGETHER, GEEKING OUT OVER THE FOOD AND THE ART, AND HAVING THE TIME OF OUR LIVES.
I MISS HER CONSTANTLY.

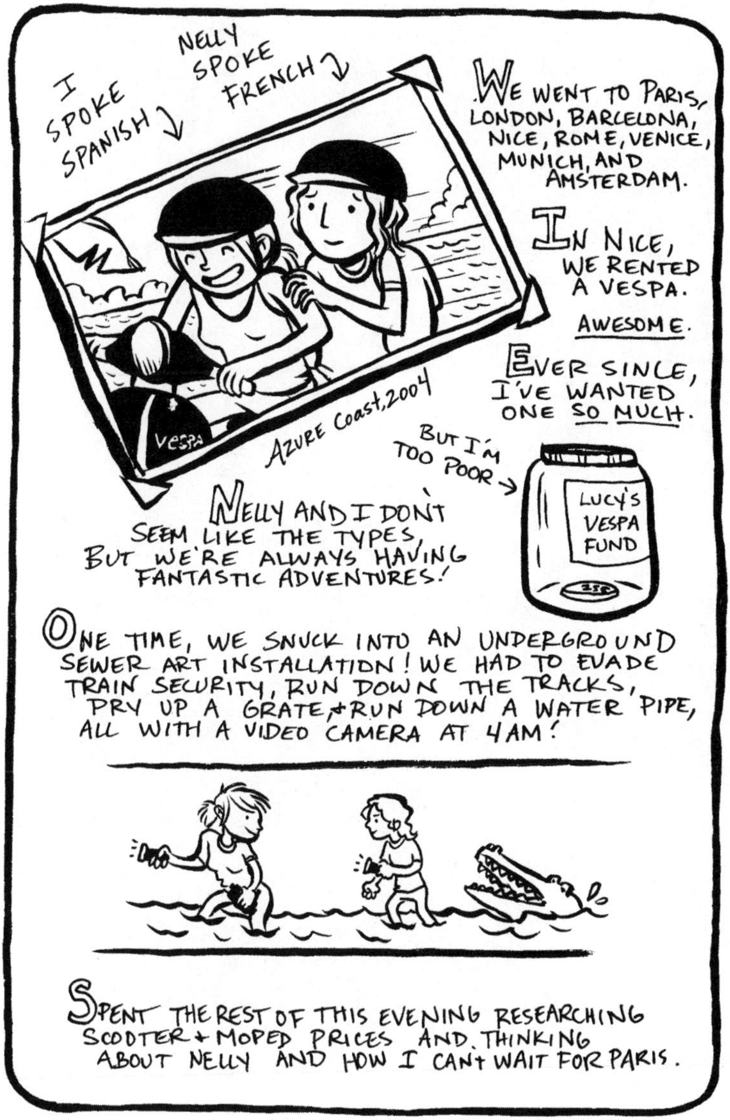
I SPOKE SPANISH
NELLY SPOKE FRENCH
WE WENT TO PARIS, LONDON, BARCELONA, NICE, ROME, VENICE, MUNICH, AND AMSTERDAM.
IN NICE, WE RENTED A VESPA.
AWESOME.
EVER SINCE, I'VE WANTED ONE SO MUCH.
VESPA
Azure Coast, 2004
BUT I'M TOO POOR
LUCY'S VESPA FUND
NELLY AND I DON'T SEEM LIKE THE TYPES, BUT WE'RE ALWAYS HAVING FANTASTIC ADVENTURES!
ONE TIME, WE SNUCK INTO AN UNDERGROUND SEWER ART INSTALLATION! WE HAD TO EVADE TRAIN SECURITY, RUN DOWN THE TRACKS, PRY UP A GRATE + RUN DOWN A WATER PIPE, ALL WITH A VIDEO CAMERA AT 4AM!
SPENT THE REST OF THIS EVENING RESEARCHING SCOOTER + MOPED PRICES AND THINKING ABOUT NELLY AND HOW I CAN'T WAIT FOR PARIS.

NELLY AND I,
PARIS: 2004

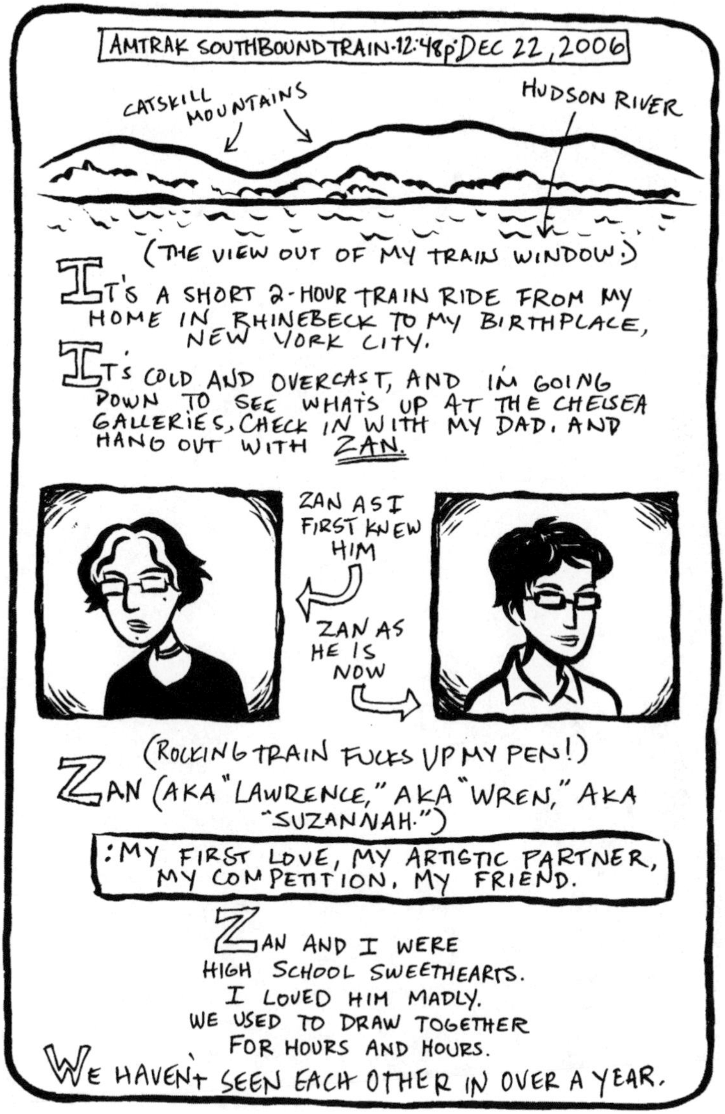
AMTRAK SOUTHBOUND TRAIN · 12:48p · DEC 22, 2006
CATSKILL MOUNTAINS
HUDSON RIVER
(THE VIEW OUT OF MY TRAIN WINDOW.)
IT'S A SHORT 2-HOUR TRAIN RIDE FROM MY HOME IN RHINEBECK TO MY BIRTHPLACE, NEW YORK CITY.
IT'S COLD AND OVERCAST, AND I'M GOING DOWN TO SEE WHAT'S UP AT THE CHELSEA GALLERIES, CHECK IN WITH MY DAD, AND HANG OUT WITH ZAN.
ZAN AS I FIRST KNEW HIM
ZAN AS HE IS NOW
(ROCKING TRAIN FUCKS UP MY PEN!)
ZAN (AKA "LAWRENCE," AKA "WREN," AKA "SUZANNAH.")
: MY FIRST LOVE, MY ARTISTIC PARTNER, MY COMPETITION, MY FRIEND.
ZAN AND I WERE HIGH SCHOOL SWEETHEARTS.
I LOVED HIM MADLY.
WE USED TO DRAW TOGETHER FOR HOURS AND HOURS.
WE HAVEN'T SEEN EACH OTHER IN OVER A YEAR.

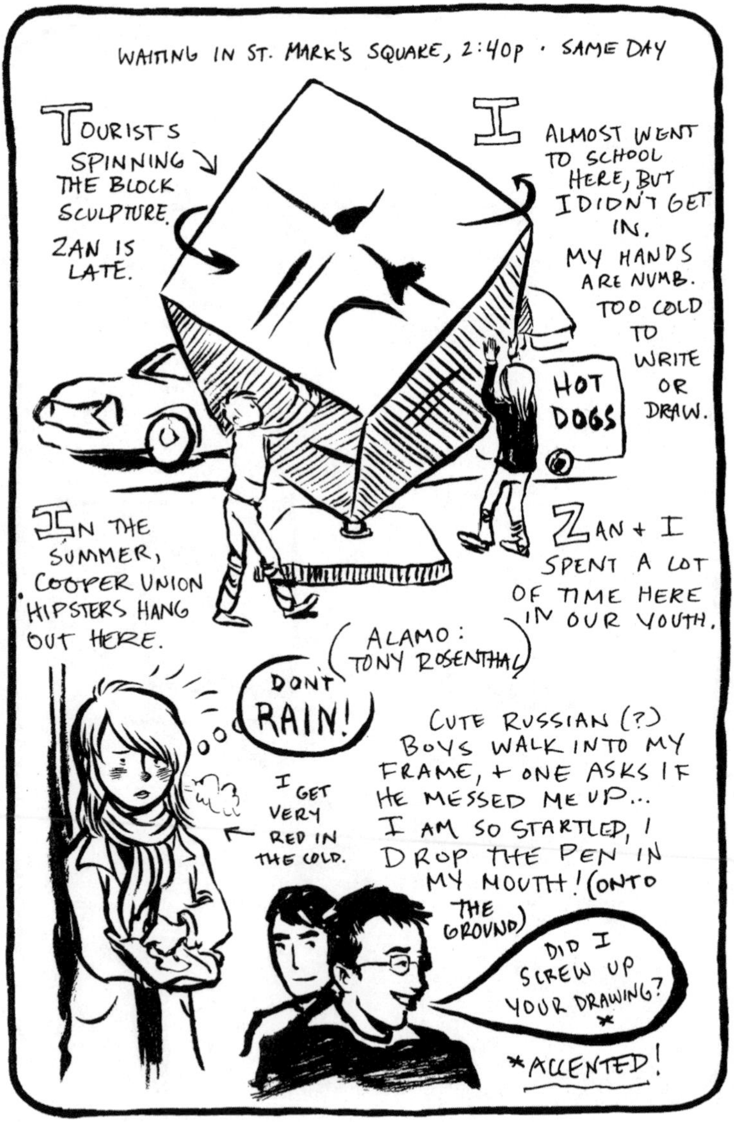
WAITING IN ST. MARK'S SQUARE, 2:40P · SAME DAY
TOURISTS SPINNING THE BLOCK SCULPTURE.
ZAN IS LATE.
I ALMOST WENT TO SCHOOL HERE, BUT I DIDN'T GET IN.
MY HANDS ARE NUMB. TOO COLD TO WRITE OR DRAW.
HOT DOGS
IN THE SUMMER, COOPER UNION HIPSTERS HANG OUT HERE.
ZAN + I SPENT A LOT OF TIME HERE IN OUR YOUTH.
(ALAMO: TONY ROSENTHAL)
DON'T RAIN!
I GET VERY RED IN THE COLD.
CUTE RUSSIAN (?) BOYS WALK INTO MY FRAME, + ONE ASKS IF HE MESSED ME UP... I AM SO STARTLED, I DROP THE PEN IN MY MOUTH! (ONTO THE GROUND)
DID I SCREW UP YOUR DRAWING? *
*ACCENTED!

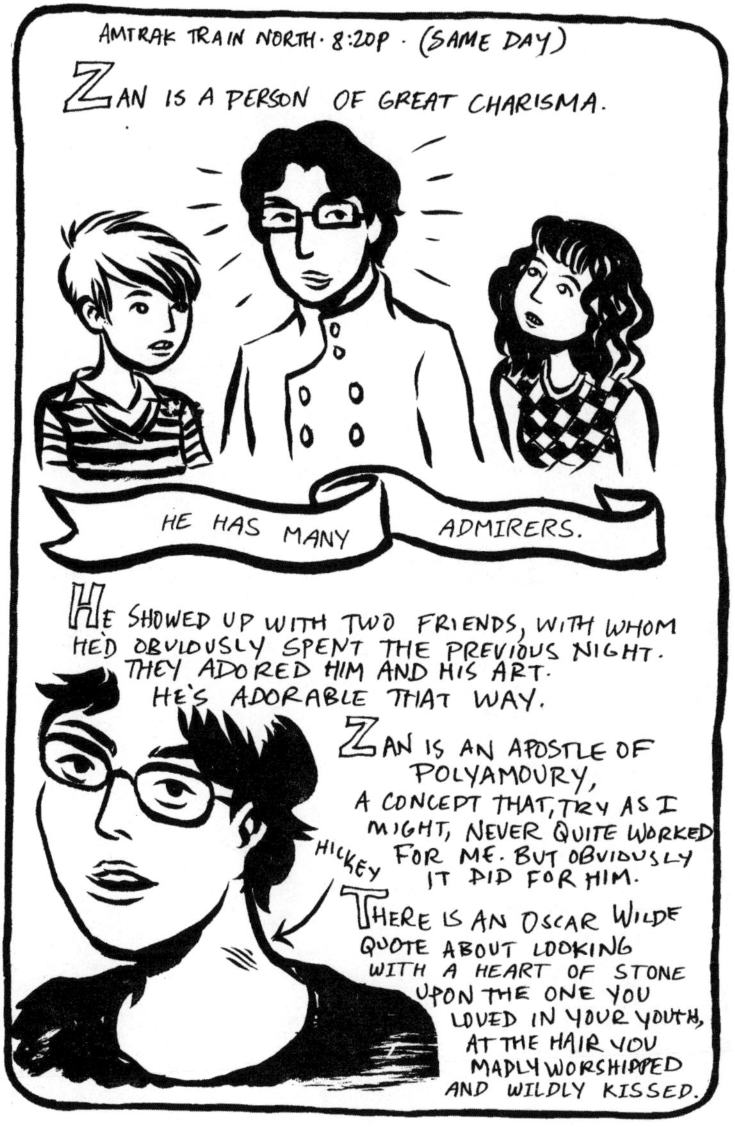
AMTRAK TRAIN NORTH · 8:20P · (SAME DAY)
ZAN IS A PERSON OF GREAT CHARISMA.
HE HAS MANY ADMIRERS.
HE SHOWED UP WITH TWO FRIENDS, WITH WHOM HE'D OBVIOUSLY SPENT THE PREVIOUS NIGHT. THEY ADORED HIM AND HIS ART. HE'S ADORABLE THAT WAY.
ZAN IS AN APOSTLE OF POLYAMOURY, A CONCEPT THAT, TRY AS I MIGHT, NEVER QUITE WORKED FOR ME. BUT OBVIOUSLY IT DID FOR HIM.
HICKEY
THERE IS AN OSCAR WILDE QUOTE ABOUT LOOKING WITH A HEART OF STONE UPON THE ONE YOU LOVED IN YOUR YOUTH, AT THE HAIR YOU MADLY WORSHIPPED AND WILDLY KISSED.

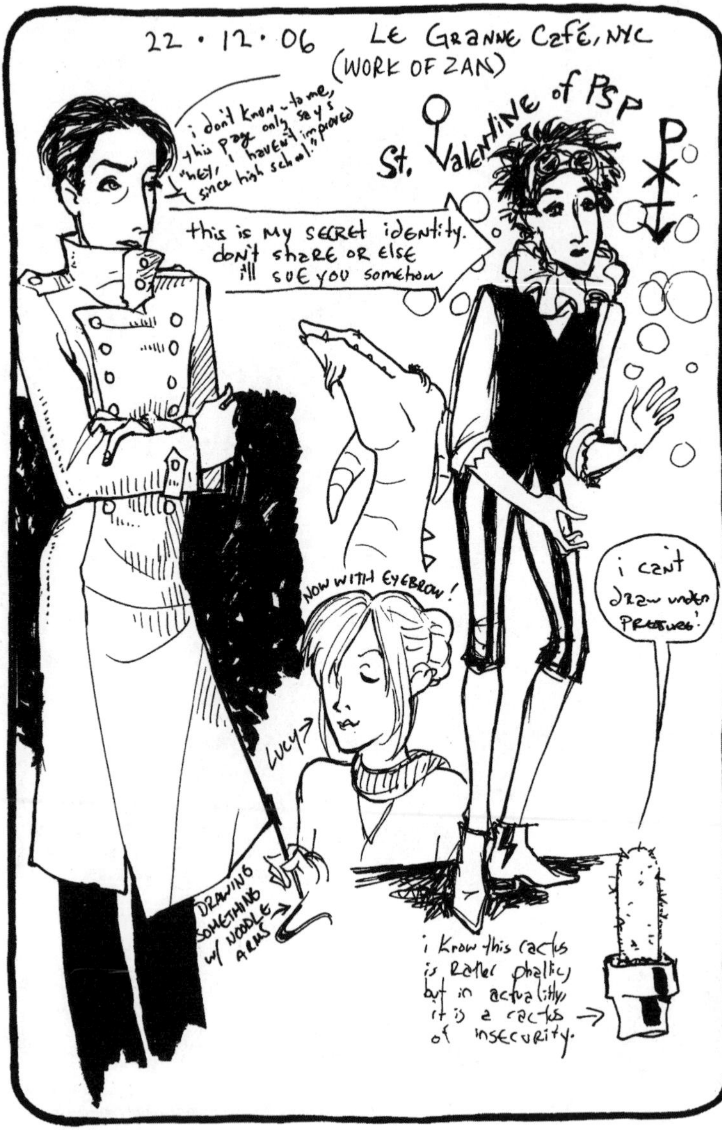
22 • 12 • 06
LE GRANNE Café, NYC
(WORK OF ZAN)
i don't know — to me, this page only says "hey, i haven't improved since high school!"
St. Valentine of PSP
this is my secret identity. don't share or else i'll sue you somehow
NOW WITH EYEBROW!
i can't draw under pressure!
LUCY
DRAWING SOMETHING W/ NOODLE ARMS
i know this cactus is rather phallic, but in actuality, it is a cactus of insecurity.

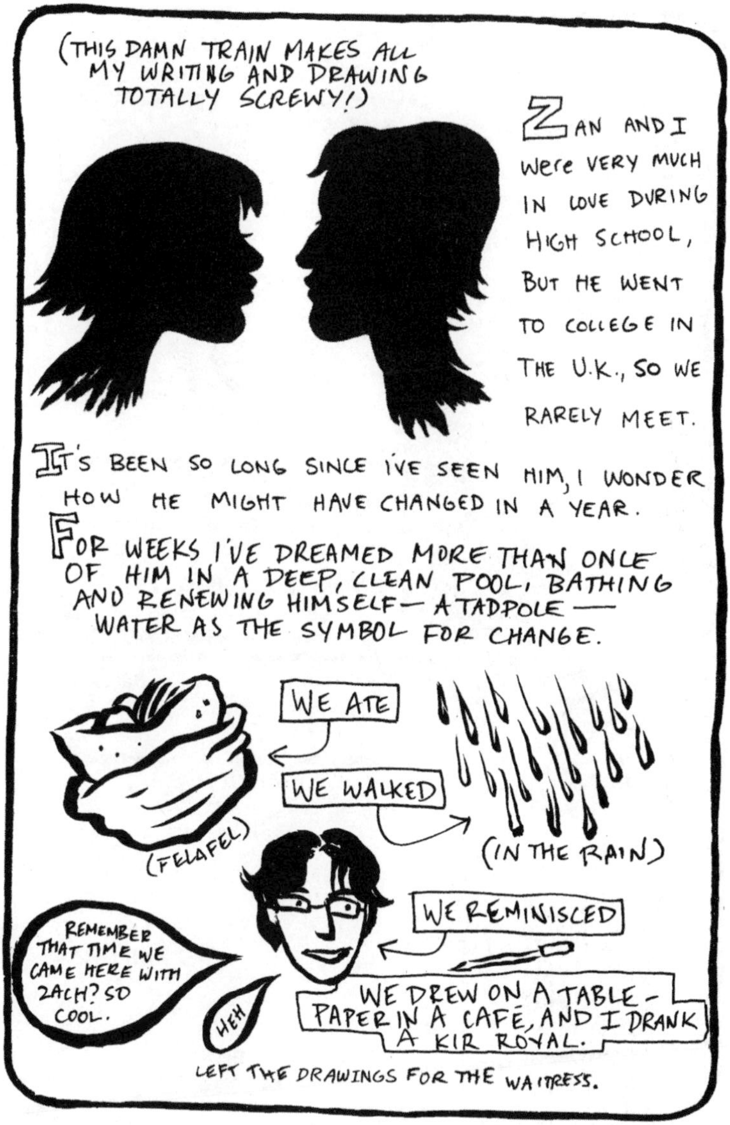
(THIS DAMN TRAIN MAKES ALL MY WRITING AND DRAWING TOTALLY SCREWY!)
ZAN AND I WERE VERY MUCH IN LOVE DURING HIGH SCHOOL, BUT HE WENT TO COLLEGE IN THE U.K., SO WE RARELY MEET.
IT'S BEEN SO LONG SINCE I'VE SEEN HIM, I WONDER HOW HE MIGHT HAVE CHANGED IN A YEAR.
FOR WEEKS I'VE DREAMED MORE THAN ONCE OF HIM IN A DEEP, CLEAN POOL, BATHING AND RENEWING HIMSELF— A TADPOLE— WATER AS THE SYMBOL FOR CHANGE.
WE ATE
(FELAFEL)
WE WALKED
(IN THE RAIN)
WE REMINISCED
REMEMBER THAT TIME WE CAME HERE WITH ZACH? SO COOL.
HEH
WE DREW ON A TABLE-PAPER IN A CAFÉ, AND I DRANK A KIR ROYAL.
LEFT THE DRAWINGS FOR THE WAITRESS.

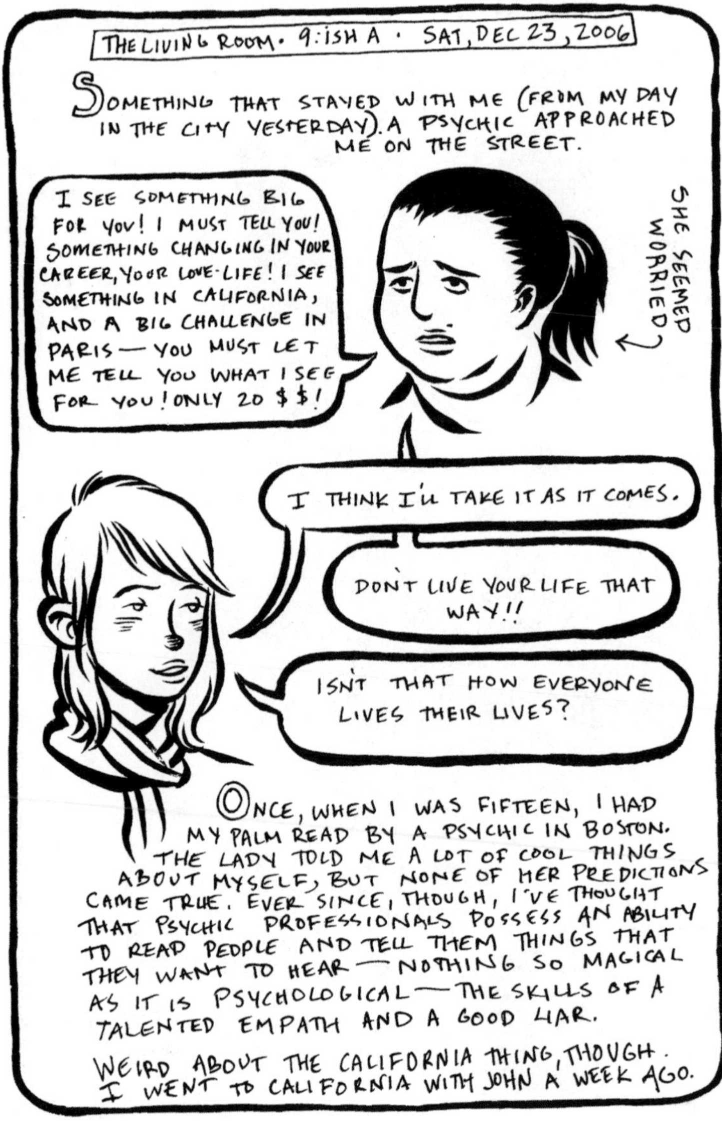
THE LIVING ROOM • 9:ISH A • SAT, DEC 23, 2006
SOMETHING THAT STAYED WITH ME (FROM MY DAY IN THE CITY YESTERDAY). A PSYCHIC APPROACHED ME ON THE STREET.
I SEE SOMETHING BIG FOR YOU! I MUST TELL YOU! SOMETHING CHANGING IN YOUR CAREER, YOUR LOVE-LIFE! I SEE SOMETHING IN CALIFORNIA, AND A BIG CHALLENGE IN PARIS — YOU MUST LET ME TELL YOU WHAT I SEE FOR YOU! ONLY 20 $$!
SHE SEEMED WORRIED
I THINK I'LL TAKE IT AS IT COMES.
DON'T LIVE YOUR LIFE THAT WAY!!
ISN'T THAT HOW EVERYONE LIVES THEIR LIVES?
ONCE, WHEN I WAS FIFTEEN, I HAD MY PALM READ BY A PSYCHIC IN BOSTON. THE LADY TOLD ME A LOT OF COOL THINGS ABOUT MYSELF, BUT NONE OF HER PREDICTIONS CAME TRUE. EVER SINCE, THOUGH, I'VE THOUGHT THAT PSYCHIC PROFESSIONALS POSSESS AN ABILITY TO READ PEOPLE AND TELL THEM THINGS THAT THEY WANT TO HEAR — NOTHING SO MAGICAL AS IT IS PSYCHOLOGICAL — THE SKILLS OF A TALENTED EMPATH AND A GOOD LIAR.
WEIRD ABOUT THE CALIFORNIA THING, THOUGH. I WENT TO CALIFORNIA WITH JOHN A WEEK AGO.

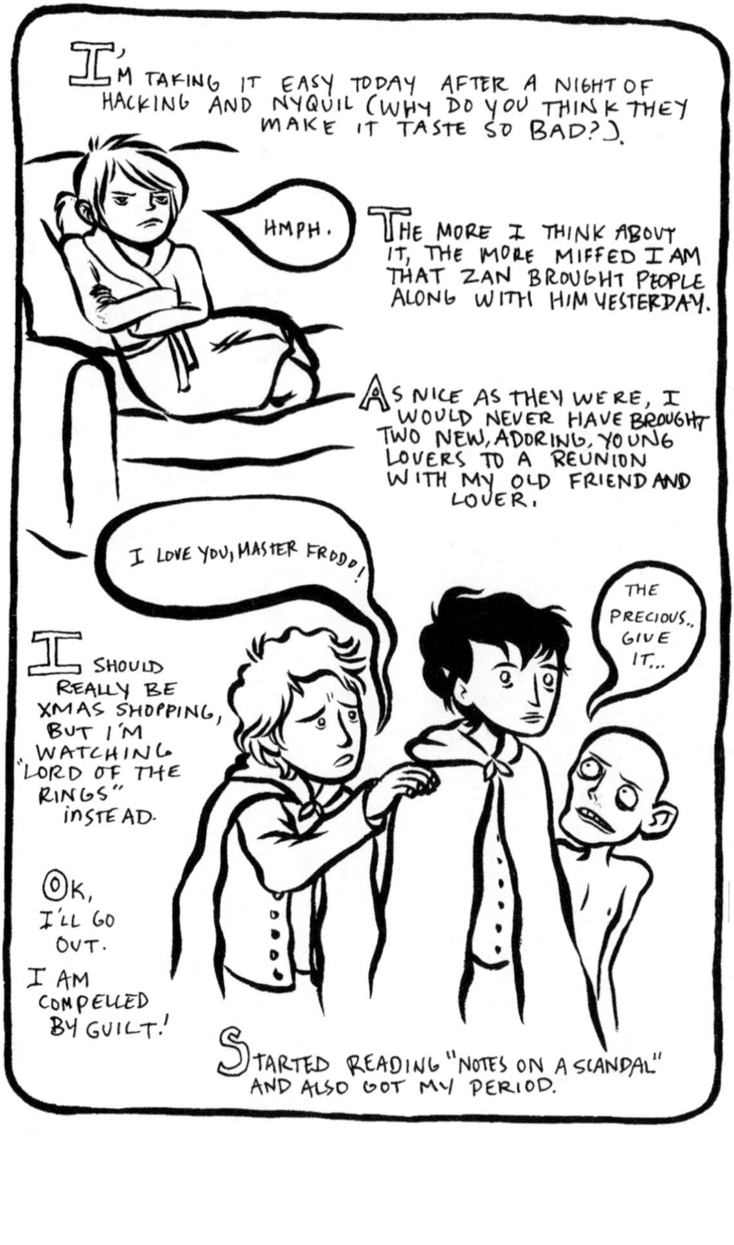
I'M TAKING IT EASY TODAY AFTER A NIGHT OF HACKING AND NYQUIL (WHY DO YOU THINK THEY MAKE IT TASTE SO BAD?).
HMPH.
THE MORE I THINK ABOUT IT, THE MORE MIFFED I AM THAT ZAN BROUGHT PEOPLE ALONG WITH HIM YESTERDAY.
AS NICE AS THEY WERE, I WOULD NEVER HAVE BROUGHT TWO NEW, ADORING, YOUNG LOVERS TO A REUNION WITH MY OLD FRIEND AND LOVER.
I LOVE YOU, MASTER FRODO!
THE PRECIOUS.. GIVE IT...
I SHOULD REALLY BE XMAS SHOPPING, BUT I'M WATCHING "LORD OF THE RINGS" INSTEAD.
OK, I'LL GO OUT.
I AM COMPELLED BY GUILT!
STARTED READING "NOTES ON A SCANDAL" AND ALSO GOT MY PERIOD.

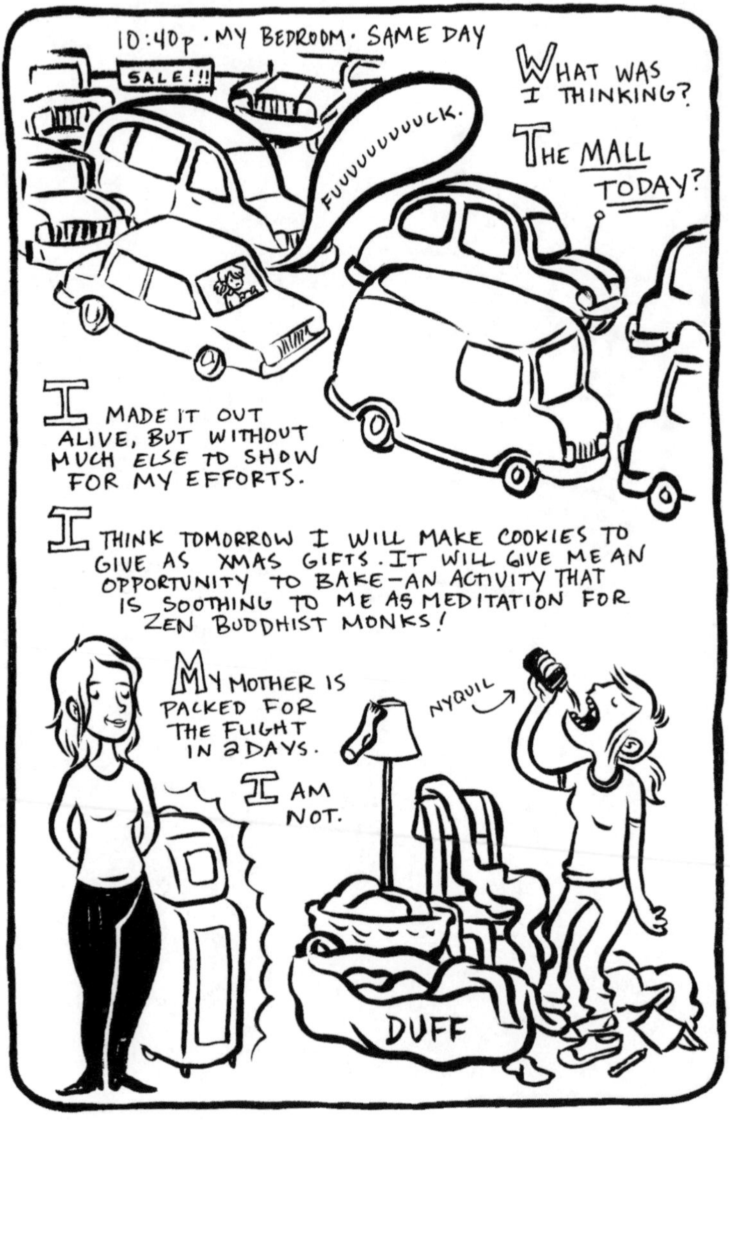
10:40p · MY BEDROOM · SAME DAY
SALE!!!
FUUUUUUUUUUCK.
WHAT WAS I THINKING?
THE MALL TODAY?
I MADE IT OUT ALIVE, BUT WITHOUT MUCH ELSE TO SHOW FOR MY EFFORTS.
I THINK TOMORROW I WILL MAKE COOKIES TO GIVE AS XMAS GIFTS. IT WILL GIVE ME AN OPPORTUNITY TO BAKE—AN ACTIVITY THAT IS SOOTHING TO ME AS MEDITATION FOR ZEN BUDDHIST MONKS!
MY MOTHER IS PACKED FOR THE FLIGHT IN 2 DAYS.
I AM NOT.
NYQUIL
DUFF

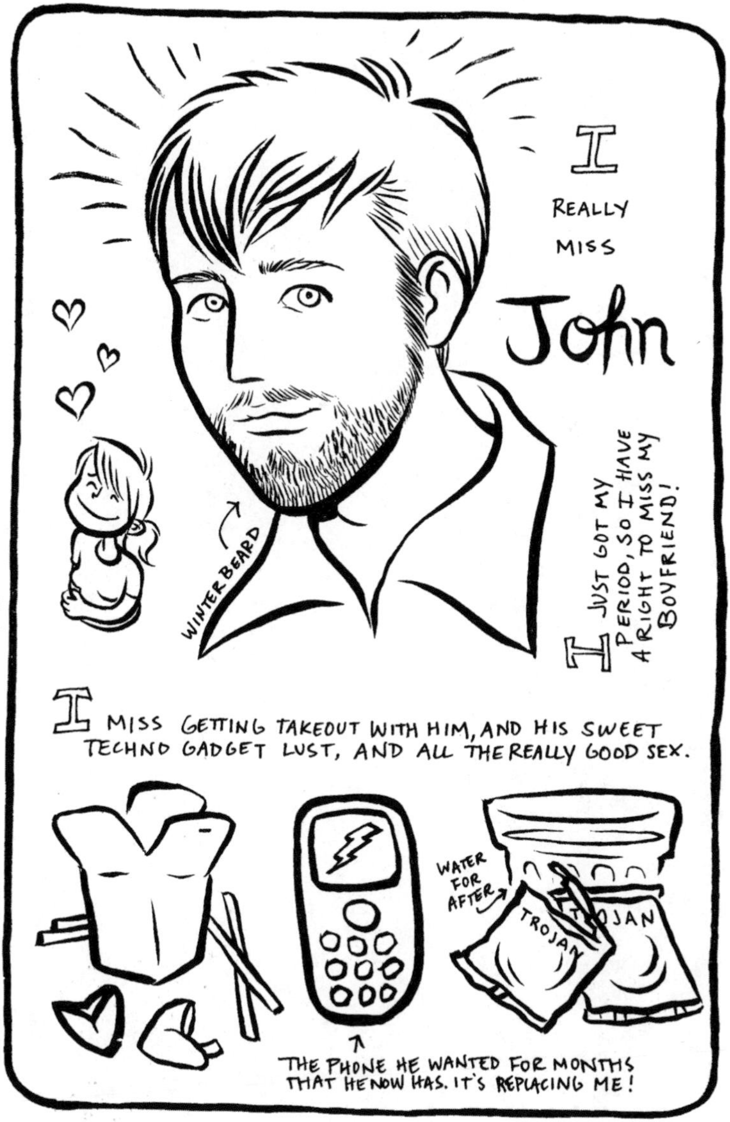
I REALLY MISS John
WINTER BEARD
I JUST GOT MY PERIOD, SO I HAVE A RIGHT TO MISS MY BOYFRIEND!
I MISS GETTING TAKEOUT WITH HIM, AND HIS SWEET TECHNO GADGET LUST, AND ALL THE REALLY GOOD SEX.
WATER FOR AFTER
TROJAN
TROJAN
THE PHONE HE WANTED FOR MONTHS THAT HE NOW HAS. IT'S REPLACING ME!

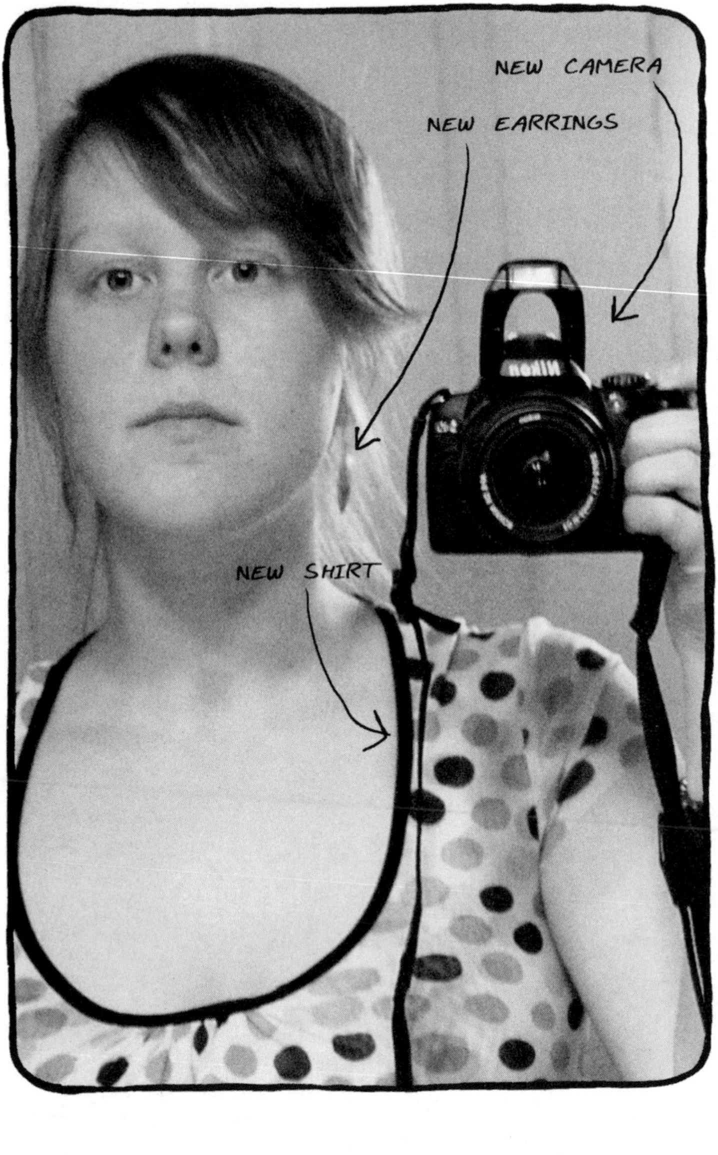
NEW CAMERA
NEW EARRINGS
NEW SHIRT

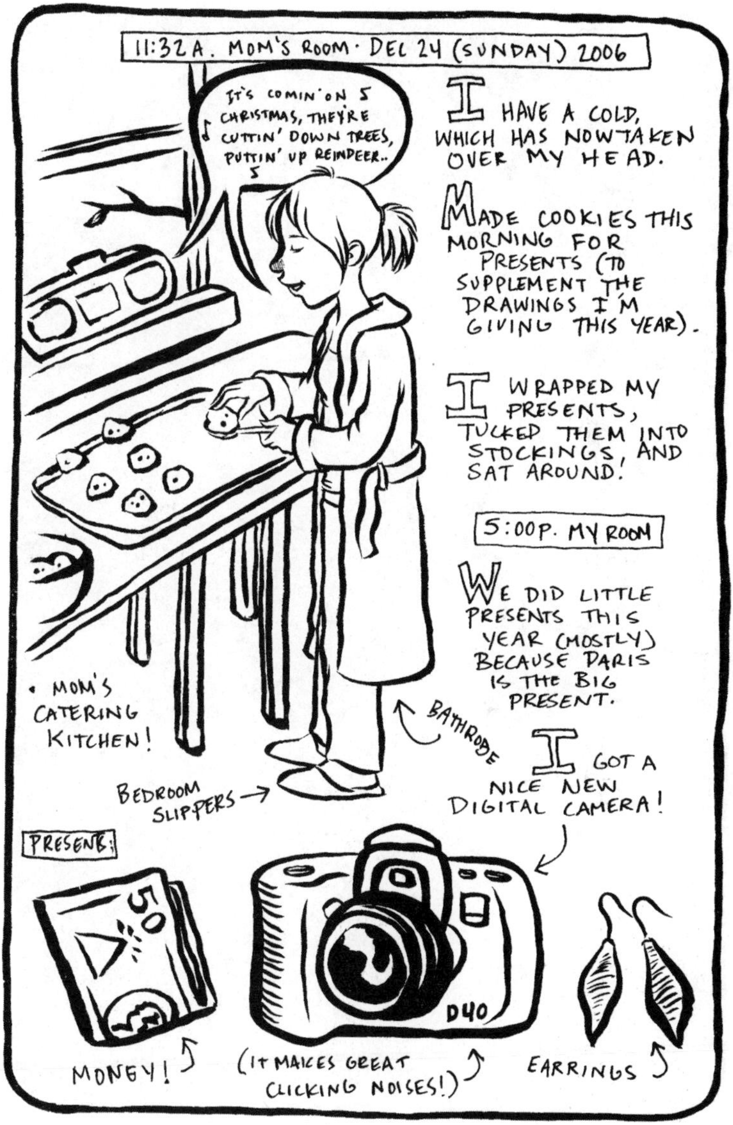
11:32A. MOM'S ROOM · DEC 24 (SUNDAY) 2006
IT'S COMIN' ON CHRISTMAS, THEY'RE CUTTIN' DOWN TREES, PUTTIN' UP REINDEER..
I HAVE A COLD, WHICH HAS NOW TAKEN OVER MY HEAD.
MADE COOKIES THIS MORNING FOR PRESENTS (TO SUPPLEMENT THE DRAWINGS I'M GIVING THIS YEAR).
I WRAPPED MY PRESENTS, TUCKED THEM INTO STOCKINGS, AND SAT AROUND!
5:00P. MY ROOM
WE DID LITTLE PRESENTS THIS YEAR (MOSTLY) BECAUSE PARIS IS THE BIG PRESENT.
· MOM'S CATERING KITCHEN!
BATHROBE
BEDROOM SLIPPERS
I GOT A NICE NEW DIGITAL CAMERA!
PRESENTS:
50
D40
MONEY!
(IT MAKES GREAT CLICKING NOISES!)
EARRINGS

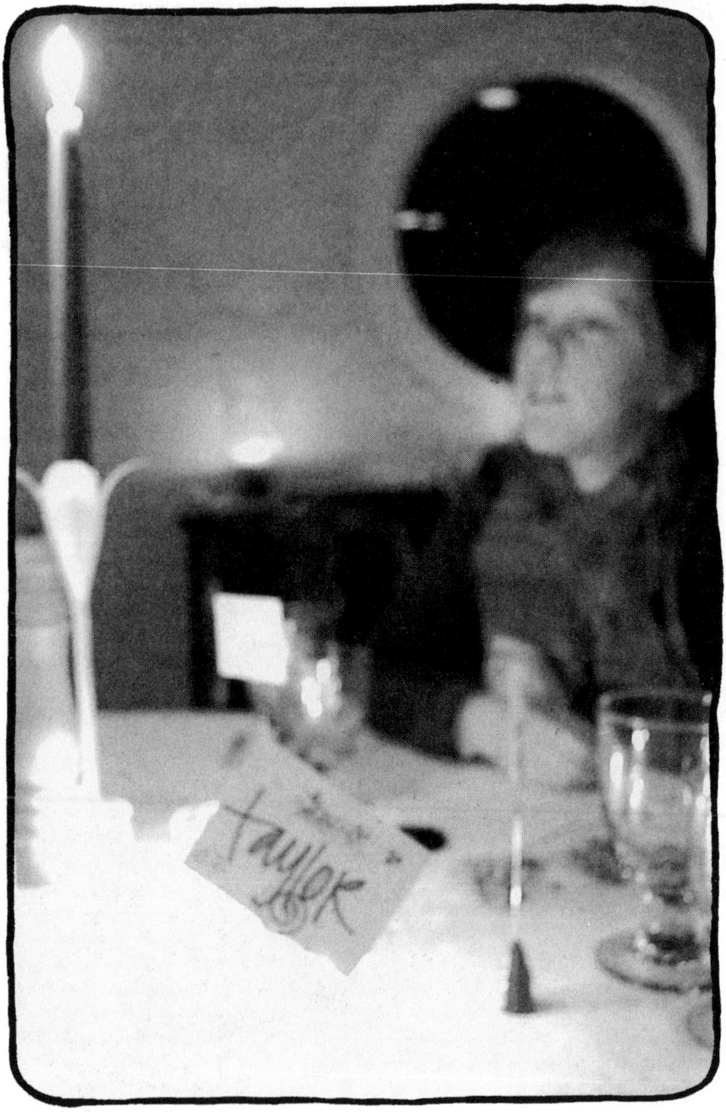
taylor

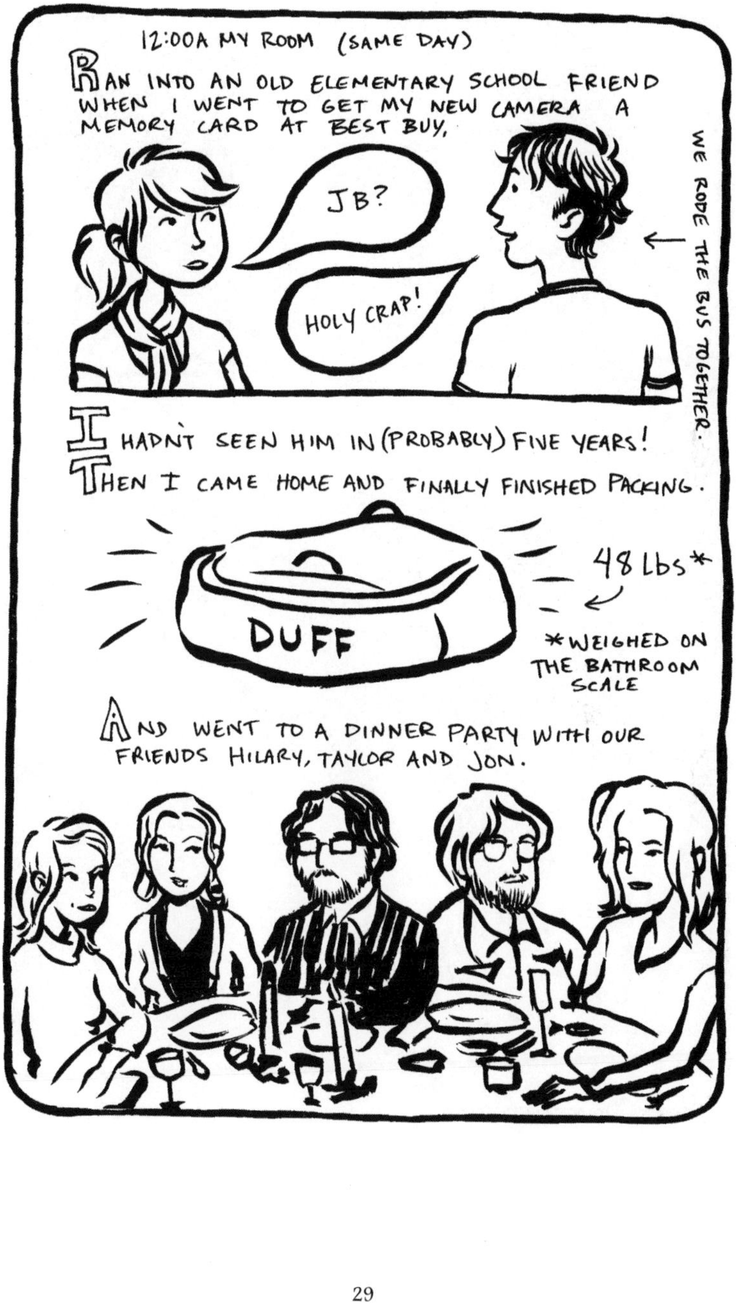
12:00A MY ROOM (SAME DAY)
RAN INTO AN OLD ELEMENTARY SCHOOL FRIEND WHEN I WENT TO GET MY NEW CAMERA A MEMORY CARD AT BEST BUY,
JB?
HOLY CRAP!
WE RODE THE BUS TOGETHER.
I HADN'T SEEN HIM IN (PROBABLY) FIVE YEARS!
THEN I CAME HOME AND FINALLY FINISHED PACKING.
DUFF
48 Lbs*
*WEIGHED ON THE BATHROOM SCALE
AND WENT TO A DINNER PARTY WITH OUR FRIENDS HILARY, TAYLOR AND JON.

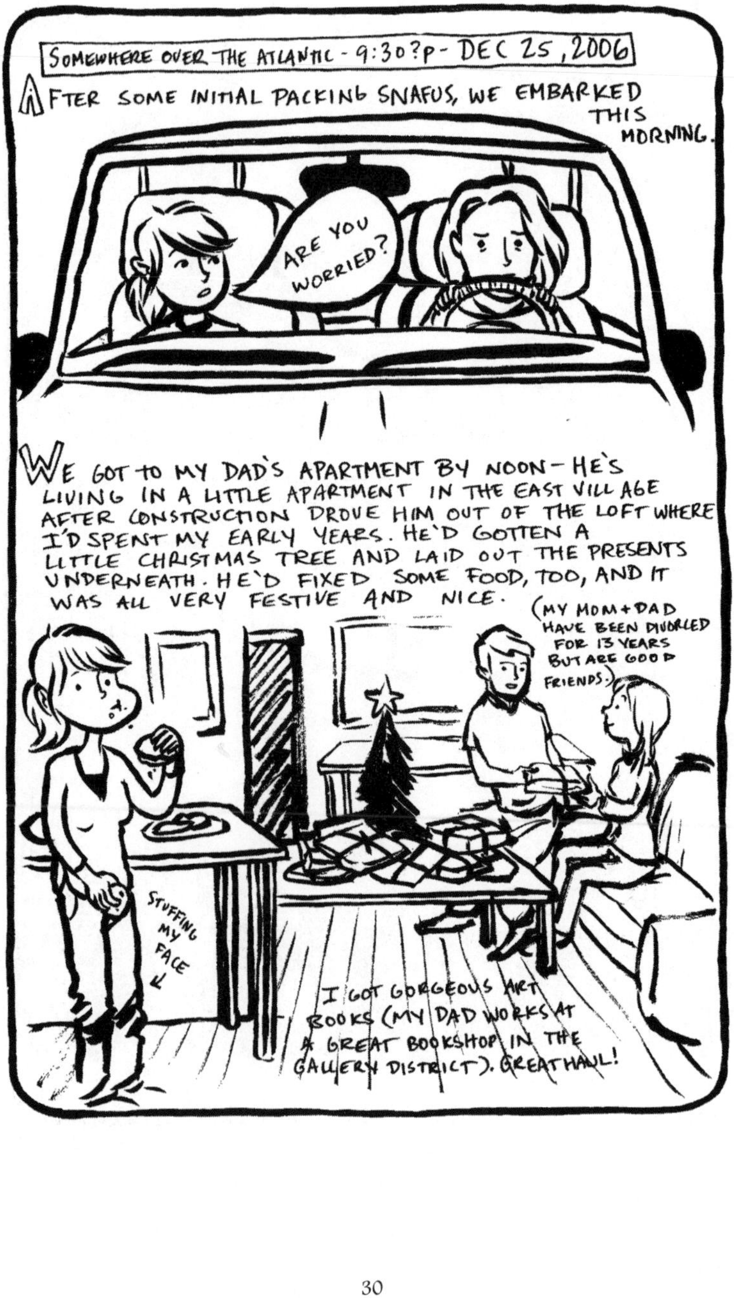
SOMEWHERE OVER THE ATLANTIC - 9:30?P - DEC 25, 2006
AFTER SOME INITIAL PACKING SNAFUS, WE EMBARKED THIS MORNING.
ARE YOU WORRIED?
WE GOT TO MY DAD'S APARTMENT BY NOON - HE'S LIVING IN A LITTLE APARTMENT IN THE EAST VILLAGE AFTER CONSTRUCTION DROVE HIM OUT OF THE LOFT WHERE I'D SPENT MY EARLY YEARS. HE'D GOTTEN A LITTLE CHRISTMAS TREE AND LAID OUT THE PRESENTS UNDERNEATH. HE'D FIXED SOME FOOD, TOO, AND IT WAS ALL VERY FESTIVE AND NICE.
(MY MOM + DAD HAVE BEEN DIVORCED FOR 13 YEARS BUT ARE GOOD FRIENDS.)
STUFFING MY FACE
I GOT GORGEOUS ART BOOKS (MY DAD WORKS AT A GREAT BOOKSHOP IN THE GALLERY DISTRICT). GREAT HAUL!

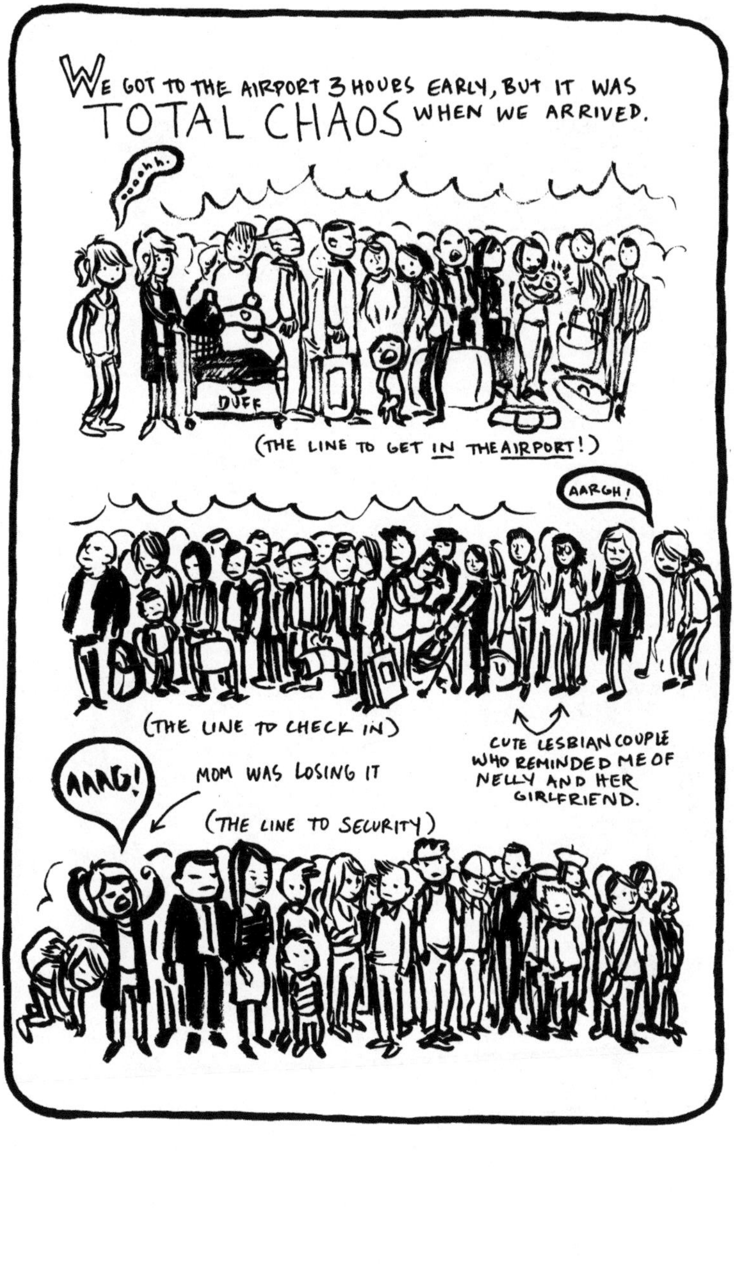
WE GOT TO THE AIRPORT 3 HOURS EARLY, BUT IT WAS TOTAL CHAOS WHEN WE ARRIVED.
oooohh.
DUFF
(THE LINE TO GET IN THE AIRPORT!)
AARGH!
(THE LINE TO CHECK IN)
CUTE LESBIAN COUPLE WHO REMINDED ME OF NELLY AND HER GIRLFRIEND.
AAAG!
MOM WAS LOSING IT
(THE LINE TO SECURITY)

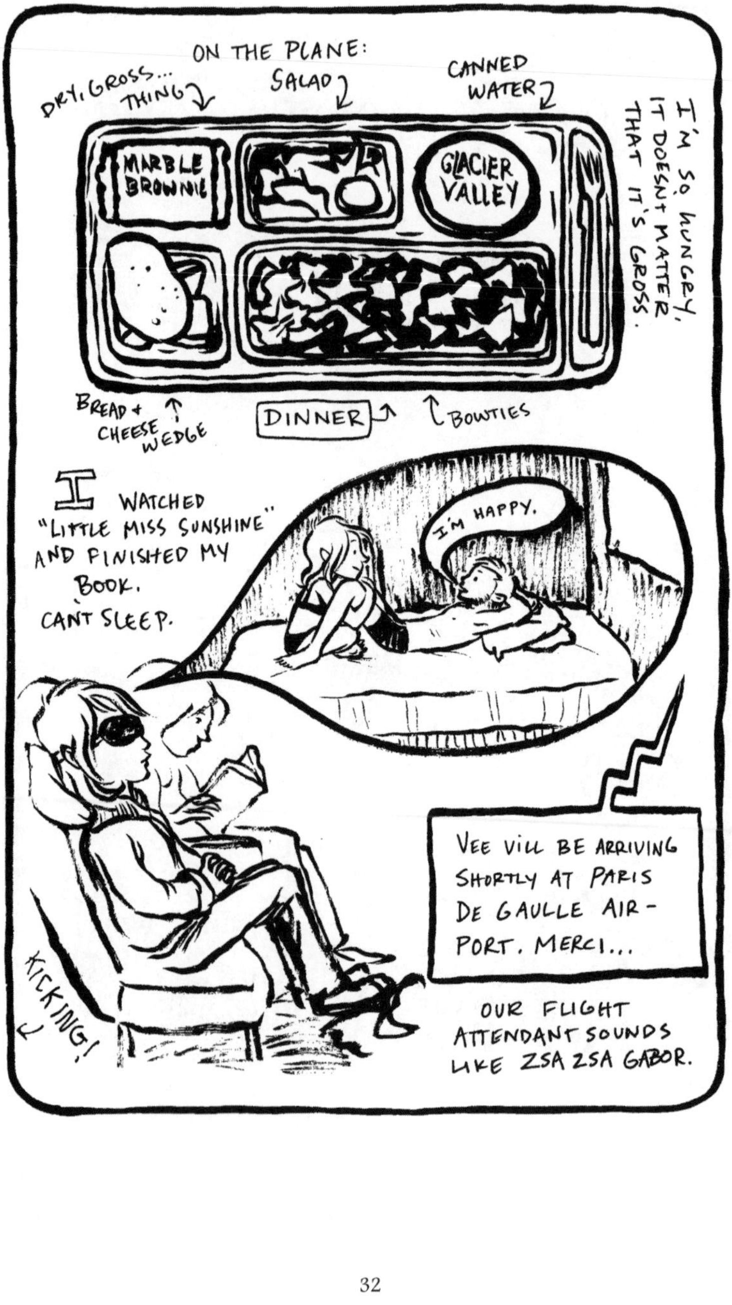
ON THE PLANE:
DRY, GROSS... THING
SALAD
CANNED WATER
MARBLE BROWNIE
GLACIER VALLEY
I'M SO HUNGRY, IT DOESN'T MATTER THAT IT'S GROSS.
BREAD + CHEESE WEDGE
DINNER
BOWTIES
I WATCHED "LITTLE MISS SUNSHINE" AND FINISHED MY BOOK.
CAN'T SLEEP.
I'M HAPPY.
VEE VILL BE ARRIVING SHORTLY AT PARIS DE GAULLE AIR-PORT. MERCI...
OUR FLIGHT ATTENDANT SOUNDS LIKE ZSA ZSA GABOR.
KICKING!

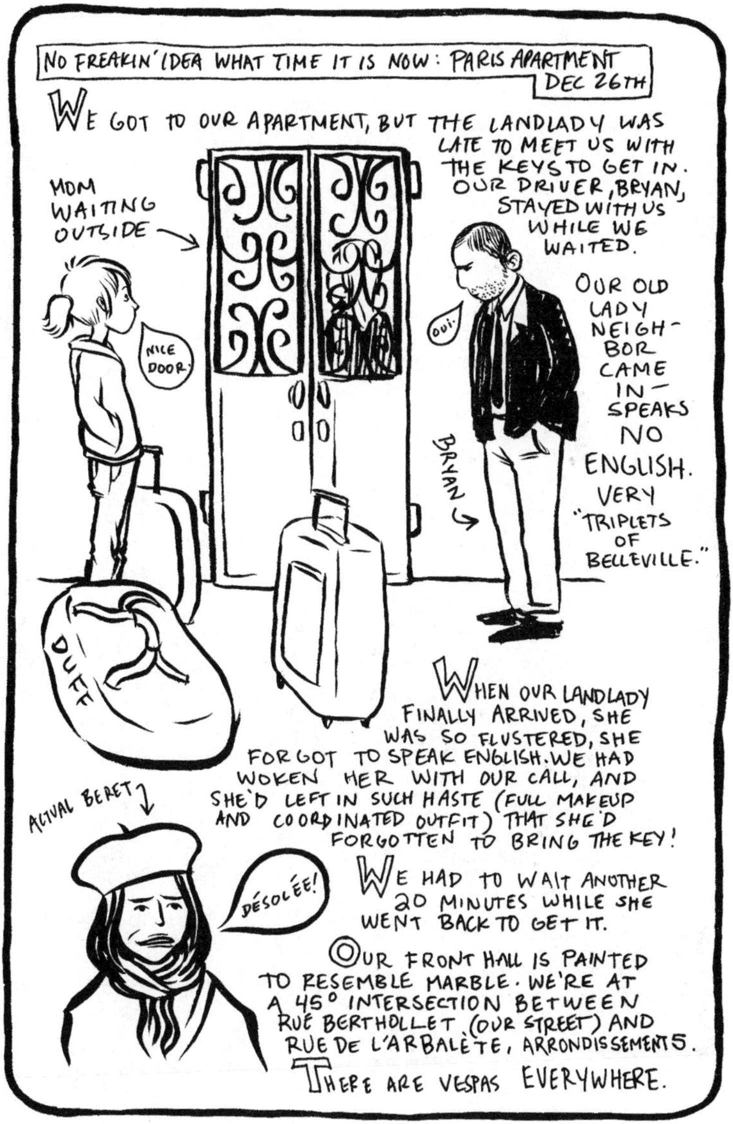
NO FREAKIN' IDEA WHAT TIME IT IS NOW: PARIS APARTMENT DEC 26TH
WE GOT TO OUR APARTMENT, BUT THE LANDLADY WAS LATE TO MEET US WITH THE KEYS TO GET IN. OUR DRIVER, BRYAN, STAYED WITH US WHILE WE WAITED.
MOM WAITING OUTSIDE
NICE DOOR.
OUI.
OUR OLD LADY NEIGHBOR CAME IN — SPEAKS NO ENGLISH. VERY "TRIPLETS OF BELLEVILLE."
BRYAN
DUFF
WHEN OUR LANDLADY FINALLY ARRIVED, SHE WAS SO FLUSTERED, SHE FORGOT TO SPEAK ENGLISH. WE HAD WOKEN HER WITH OUR CALL, AND SHE'D LEFT IN SUCH HASTE (FULL MAKEUP AND COORDINATED OUTFIT) THAT SHE'D FORGOTTEN TO BRING THE KEY!
ACTUAL BERET
DÉSOLÉE!
WE HAD TO WAIT ANOTHER 20 MINUTES WHILE SHE WENT BACK TO GET IT.
OUR FRONT HALL IS PAINTED TO RESEMBLE MARBLE. WE'RE AT A 45° INTERSECTION BETWEEN RUE BERTHOLLET (OUR STREET) AND RUE DE L'ARBALÈTE, ARRONDISSEMENT 5.
THERE ARE VESPAS EVERYWHERE.

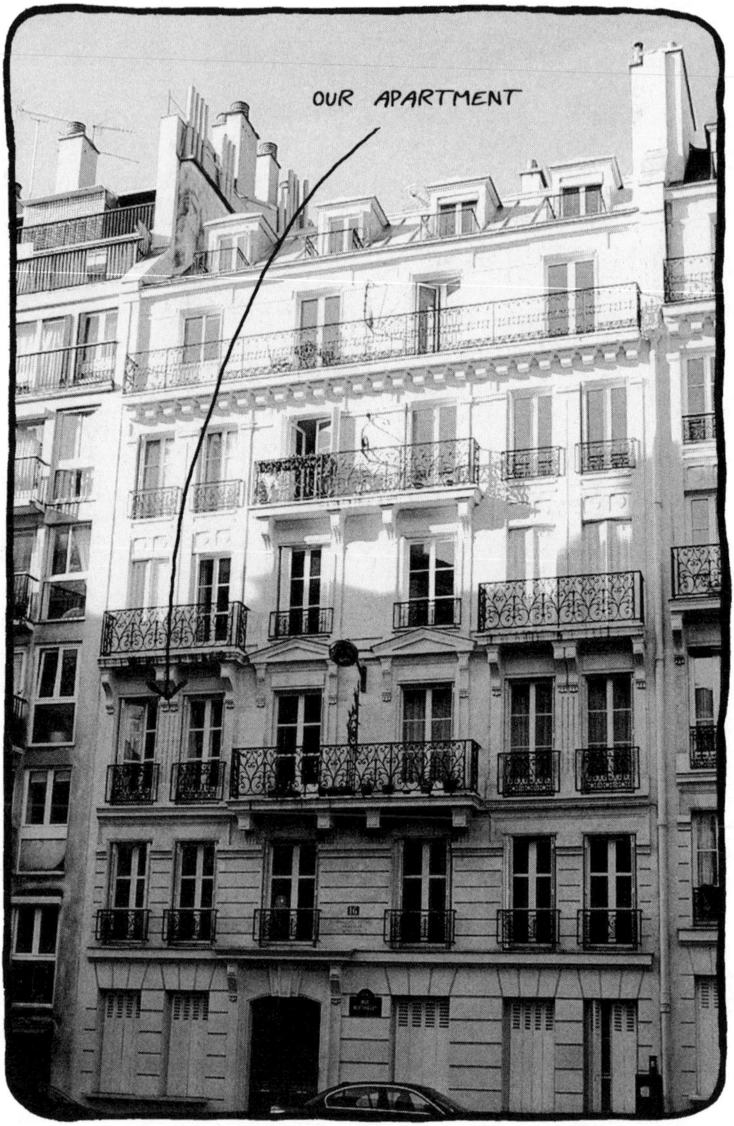
OUR APARTMENT

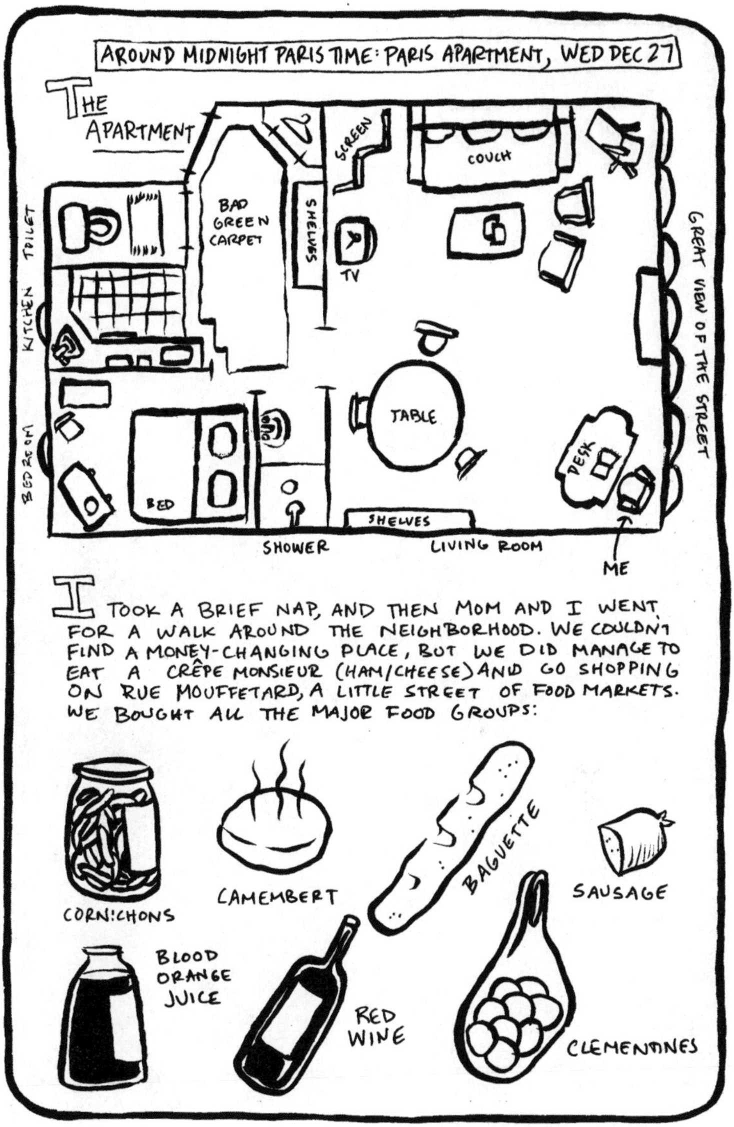
AROUND MIDNIGHT PARIS TIME: PARIS APARTMENT, WED DEC 27
THE APARTMENT
SCREEN
COUCH
BAD GREEN CARPET
SHELVES
TV
TOILET
KITCHEN
BEDROOM
GREAT VIEW OF THE STREET
TABLE
DESK
BED
SHELVES
SHOWER
LIVING ROOM
ME
I TOOK A BRIEF NAP, AND THEN MOM AND I WENT FOR A WALK AROUND THE NEIGHBORHOOD. WE COULDN'T FIND A MONEY-CHANGING PLACE, BUT WE DID MANAGE TO EAT A CRÊPE MONSIEUR (HAM/CHEESE) AND GO SHOPPING ON RUE MOUFFETARD, A LITTLE STREET OF FOOD MARKETS. WE BOUGHT ALL THE MAJOR FOOD GROUPS:
CORNICHONS
CAMEMBERT
BAGUETTE
SAUSAGE
BLOOD ORANGE JUICE
RED WINE
CLEMENTINES

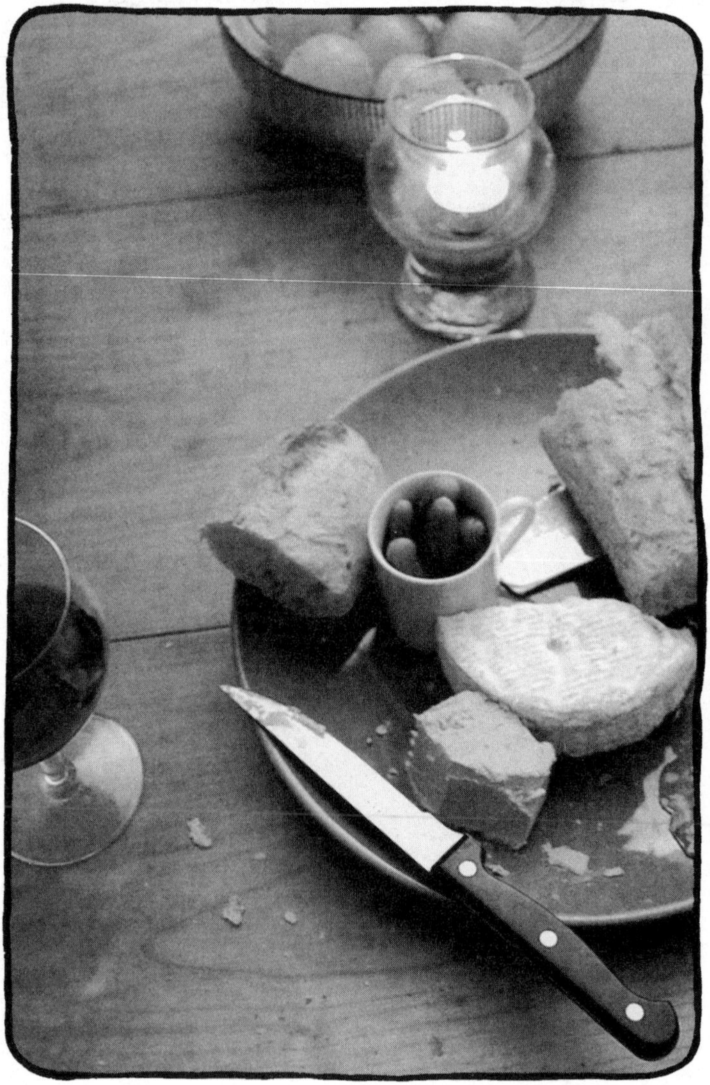

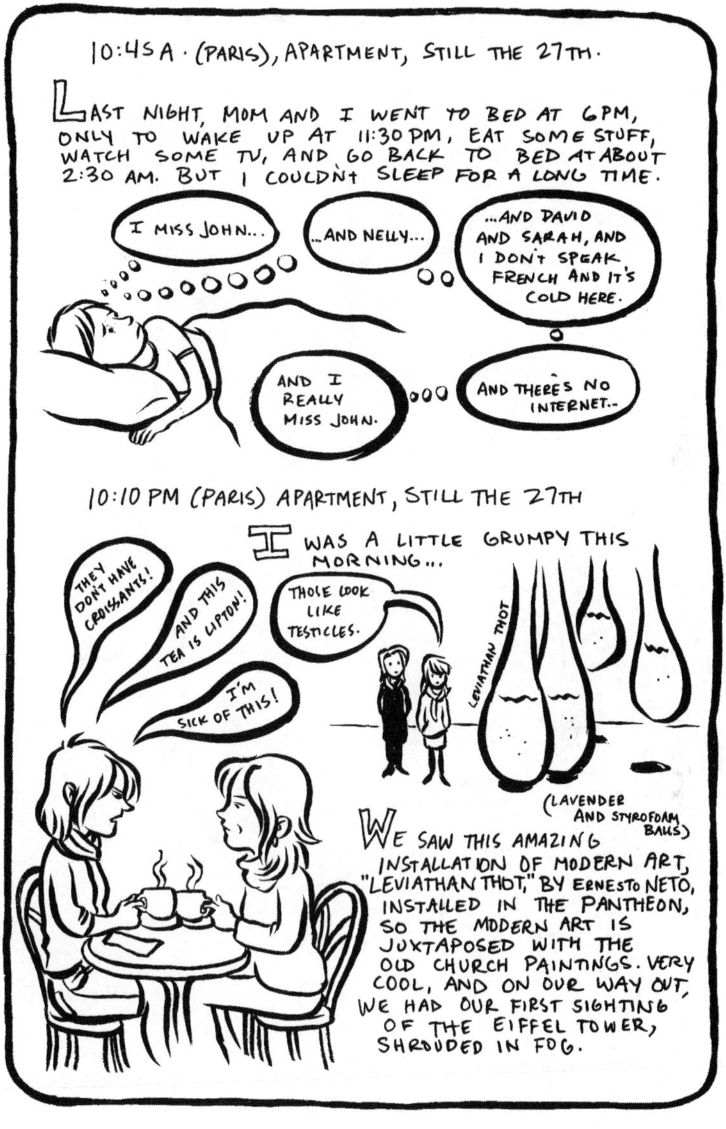

10:45 A. (PARIS), APARTMENT, STILL THE 27TH.
LAST NIGHT, MOM AND I WENT TO BED AT 6PM, ONLY TO WAKE UP AT 11:30 PM, EAT SOME STUFF, WATCH SOME TV, AND GO BACK TO BED AT ABOUT 2:30 AM. BUT I COULDN'T SLEEP FOR A LONG TIME.
I MISS JOHN...
...AND NELLY...
...AND DAVID AND SARAH, AND I DON'T SPEAK FRENCH AND IT'S COLD HERE.
AND THERE'S NO INTERNET..
AND I REALLY MISS JOHN.
10:10 PM (PARIS) APARTMENT, STILL THE 27TH
I WAS A LITTLE GRUMPY THIS MORNING...
THEY DON'T HAVE CROISSANTS!
AND THIS TEA IS LIPTON!
I'M SICK OF THIS!
THOSE LOOK LIKE TESTICLES.
LEVIATHAN THOT
(LAVENDER AND STYROFOAM BALLS)
WE SAW THIS AMAZING INSTALLATION OF MODERN ART, "LEVIATHAN THOT," BY ERNESTO NETO, INSTALLED IN THE PANTHEON, SO THE MODERN ART IS JUXTAPOSED WITH THE OLD CHURCH PAINTINGS. VERY COOL, AND ON OUR WAY OUT, WE HAD OUR FIRST SIGHTING OF THE EIFFEL TOWER, SHROUDED IN FOG.

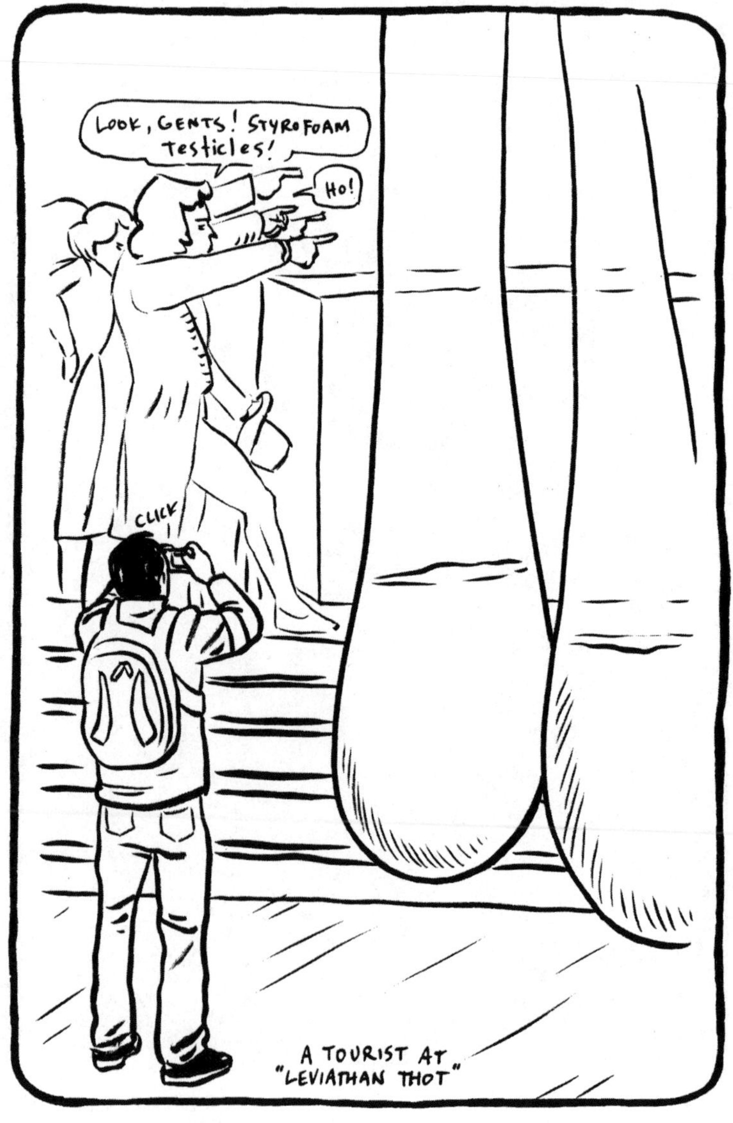

LOOK, GENTS! STYROFOAM testicles!
Ho!
CLICK
A TOURIST AT "LEVIATHAN THOT"

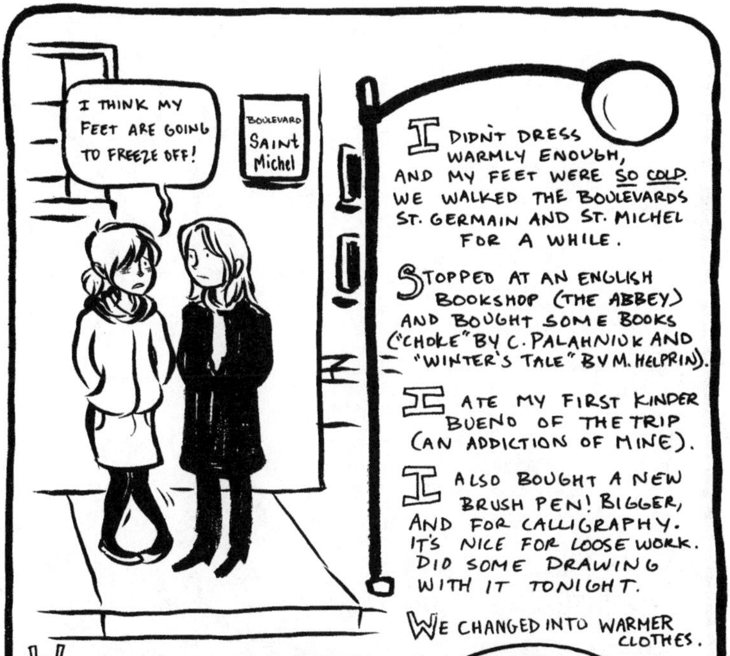

I THINK MY FEET ARE GOING TO FREEZE OFF!
BOULEVARD Saint Michel
I DIDN'T DRESS WARMLY ENOUGH, AND MY FEET WERE SO COLD. WE WALKED THE BOULEVARDS ST. GERMAIN AND ST. MICHEL FOR A WHILE.
STOPPED AT AN ENGLISH BOOKSHOP (THE ABBEY) AND BOUGHT SOME BOOKS ("CHOKE" BY C. PALAHNIUK AND "WINTER'S TALE" BY M. HELPRIN).
I ATE MY FIRST KINDER BUENO OF THE TRIP (AN ADDICTION OF MINE).
I ALSO BOUGHT A NEW BRUSH PEN! BIGGER, AND FOR CALLIGRAPHY. IT'S NICE FOR LOOSE WORK. DID SOME DRAWING WITH IT TONIGHT.
WE CHANGED INTO WARMER CLOTHES.

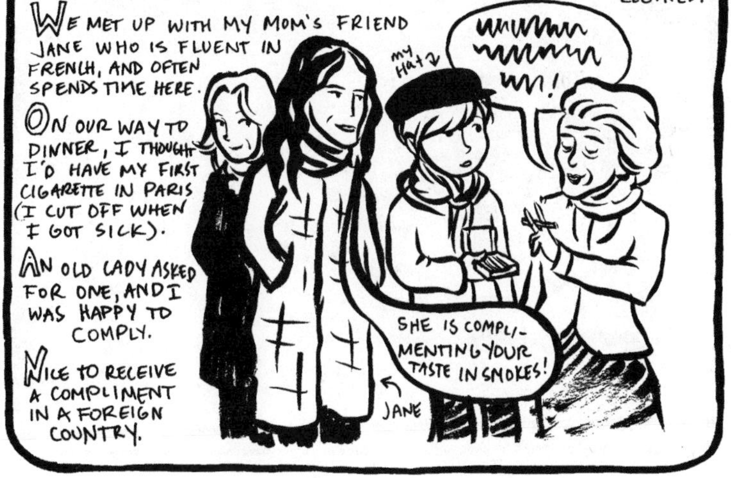

WE MET UP WITH MY MOM'S FRIEND JANE WHO IS FLUENT IN FRENCH, AND OFTEN SPENDS TIME HERE.
ON OUR WAY TO DINNER, I THOUGHT I'D HAVE MY FIRST CIGARETTE IN PARIS (I CUT OFF WHEN I GOT SICK).
AN OLD LADY ASKED FOR ONE, AND I WAS HAPPY TO COMPLY.
NICE TO RECEIVE A COMPLIMENT IN A FOREIGN COUNTRY.
MY HAT
SHE IS COMPLIMENTING YOUR TASTE IN SMOKES!
JANE

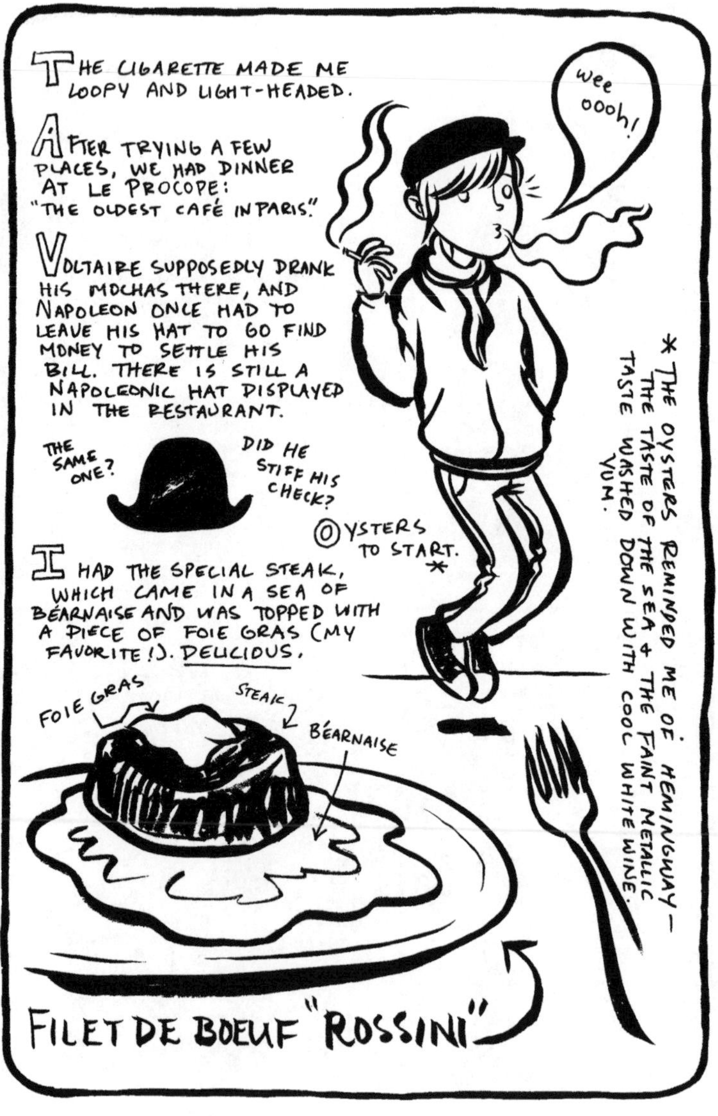
THE CIGARETTE MADE ME LOOPY AND LIGHT-HEADED.
wee oooh!
AFTER TRYING A FEW PLACES, WE HAD DINNER AT LE PROCOPE: "THE OLDEST CAFÉ IN PARIS."
VOLTAIRE SUPPOSEDLY DRANK HIS MOCHAS THERE, AND NAPOLEON ONCE HAD TO LEAVE HIS HAT TO GO FIND MONEY TO SETTLE HIS BILL. THERE IS STILL A NAPOLEONIC HAT DISPLAYED IN THE RESTAURANT.
THE SAME ONE?
DID HE STIFF HIS CHECK?
OYSTERS TO START. *
* THE OYSTERS REMINDED ME OF HEMINGWAY — THE TASTE OF THE SEA & THE FAINT METALLIC TASTE WASHED DOWN WITH COOL WHITE WINE. YUM.
I HAD THE SPECIAL STEAK, WHICH CAME IN A SEA OF BÉARNAISE AND WAS TOPPED WITH A PIECE OF FOIE GRAS (MY FAVORITE!). DELICIOUS.
FOIE GRAS
STEAK
BÉARNAISE
FILET DE BOEUF "ROSSINI"

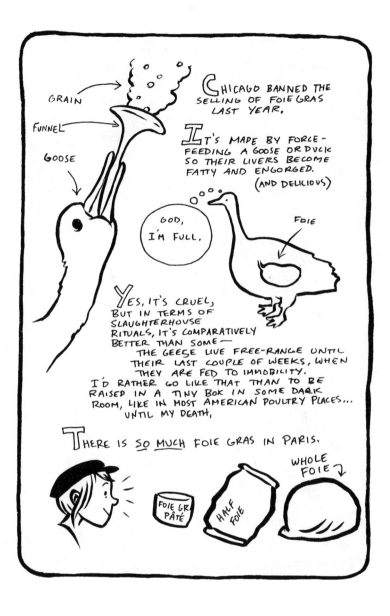

GRAIN

FUNNEL

GOOSE

CHICAGO BANNED THE SELLING OF FOIE GRAS LAST YEAR.

IT'S MADE BY FORCE-FEEDING A GOOSE OR DUCK SO THEIR LIVERS BECOME FATTY AND ENGORGED.

(AND DELICIOUS)

GOD, I'M FULL.

FOIE

YES, IT'S CRUEL, BUT IN TERMS OF SLAUGHTERHOUSE RITUALS, IT'S COMPARATIVELY BETTER THAN SOME—
THE GEESE LIVE FREE-RANGE UNTIL THEIR LAST COUPLE OF WEEKS, WHEN THEY ARE FED TO IMMOBILITY.
I'D RATHER GO LIKE THAT THAN TO BE RAISED IN A TINY BOX IN SOME DARK ROOM, LIKE IN MOST AMERICAN POULTRY PLACES... UNTIL MY DEATH,

THERE IS SO MUCH FOIE GRAS IN PARIS.

FOIE GR PÂTÉ

HALF FOIE

WHOLE FOIE

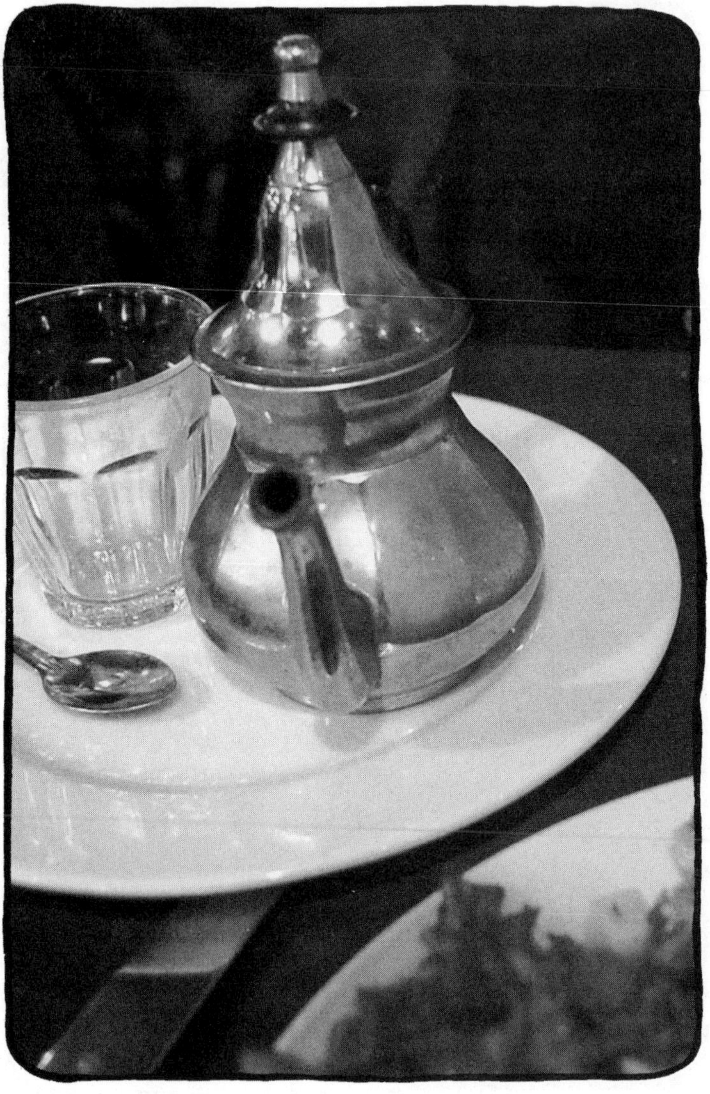

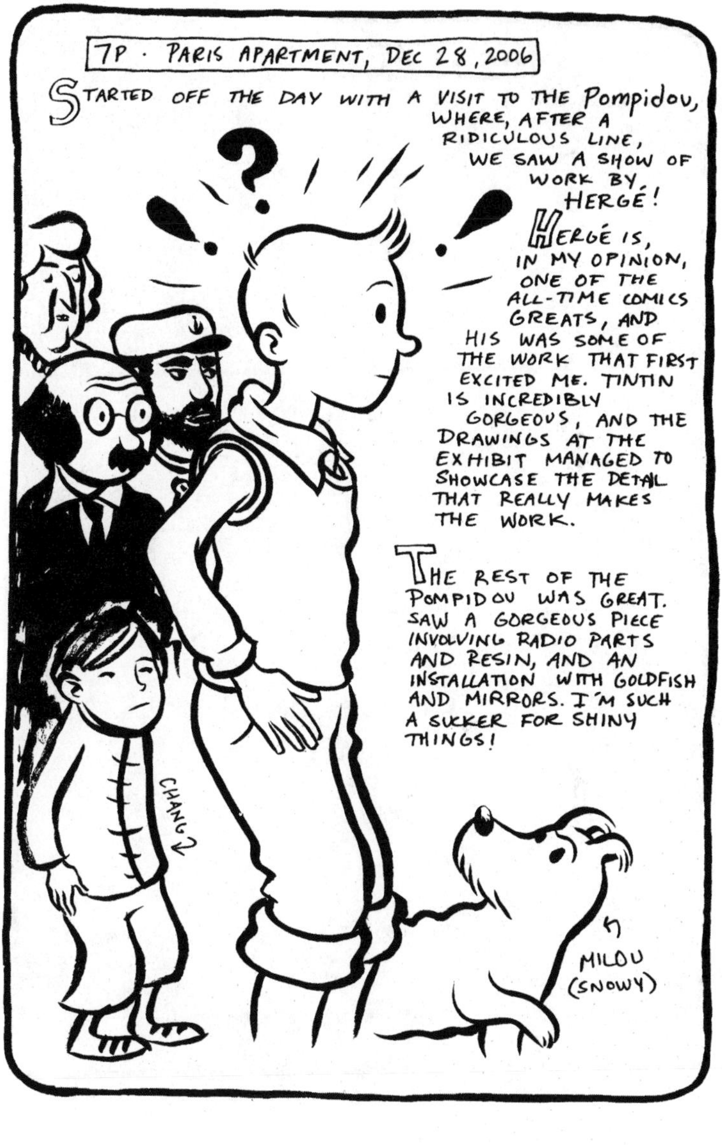
7P · PARIS APARTMENT, DEC 28, 2006
STARTED OFF THE DAY WITH A VISIT TO THE Pompidou, WHERE, AFTER A RIDICULOUS LINE, WE SAW A SHOW OF WORK BY HERGÉ!
HERGÉ IS, IN MY OPINION, ONE OF THE ALL-TIME COMICS GREATS, AND HIS WAS SOME OF THE WORK THAT FIRST EXCITED ME. TINTIN IS INCREDIBLY GORGEOUS, AND THE DRAWINGS AT THE EXHIBIT MANAGED TO SHOWCASE THE DETAIL THAT REALLY MAKES THE WORK.
THE REST OF THE POMPIDOU WAS GREAT. SAW A GORGEOUS PIECE INVOLVING RADIO PARTS AND RESIN, AND AN INSTALLATION WITH GOLDFISH AND MIRRORS. I'M SUCH A SUCKER FOR SHINY THINGS!
CHANG
MILOU (SNOWY)

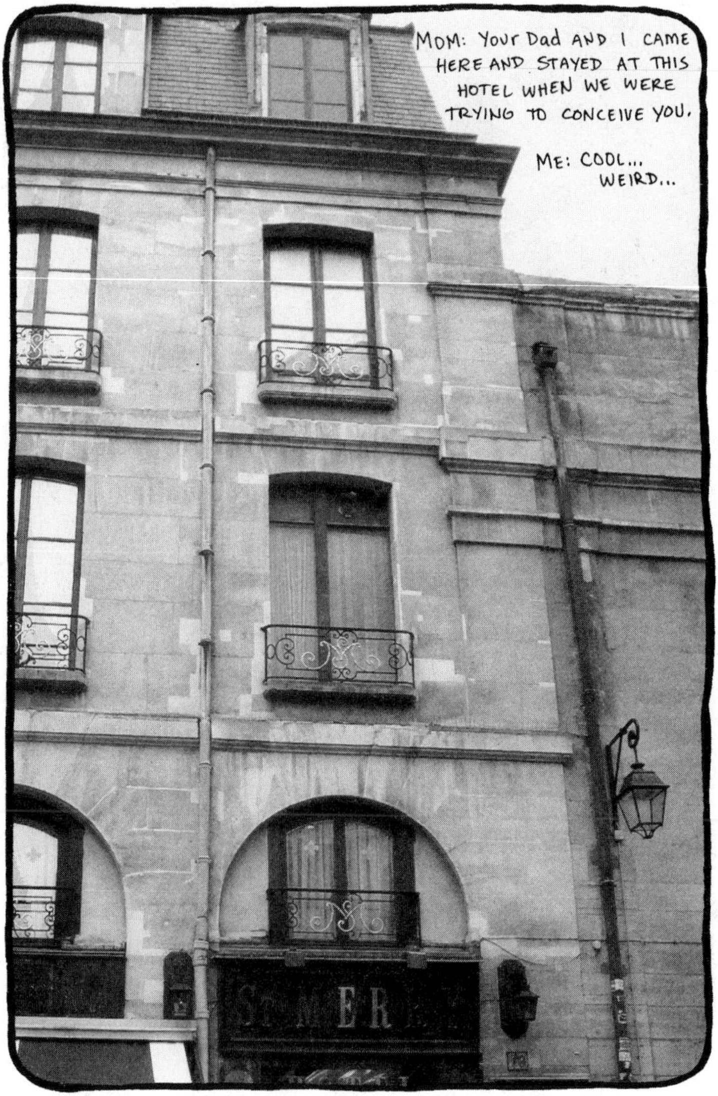
MOM: Your Dad AND I CAME HERE AND STAYED AT THIS HOTEL WHEN WE WERE TRYING TO CONCEIVE YOU.
ME: COOL... WEIRD...

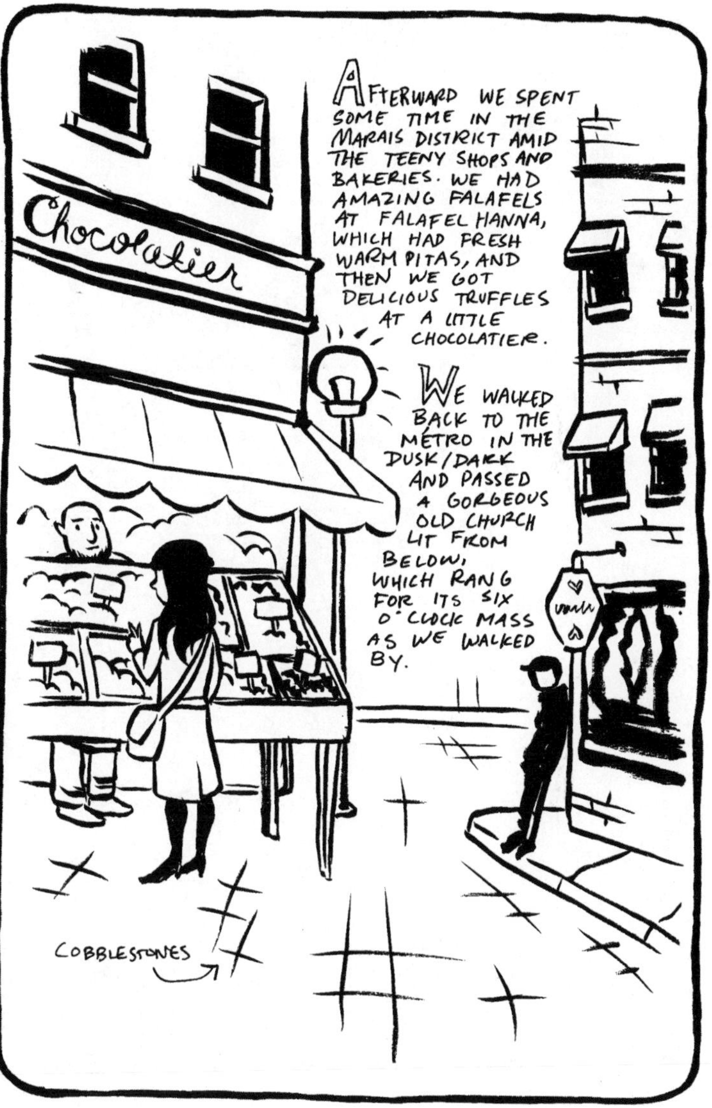
Chocolatier
AFTERWARD WE SPENT SOME TIME IN THE MARAIS DISTRICT AMID THE TEENY SHOPS AND BAKERIES. WE HAD AMAZING FALAFELS AT FALAFEL HANNA, WHICH HAD FRESH WARM PITAS, AND THEN WE GOT DELICIOUS TRUFFLES AT A LITTLE CHOCOLATIER.
WE WALKED BACK TO THE MÉTRO IN THE DUSK/DARK AND PASSED A GORGEOUS OLD CHURCH LIT FROM BELOW, WHICH RANG FOR ITS SIX O' CLOCK MASS AS WE WALKED BY.
COBBLESTONES

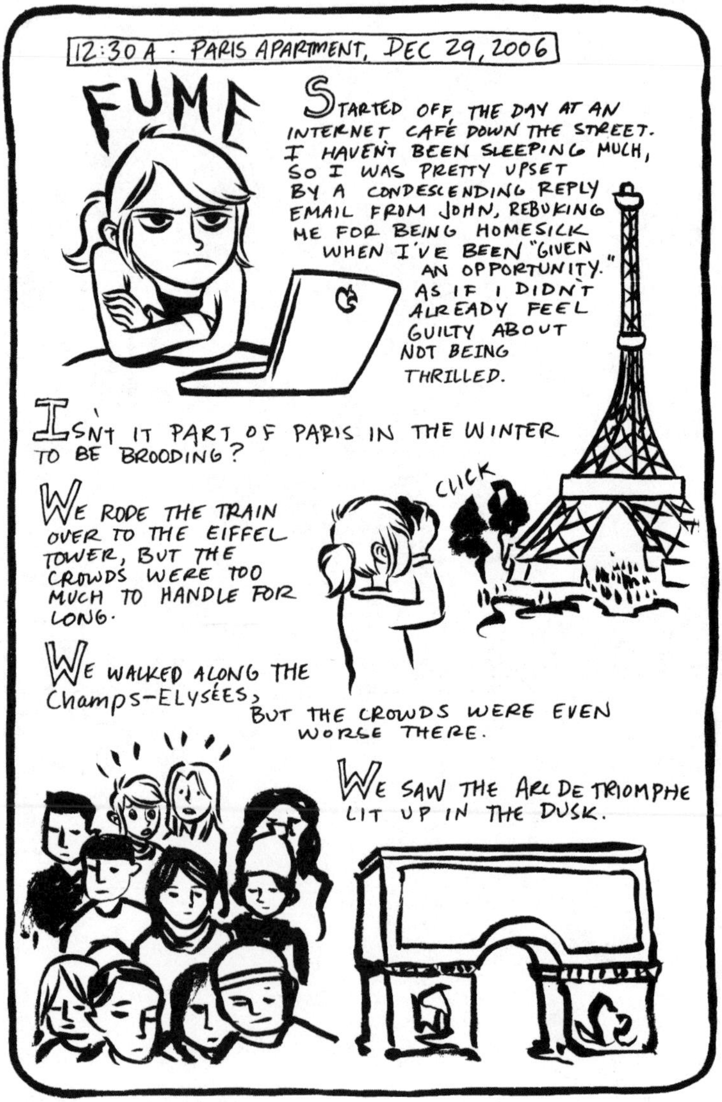
12:30A · PARIS APARTMENT, DEC 29, 2006
FUME
STARTED OFF THE DAY AT AN INTERNET CAFÉ DOWN THE STREET. I HAVEN'T BEEN SLEEPING MUCH, SO I WAS PRETTY UPSET BY A CONDESCENDING REPLY EMAIL FROM JOHN, REBUKING ME FOR BEING HOMESICK WHEN I'VE BEEN "GIVEN AN OPPORTUNITY." AS IF I DIDN'T ALREADY FEEL GUILTY ABOUT NOT BEING THRILLED.
ISN'T IT PART OF PARIS IN THE WINTER TO BE BROODING?
WE RODE THE TRAIN OVER TO THE EIFFEL TOWER, BUT THE CROWDS WERE TOO MUCH TO HANDLE FOR LONG.
CLICK
WE WALKED ALONG THE Champs-ELYSÉES, BUT THE CROWDS WERE EVEN WORSE THERE.
WE SAW THE ARC DE TRIOMPHE LIT UP IN THE DUSK.

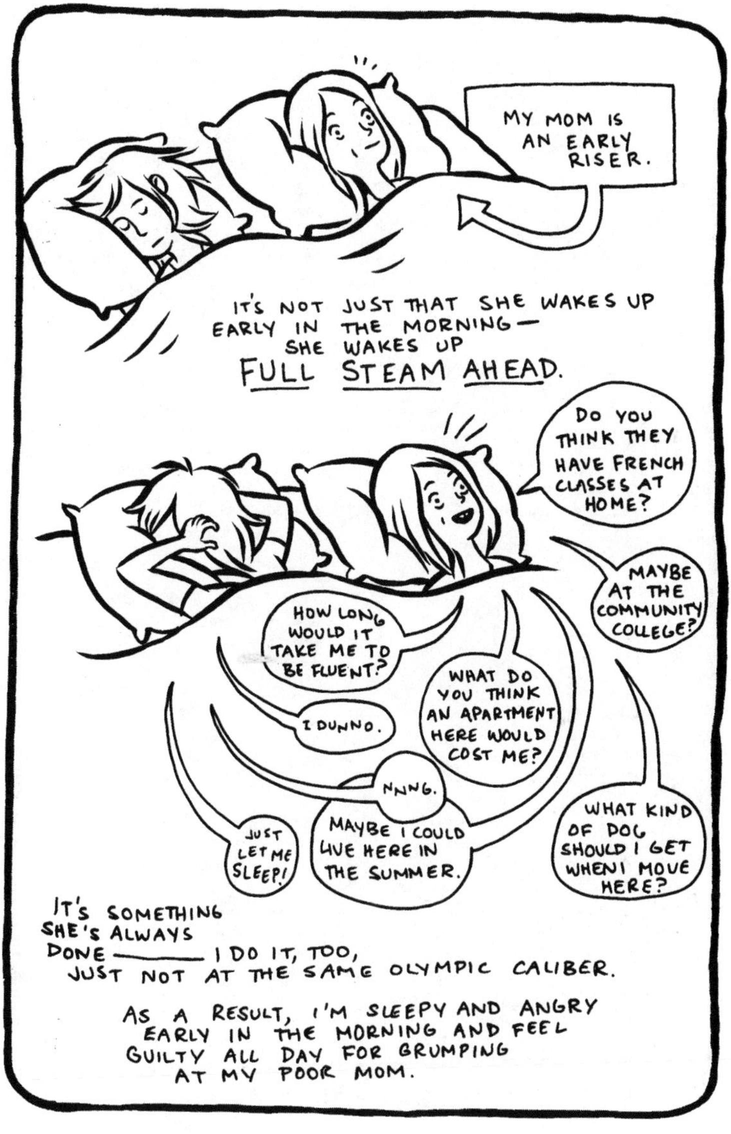
MY MOM IS AN EARLY RISER.
IT'S NOT JUST THAT SHE WAKES UP EARLY IN THE MORNING— SHE WAKES UP FULL STEAM AHEAD.
DO YOU THINK THEY HAVE FRENCH CLASSES AT HOME?
MAYBE AT THE COMMUNITY COLLEGE?
HOW LONG WOULD IT TAKE ME TO BE FLUENT?
I DUNNO.
WHAT DO YOU THINK AN APARTMENT HERE WOULD COST ME?
NNNG.
WHAT KIND OF DOG SHOULD I GET WHEN I MOVE HERE?
MAYBE I COULD LIVE HERE IN THE SUMMER.
JUST LET ME SLEEP!
IT'S SOMETHING SHE'S ALWAYS DONE — I DO IT, TOO, JUST NOT AT THE SAME OLYMPIC CALIBER.
AS A RESULT, I'M SLEEPY AND ANGRY EARLY IN THE MORNING AND FEEL GUILTY ALL DAY FOR GRUMPING AT MY POOR MOM.

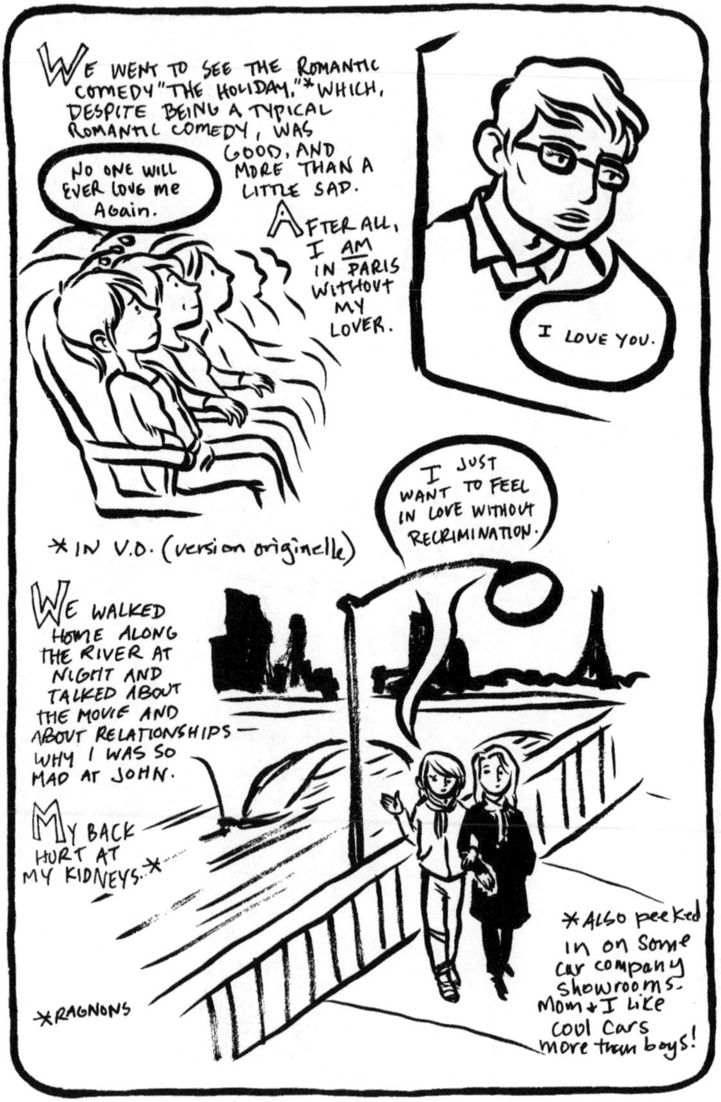
WE WENT TO SEE THE ROMANTIC COMEDY "THE HOLIDAY,"* WHICH, DESPITE BEING A TYPICAL ROMANTIC COMEDY, WAS GOOD, AND MORE THAN A LITTLE SAD.
NO ONE WILL EVER LOVE ME AGAIN.
AFTER ALL, I AM IN PARIS WITHOUT MY LOVER.
I LOVE YOU.
*IN V.O. (version originelle)
I JUST WANT TO FEEL IN LOVE WITHOUT RECRIMINATION.
WE WALKED HOME ALONG THE RIVER AT NIGHT AND TALKED ABOUT THE MOVIE AND ABOUT RELATIONSHIPS— WHY I WAS SO MAD AT JOHN.
MY BACK HURT AT MY KIDNEYS.*
*RAGNONS
*ALSO peeked in on some car company showrooms. Mom + I like cool cars more than boys!

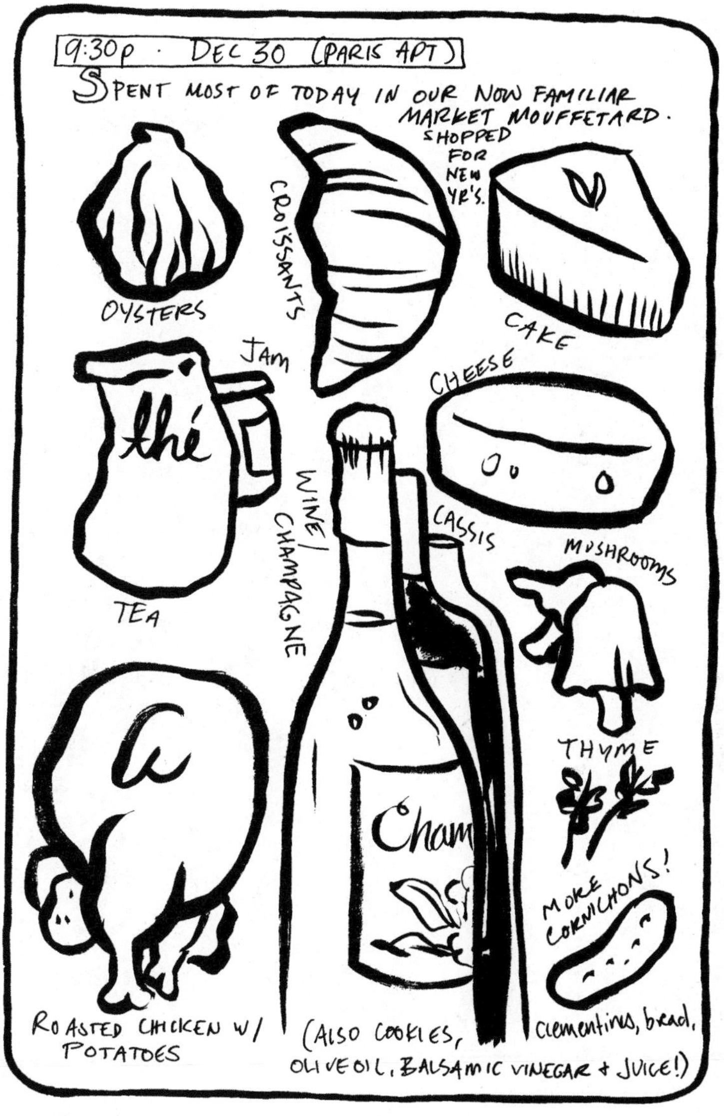
9:30p · DEC 30 (PARIS APT)
SPENT MOST OF TODAY IN OUR NOW FAMILIAR MARKET MOUFFETARD.
SHOPPED FOR NEW YR'S.
OYSTERS
CROISSANTS
CAKE
JAM
thé
TEA
CHEESE
WINE / CHAMPAGNE
CASSIS
MUSHROOMS
THYME
Cham
MORE CORNICHONS!
ROASTED CHICKEN W/ POTATOES
(ALSO COOKIES,
clementines, bread,
OLIVE OIL, BALSAMIC VINEGAR + JUICE!)

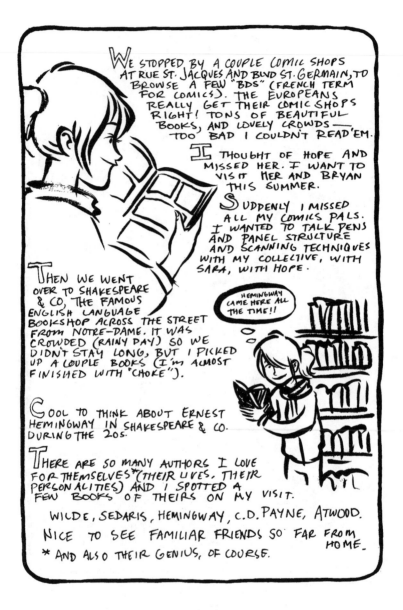

We STOPPED BY A COUPLE COMIC SHOPS AT RUE ST. JACQUES AND BLVD ST. GERMAIN, TO BROWSE A FEW "BDS" (FRENCH TERM FOR COMICS). THE EUROPEANS REALLY GET THEIR COMIC SHOPS RIGHT! TONS OF BEAUTIFUL BOOKS, AND LOVELY CROWDS— TOO BAD I COULDN'T READ 'EM.

I THOUGHT OF HOPE AND MISSED HER. I WANT TO VISIT HER AND BRYAN THIS SUMMER.

Suddenly I MISSED ALL MY COMICS PALS. I WANTED TO TALK PENS AND PANEL STRUCTURE AND SCANNING TECHNIQUES WITH MY COLLECTIVE, WITH SARA, WITH HOPE.

Then WE WENT OVER TO SHAKESPEARE & CO, THE FAMOUS ENGLISH LANGUAGE BOOKSHOP ACROSS THE STREET FROM NOTRE-DAME. IT WAS CROWDED (RAINY DAY) SO WE DIDN'T STAY LONG, BUT I PICKED UP A COUPLE BOOKS (I'm ALMOST FINISHED WITH "CHOKE").

HEMINGWAY CAME HERE ALL THE TIME!!

Cool TO THINK ABOUT ERNEST HEMINGWAY IN SHAKESPEARE & CO. DURING THE 20s.

There ARE SO MANY AUTHORS I LOVE FOR THEMSELVES* (THEIR LIVES, THEIR PERSONALITIES) AND I SPOTTED A FEW BOOKS OF THEIRS ON MY VISIT.

WILDE, SEDARIS, HEMINGWAY, C.D. PAYNE, ATWOOD.

NICE TO SEE FAMILIAR FRIENDS SO FAR FROM HOME.

* AND ALSO THEIR GENIUS, OF COURSE.

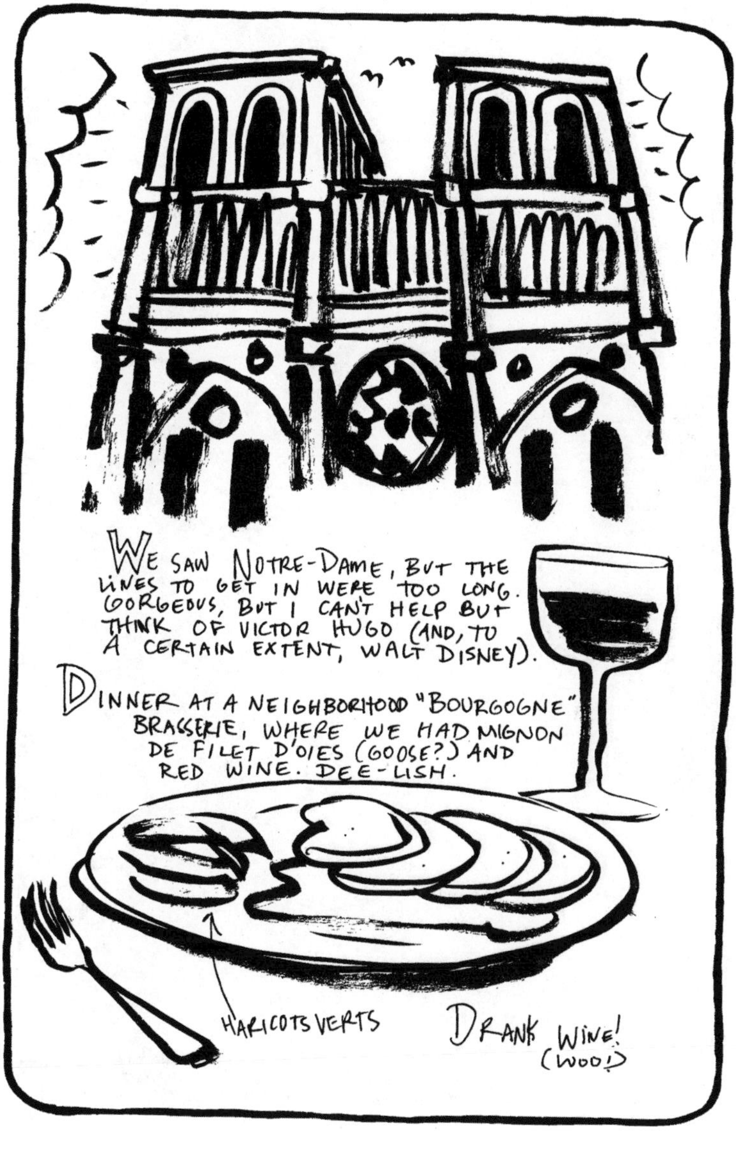

WE SAW NOTRE-DAME, BUT THE LINES TO GET IN WERE TOO LONG. GORGEOUS, BUT I CAN'T HELP BUT THINK OF VICTOR HUGO (AND, TO A CERTAIN EXTENT, WALT DISNEY).
DINNER AT A NEIGHBORHOOD "BOURGOGNE" BRASSERIE, WHERE WE HAD MIGNON DE FILET D'OIES (GOOSE?) AND RED WINE. DEE-LISH.
HARICOTS VERTS
DRANK WINE! (WOO!)

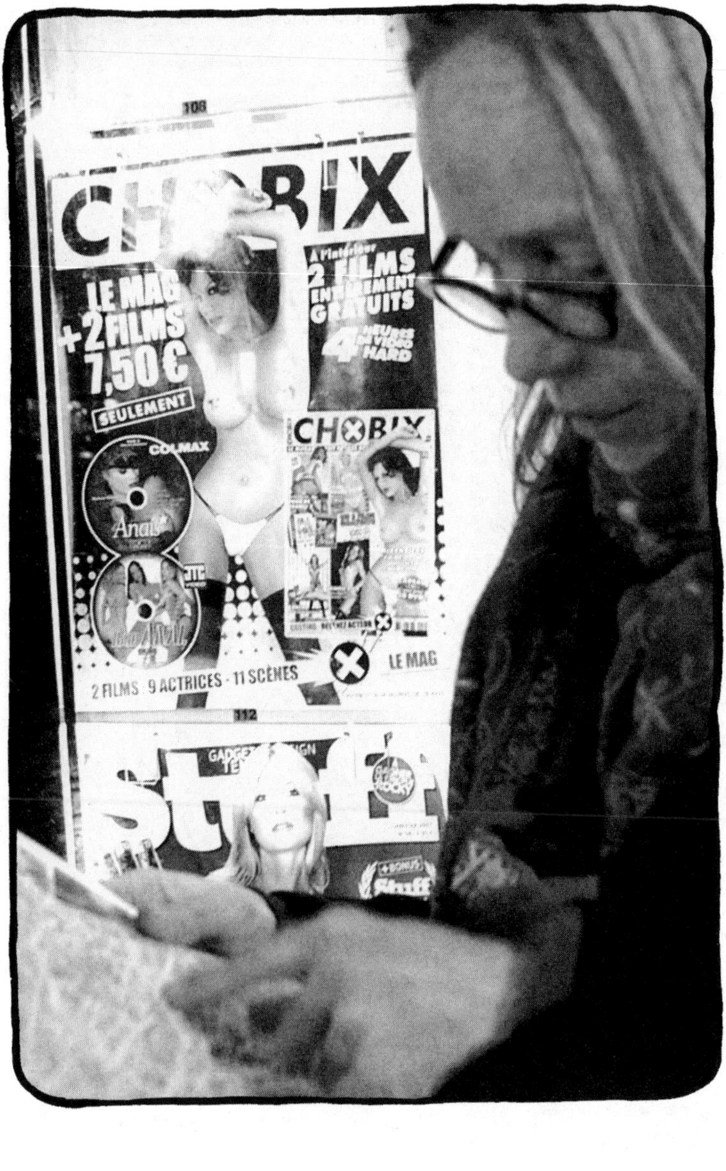
108
LE MAG
+2 FILMS
7,50 €
SEULEMENT
À l'intérieur
2 FILMS
ENTIÈREMENT
GRATUITS
4 HEURES DE VIDÉO HARD
COLMAX
Anaïs
CHOBIX
LE MAG
2 FILMS · 9 ACTRICES · 11 SCÈNES
112

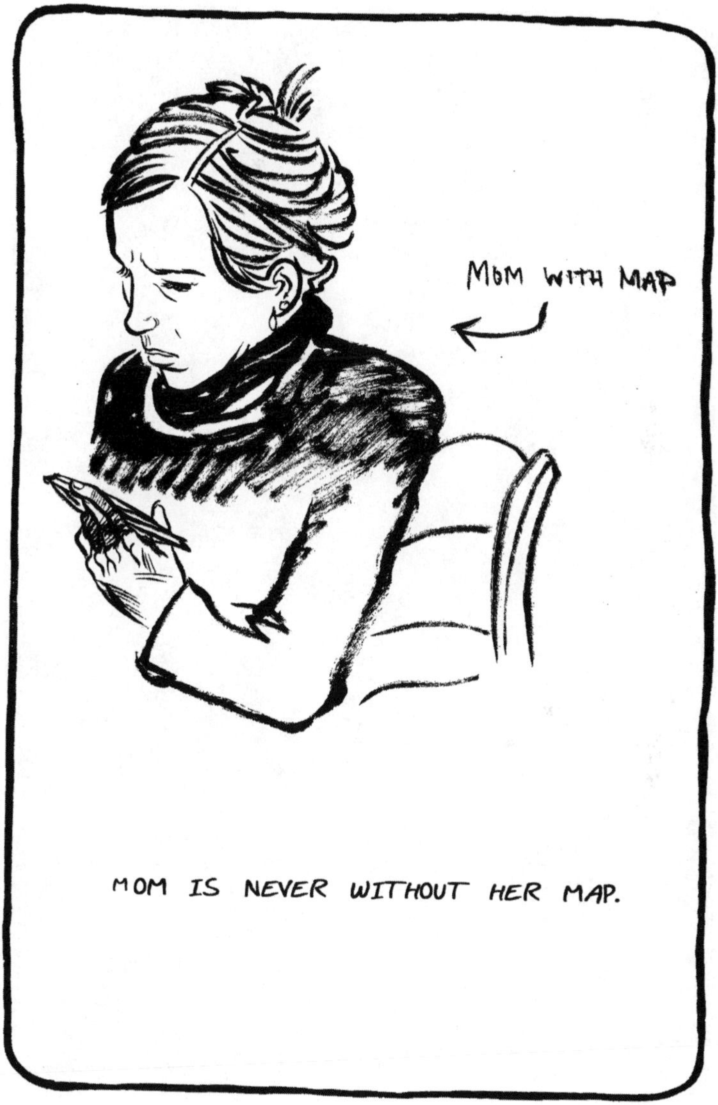
MOM WITH MAP
MOM IS NEVER WITHOUT HER MAP.

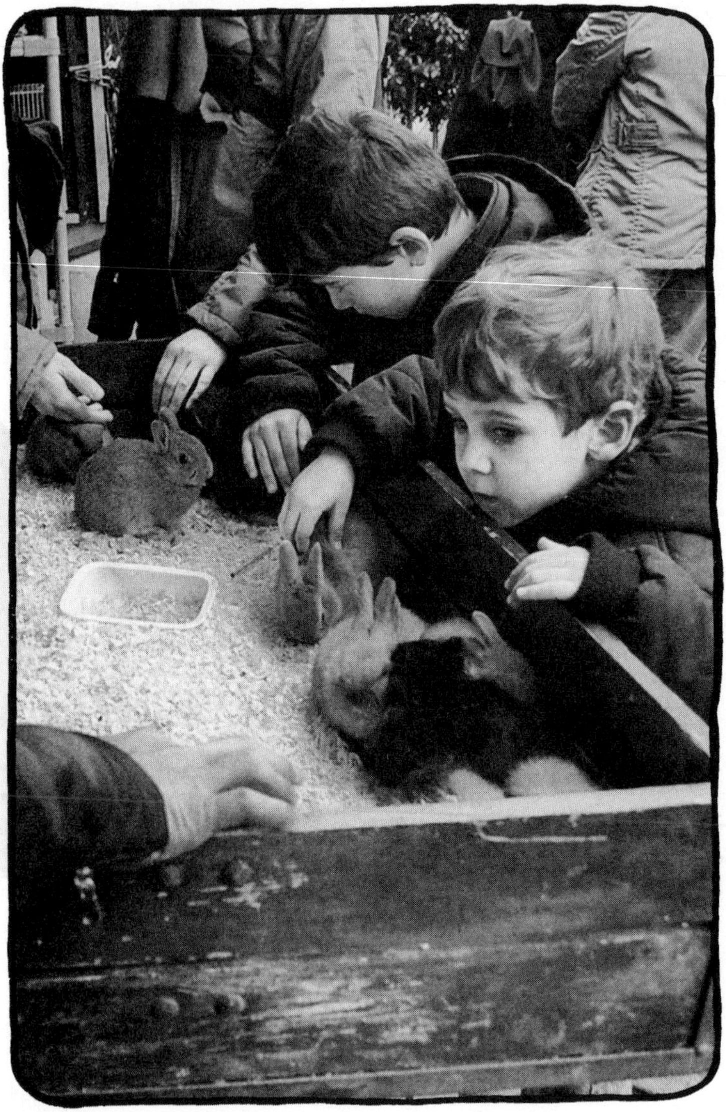

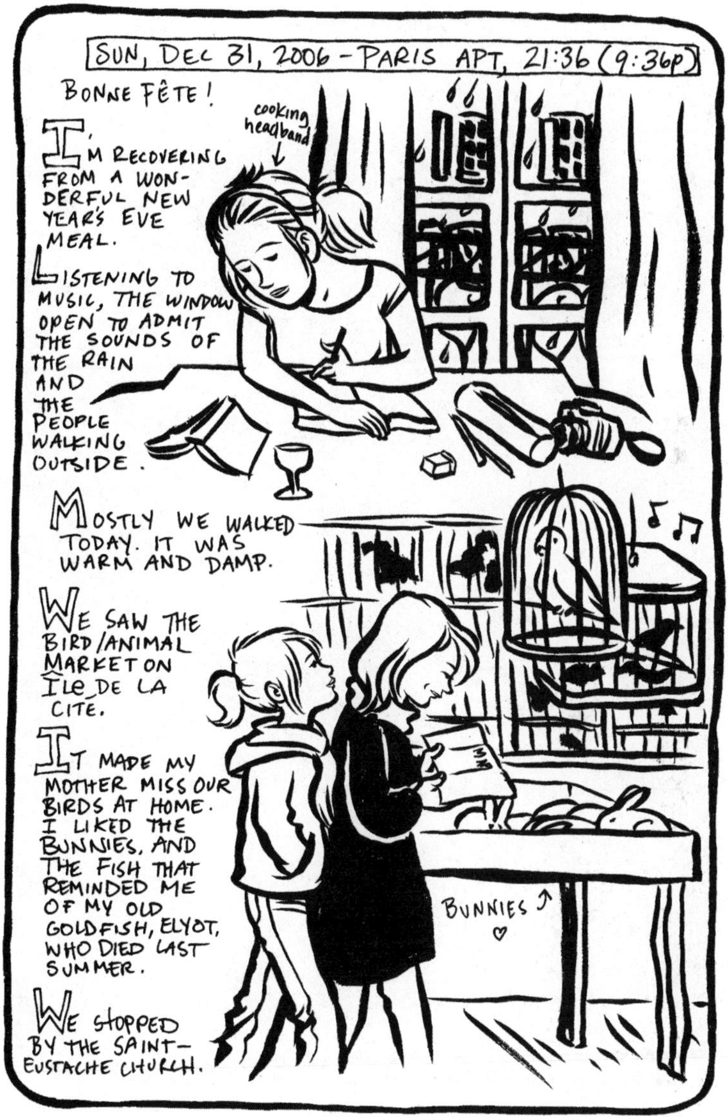
SUN, DEC 31, 2006 - PARIS APT, 21:36 (9:36p)
BONNE FÊTE!
cooking headband
I'M RECOVERING FROM A WONDERFUL NEW YEAR'S EVE MEAL.
LISTENING TO MUSIC, THE WINDOW OPEN TO ADMIT THE SOUNDS OF THE RAIN AND THE PEOPLE WALKING OUTSIDE.
MOSTLY WE WALKED TODAY. IT WAS WARM AND DAMP.
WE SAW THE BIRD/ANIMAL MARKET ON ÎLE DE LA CITÉ.
IT MADE MY MOTHER MISS OUR BIRDS AT HOME. I LIKED THE BUNNIES, AND THE FISH THAT REMINDED ME OF MY OLD GOLDFISH, ELYOT, WHO DIED LAST SUMMER.
BUNNIES ♡
WE STOPPED BY THE SAINT-EUSTACHE CHURCH.

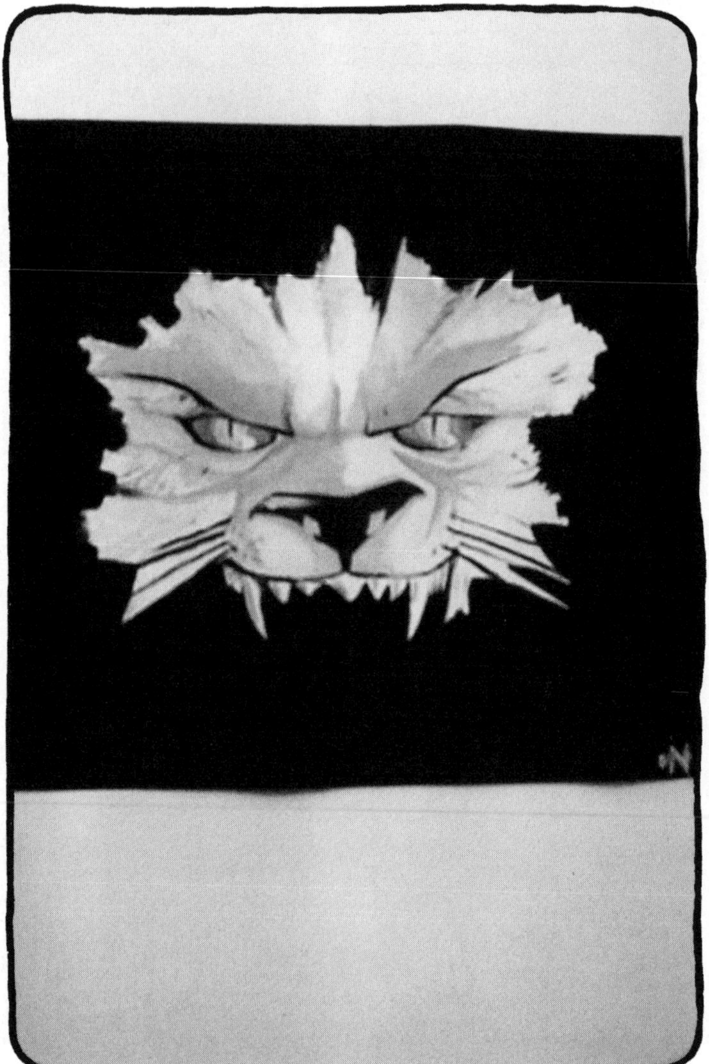

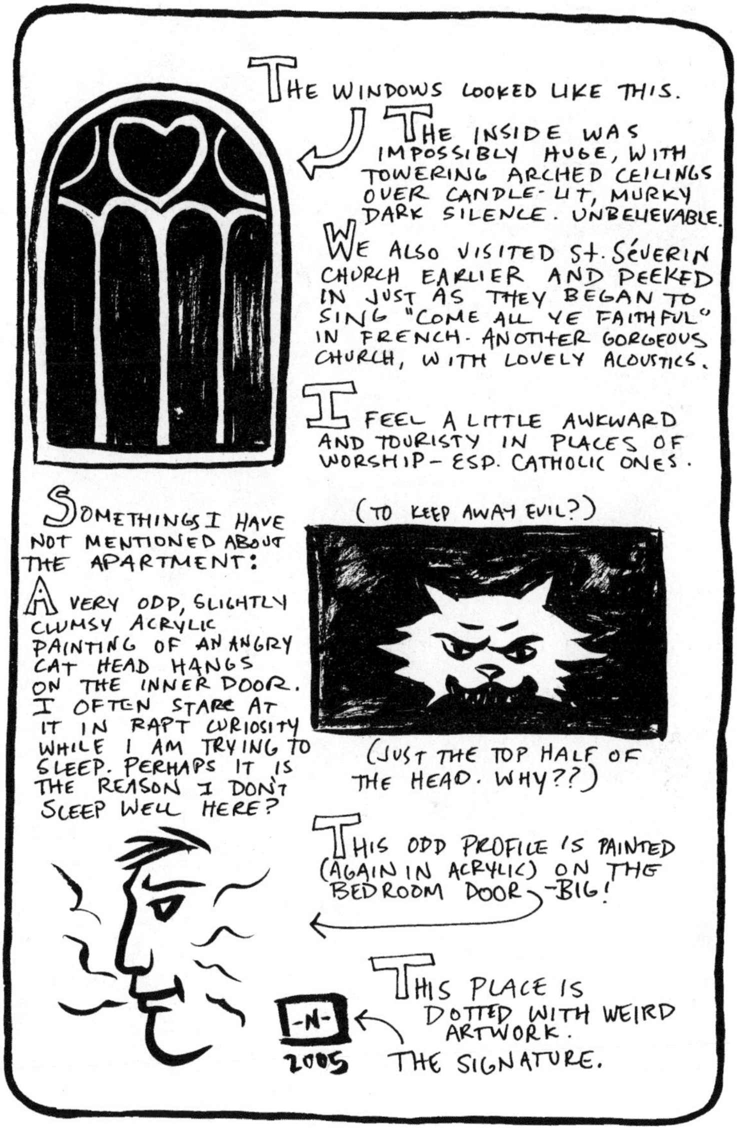
THE WINDOWS LOOKED LIKE THIS.
THE INSIDE WAS IMPOSSIBLY HUGE, WITH TOWERING ARCHED CEILINGS OVER CANDLE-LIT, MURKY DARK SILENCE. UNBELIEVABLE.
WE ALSO VISITED St. SÉVERIN CHURCH EARLIER AND PEEKED IN JUST AS THEY BEGAN TO SING "COME ALL YE FAITHFUL" IN FRENCH. ANOTHER GORGEOUS CHURCH, WITH LOVELY ACOUSTICS.
I FEEL A LITTLE AWKWARD AND TOURISTY IN PLACES OF WORSHIP – ESP. CATHOLIC ONES.
SOMETHINGS I HAVE NOT MENTIONED ABOUT THE APARTMENT:
A VERY ODD, SLIGHTLY CLUMSY ACRYLIC PAINTING OF AN ANGRY CAT HEAD HANGS ON THE INNER DOOR. I OFTEN STARE AT IT IN RAPT CURIOSITY WHILE I AM TRYING TO SLEEP. PERHAPS IT IS THE REASON I DON'T SLEEP WELL HERE?
(TO KEEP AWAY EVIL?)
(JUST THE TOP HALF OF THE HEAD. WHY??)
THIS ODD PROFILE IS PAINTED (AGAIN IN ACRYLIC) ON THE BEDROOM DOOR – BIG!
THIS PLACE IS DOTTED WITH WEIRD ARTWORK.
-N-
2005
THE SIGNATURE.

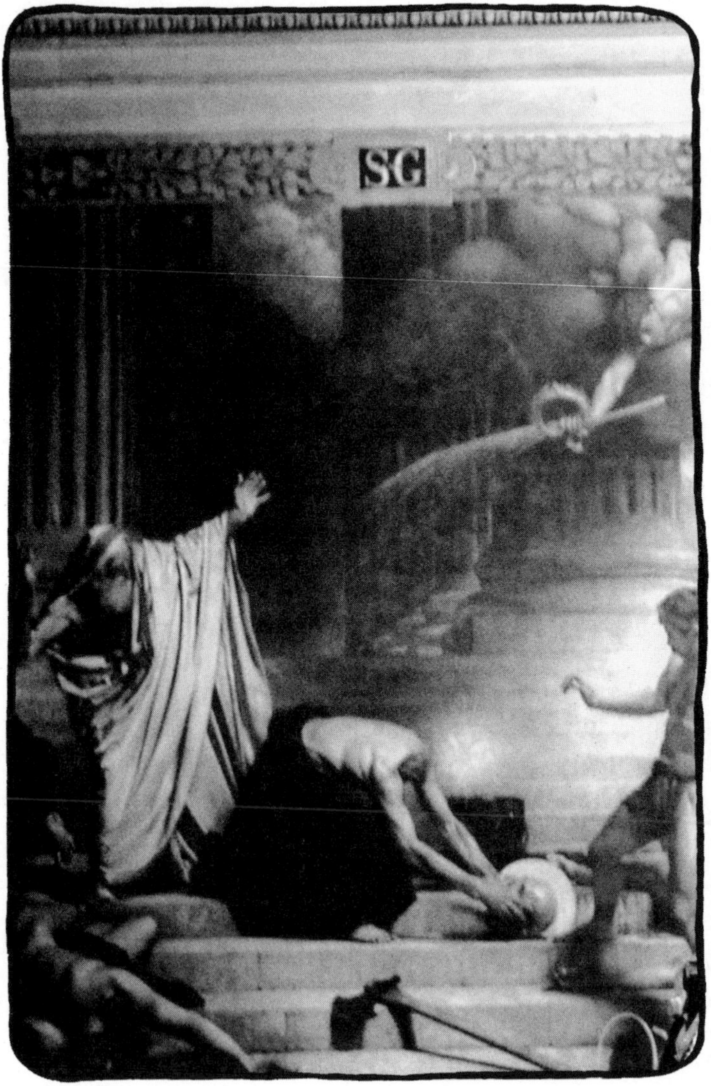
SG

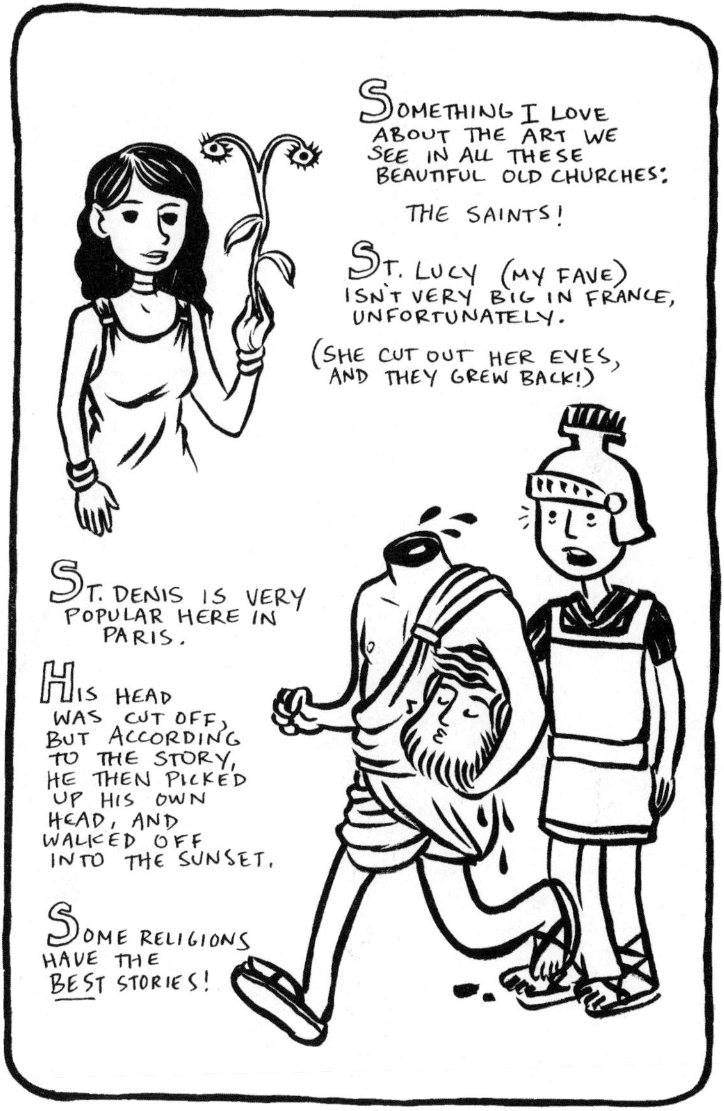
SOMETHING I LOVE ABOUT THE ART WE SEE IN ALL THESE BEAUTIFUL OLD CHURCHES:
THE SAINTS!
ST. LUCY (MY FAVE) ISN'T VERY BIG IN FRANCE, UNFORTUNATELY.
(SHE CUT OUT HER EYES, AND THEY GREW BACK!)
ST. DENIS IS VERY POPULAR HERE IN PARIS.
HIS HEAD WAS CUT OFF, BUT ACCORDING TO THE STORY, HE THEN PICKED UP HIS OWN HEAD, AND WALKED OFF INTO THE SUNSET.
SOME RELIGIONS HAVE THE BEST STORIES!

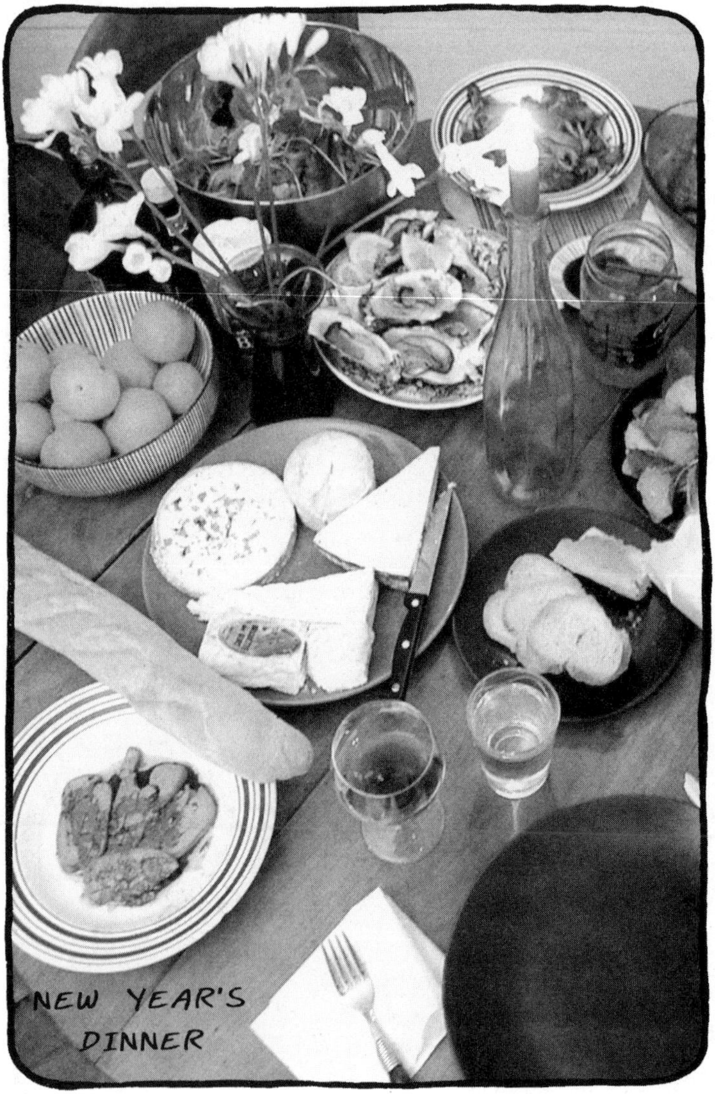
NEW YEAR'S
DINNER

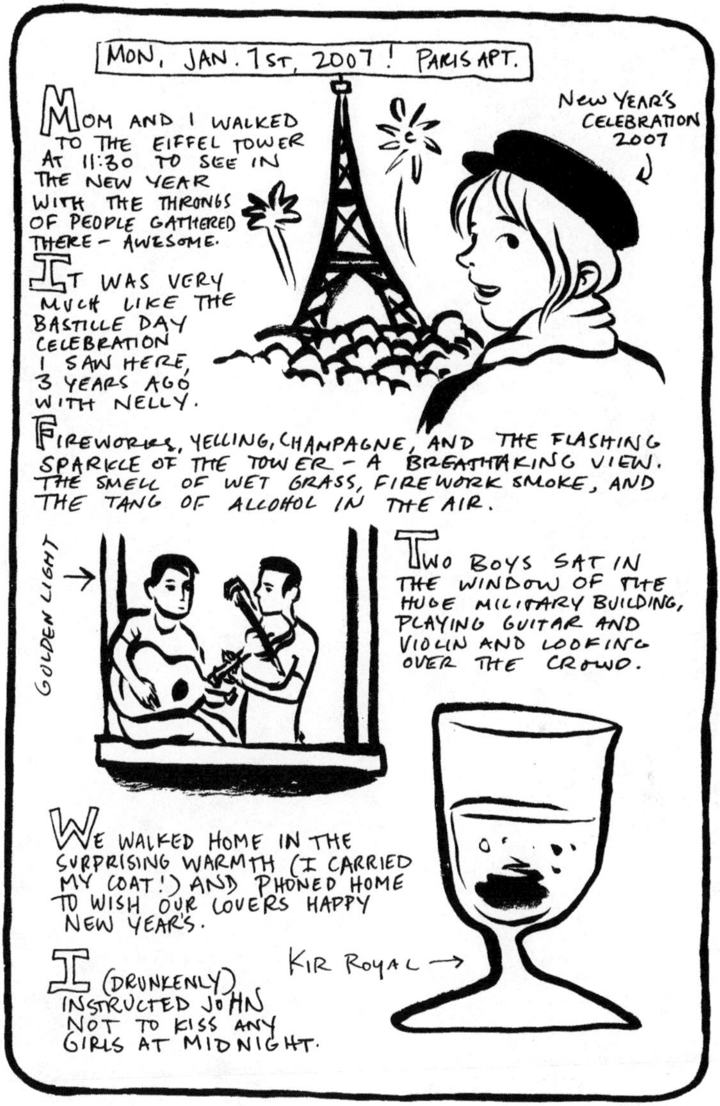
MON. JAN. 1ST, 2007! PARIS APT.
MOM AND I WALKED TO THE EIFFEL TOWER AT 11:30 TO SEE IN THE NEW YEAR WITH THE THRONGS OF PEOPLE GATHERED THERE - AWESOME.
IT WAS VERY MUCH LIKE THE BASTILLE DAY CELEBRATION I SAW HERE, 3 YEARS AGO WITH NELLY.
NEW YEAR'S CELEBRATION 2007
FIREWORKS, YELLING, CHAMPAGNE, AND THE FLASHING SPARKLE OF THE TOWER - A BREATHTAKING VIEW. THE SMELL OF WET GRASS, FIREWORK SMOKE, AND THE TANG OF ALCOHOL IN THE AIR.
GOLDEN LIGHT
TWO BOYS SAT IN THE WINDOW OF THE HUGE MILITARY BUILDING, PLAYING GUITAR AND VIOLIN AND LOOKING OVER THE CROWD.
WE WALKED HOME IN THE SURPRISING WARMTH (I CARRIED MY COAT!) AND PHONED HOME TO WISH OUR LOVERS HAPPY NEW YEAR'S.
KIR ROYAL
I (DRUNKENLY) INSTRUCTED JOHN NOT TO KISS ANY GIRLS AT MIDNIGHT.

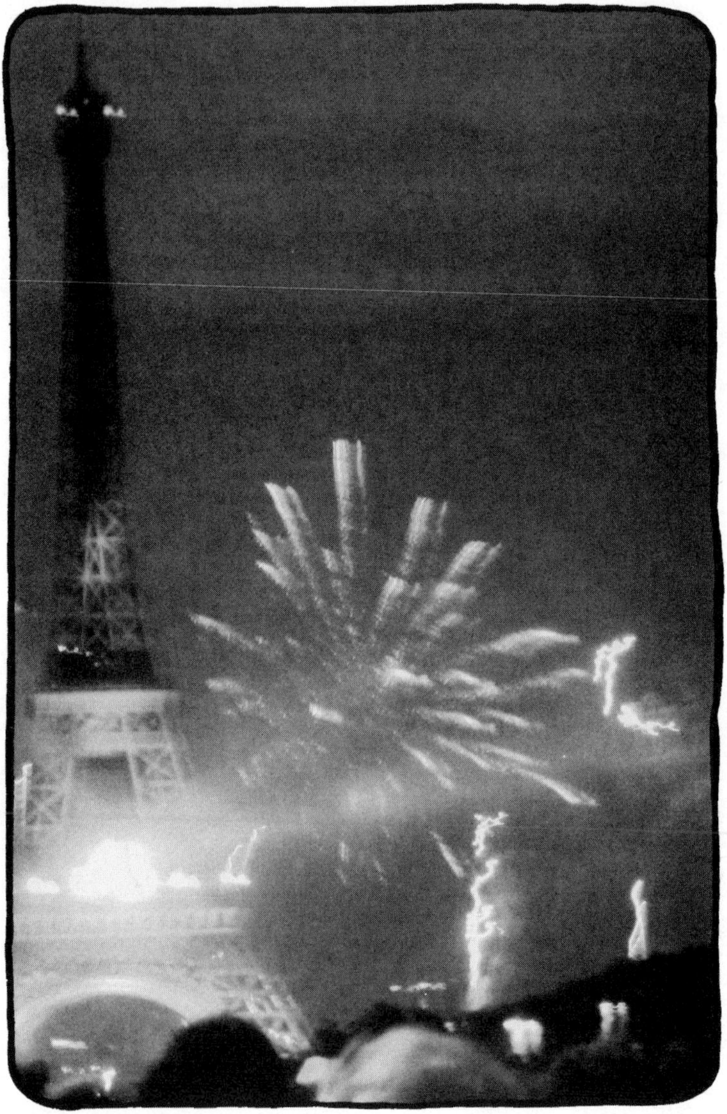

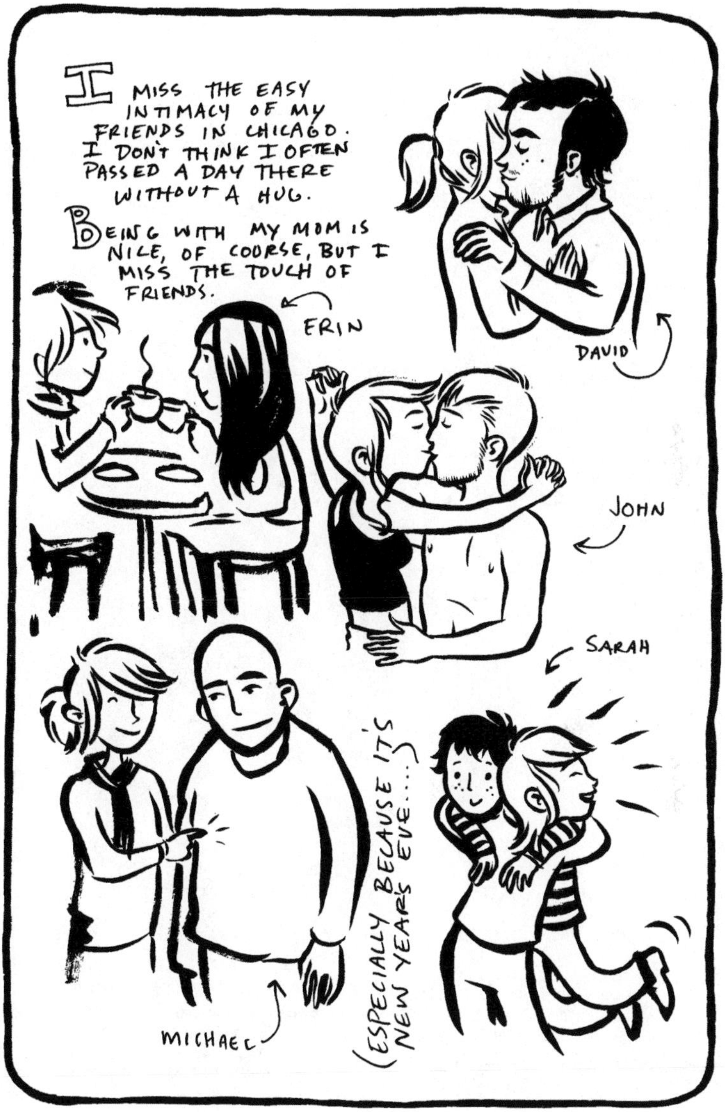
I MISS THE EASY INTIMACY OF MY FRIENDS IN CHICAGO. I DON'T THINK I OFTEN PASSED A DAY THERE WITHOUT A HUG.
BEING WITH MY MOM IS NICE, OF COURSE, BUT I MISS THE TOUCH OF FRIENDS.
ERIN
DAVID
JOHN
SARAH
MICHAEL
(ESPECIALLY BECAUSE IT'S NEW YEAR'S EVE....)

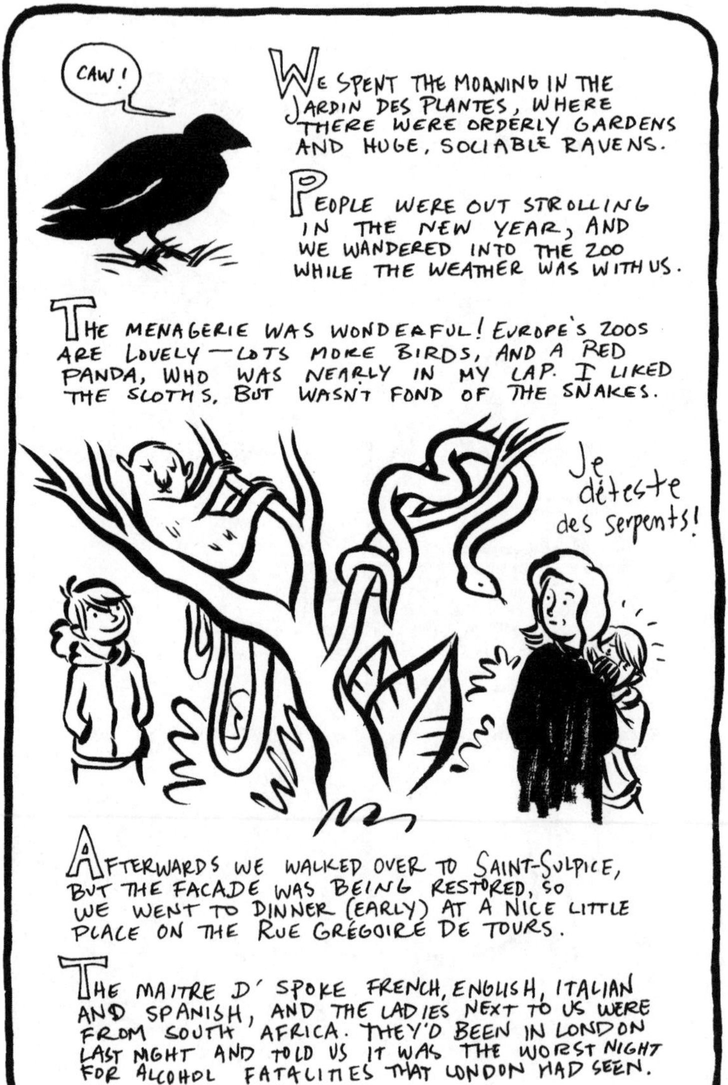
CAW!
WE SPENT THE MORNING IN THE JARDIN DES PLANTES, WHERE THERE WERE ORDERLY GARDENS AND HUGE, SOCIABLE RAVENS.
PEOPLE WERE OUT STROLLING IN THE NEW YEAR, AND WE WANDERED INTO THE ZOO WHILE THE WEATHER WAS WITH US.
THE MENAGERIE WAS WONDERFUL! EUROPE'S ZOOS ARE LOVELY—LOTS MORE BIRDS, AND A RED PANDA, WHO WAS NEARLY IN MY LAP. I LIKED THE SLOTHS, BUT WASN'T FOND OF THE SNAKES.
Je déteste des serpents!
AFTERWARDS WE WALKED OVER TO SAINT-SULPICE, BUT THE FACADE WAS BEING RESTORED, SO WE WENT TO DINNER (EARLY) AT A NICE LITTLE PLACE ON THE RUE GRÉGOIRE DE TOURS.
THE MAITRE D' SPOKE FRENCH, ENGLISH, ITALIAN AND SPANISH, AND THE LADIES NEXT TO US WERE FROM SOUTH AFRICA. THEY'D BEEN IN LONDON LAST NIGHT AND TOLD US IT WAS THE WORST NIGHT FOR ALCOHOL FATALITIES THAT LONDON HAD SEEN.

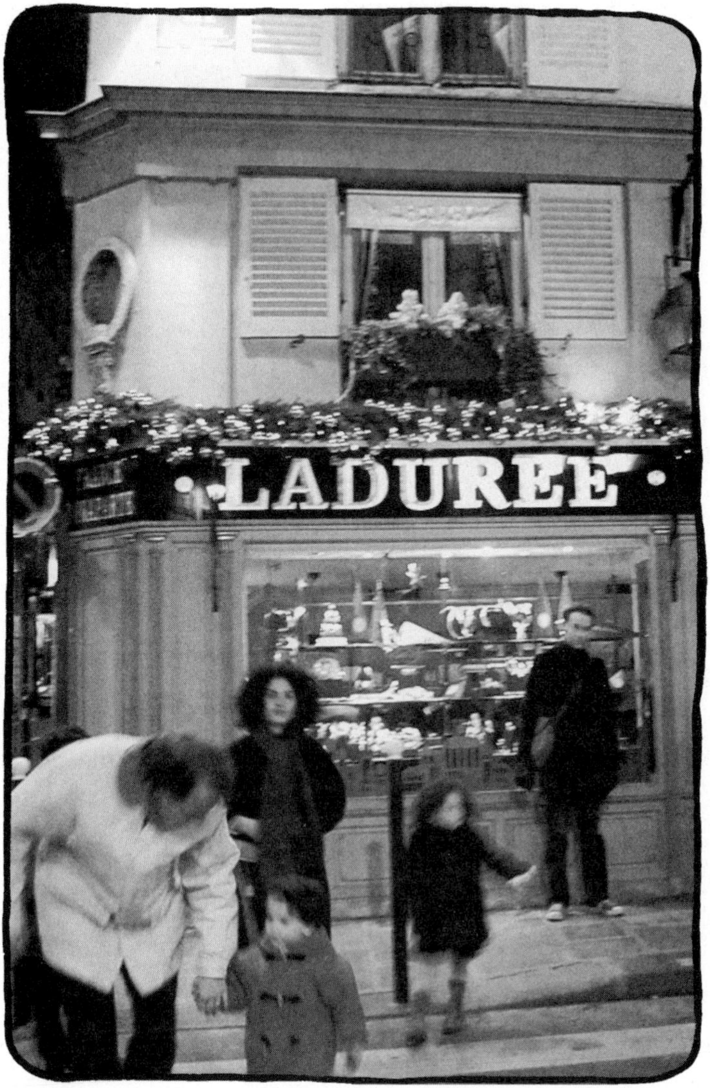
LADUREE

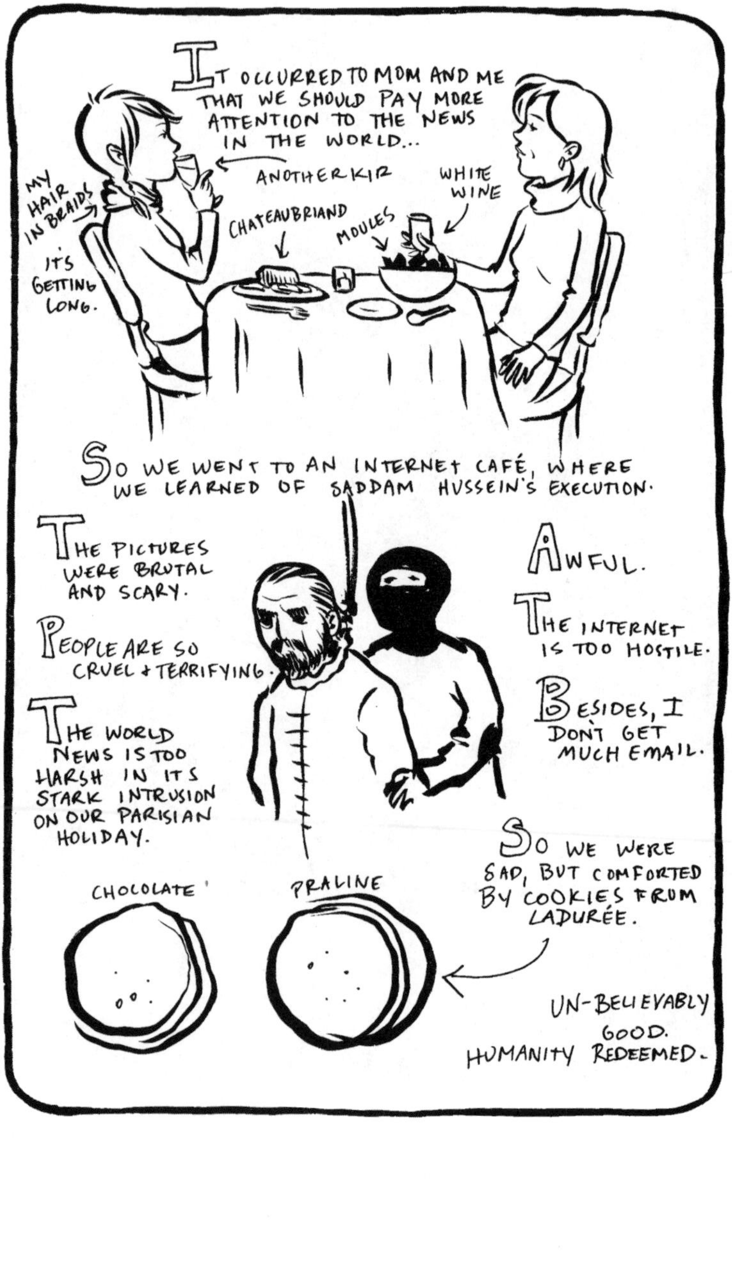

IT OCCURRED TO MOM AND ME THAT WE SHOULD PAY MORE ATTENTION TO THE NEWS IN THE WORLD...
ANOTHER KIR
WHITE WINE
MY HAIR IN BRAIDS
IT'S GETTING LONG.
CHATEAUBRIAND
MOULES
SO WE WENT TO AN INTERNET CAFÉ, WHERE WE LEARNED OF SADDAM HUSSEIN'S EXECUTION.
THE PICTURES WERE BRUTAL AND SCARY.
PEOPLE ARE SO CRUEL + TERRIFYING.
THE WORLD NEWS IS TOO HARSH IN ITS STARK INTRUSION ON OUR PARISIAN HOLIDAY.
AWFUL.
THE INTERNET IS TOO HOSTILE.
BESIDES, I DON'T GET MUCH EMAIL.
SO WE WERE SAD, BUT COMFORTED BY COOKIES FROM LADURÉE.
CHOCOLATE
PRALINE
UN-BELIEVABLY GOOD. HUMANITY REDEEMED.

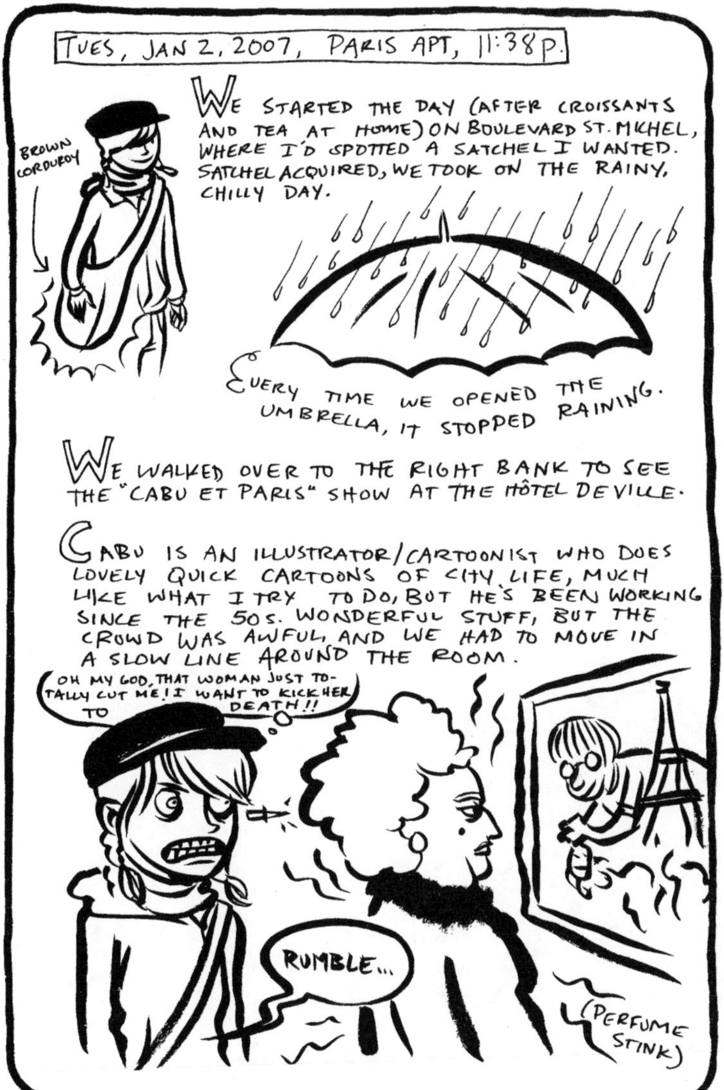
TUES, JAN 2, 2007, PARIS APT, 11:38p.
WE STARTED THE DAY (AFTER CROISSANTS AND TEA AT HOME) ON BOULEVARD ST. MICHEL, WHERE I'D SPOTTED A SATCHEL I WANTED. SATCHEL ACQUIRED, WE TOOK ON THE RAINY, CHILLY DAY.
BROWN CORDUROY
EVERY TIME WE OPENED THE UMBRELLA, IT STOPPED RAINING.
WE WALKED OVER TO THE RIGHT BANK TO SEE THE "CABU ET PARIS" SHOW AT THE HÔTEL DE VILLE.
CABU IS AN ILLUSTRATOR/CARTOONIST WHO DOES LOVELY QUICK CARTOONS OF CITY LIFE, MUCH LIKE WHAT I TRY TO DO, BUT HE'S BEEN WORKING SINCE THE 50s. WONDERFUL STUFF, BUT THE CROWD WAS AWFUL, AND WE HAD TO MOVE IN A SLOW LINE AROUND THE ROOM.
OH MY GOD, THAT WOMAN JUST TOTALLY CUT ME! I WANT TO KICK HER TO DEATH!!
RUMBLE...
(PERFUME STINK)

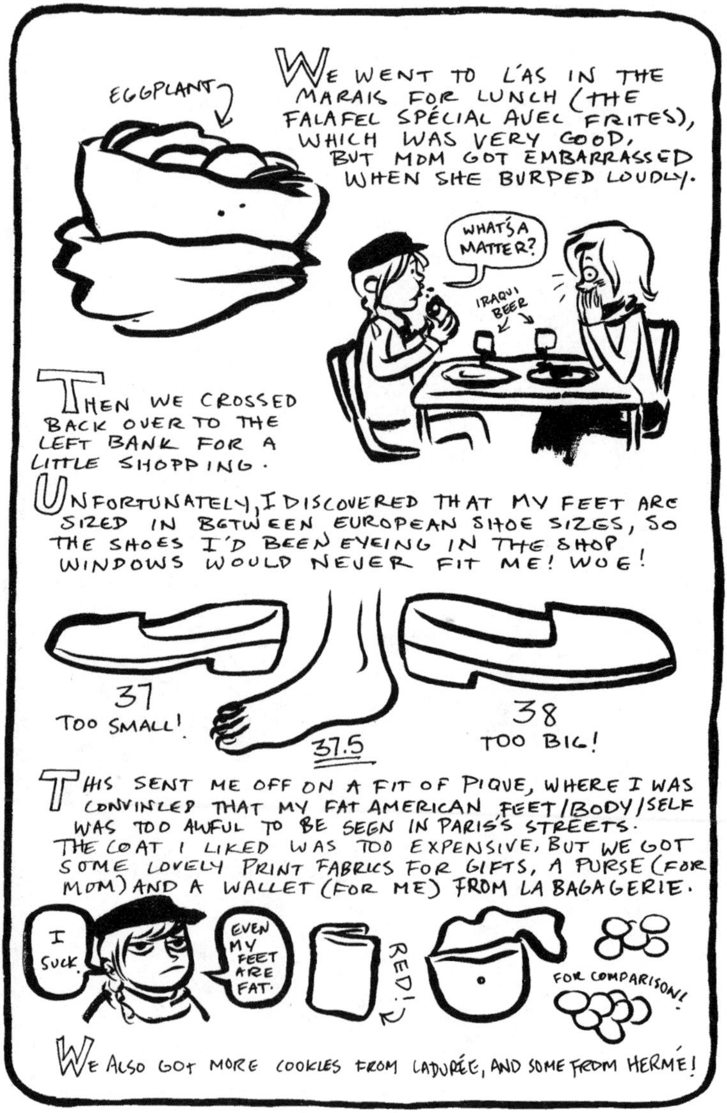
WE WENT TO L'AS IN THE MARAIS FOR LUNCH (THE FALAFEL SPÉCIAL AVEC FRITES), WHICH WAS VERY GOOD, BUT MOM GOT EMBARRASSED WHEN SHE BURPED LOUDLY.
EGGPLANT
WHAT'S A MATTER?
IRAQUI BEER
THEN WE CROSSED BACK OVER TO THE LEFT BANK FOR A LITTLE SHOPPING.
UNFORTUNATELY, I DISCOVERED THAT MY FEET ARE SIZED IN BETWEEN EUROPEAN SHOE SIZES, SO THE SHOES I'D BEEN EYEING IN THE SHOP WINDOWS WOULD NEVER FIT ME! WOE!
37
TOO SMALL!
37.5
38
TOO BIG!
THIS SENT ME OFF ON A FIT OF PIQUE, WHERE I WAS CONVINCED THAT MY FAT AMERICAN FEET/BODY/SELF WAS TOO AWFUL TO BE SEEN IN PARIS'S STREETS.
THE COAT I LIKED WAS TOO EXPENSIVE, BUT WE GOT SOME LOVELY PRINT FABRICS FOR GIFTS, A PURSE (FOR MOM) AND A WALLET (FOR ME) FROM LA BAGAGERIE.
I SUCK.
EVEN MY FEET ARE FAT.
RED!
FOR COMPARISON!
WE ALSO GOT MORE COOKIES FROM LADURÉE, AND SOME FROM HERMÉ!

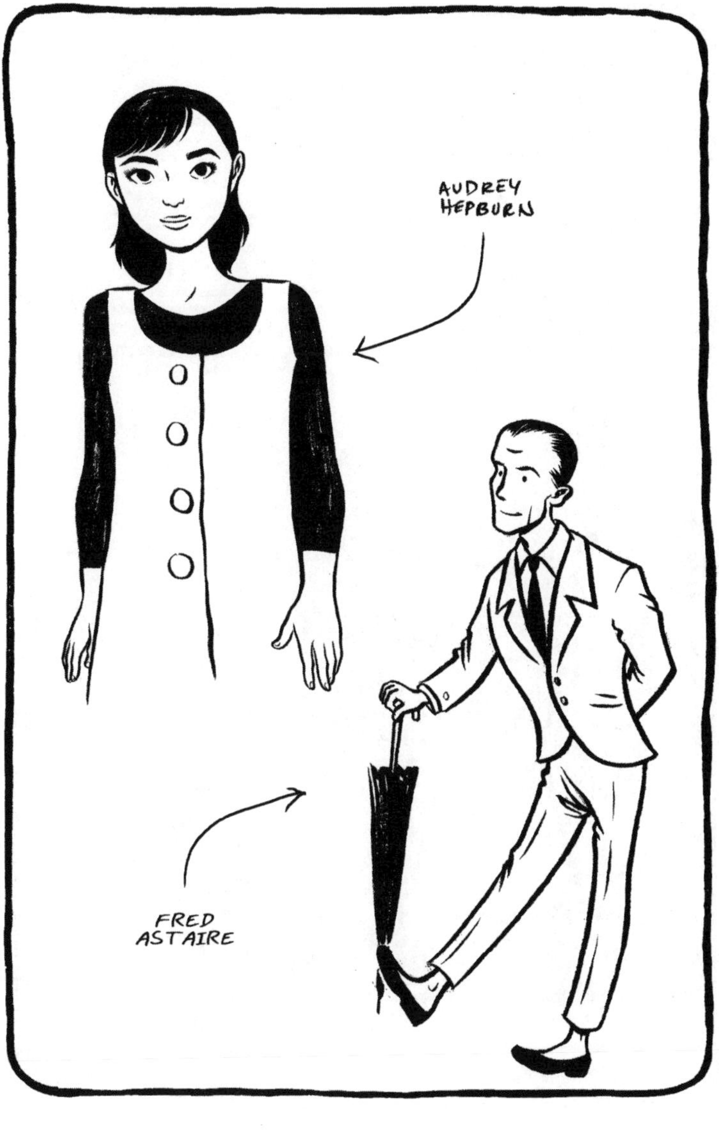
AUDREY
HEPBURN
FRED
ASTAIRE

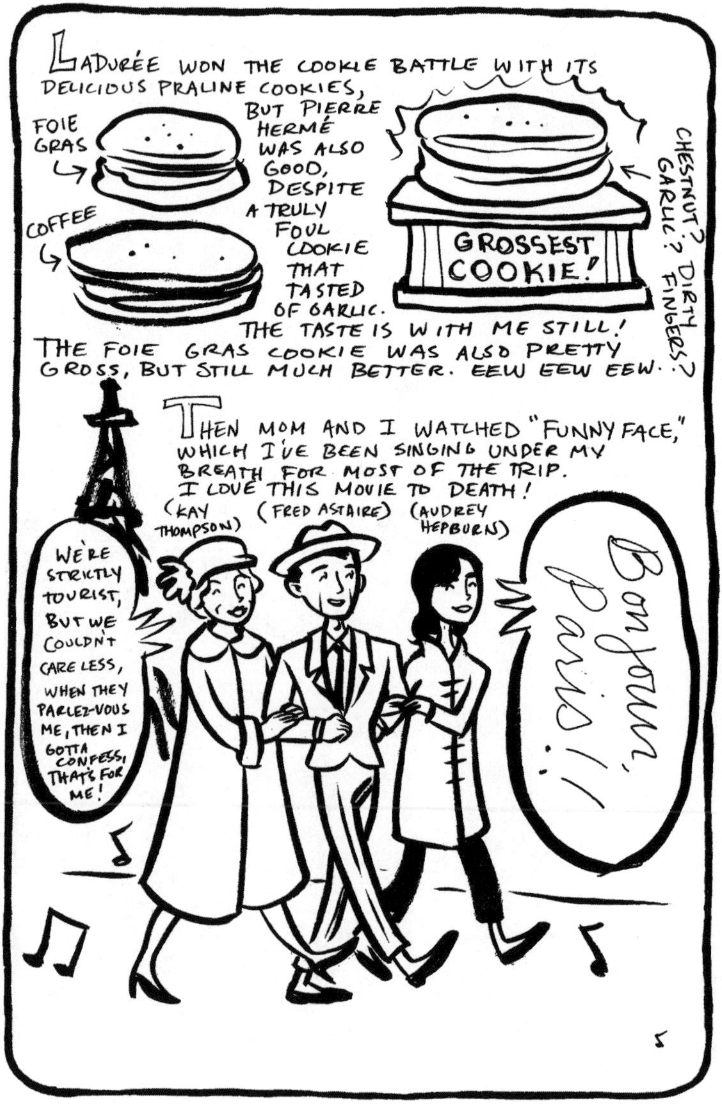
LADURÉE WON THE COOKIE BATTLE WITH ITS DELICIOUS PRALINE COOKIES,
BUT PIERRE HERMÉ WAS ALSO GOOD, DESPITE A TRULY FOUL COOKIE THAT TASTED OF GARLIC.
FOIE GRAS
COFFEE
GROSSEST COOKIE!
CHESTNUT? GARLIC? DIRTY FINGERS?
THE TASTE IS WITH ME STILL!
THE FOIE GRAS COOKIE WAS ALSO PRETTY GROSS, BUT STILL MUCH BETTER. EEW EEW EEW.
THEN MOM AND I WATCHED "FUNNY FACE," WHICH I'VE BEEN SINGING UNDER MY BREATH FOR MOST OF THE TRIP. I LOVE THIS MOVIE TO DEATH!
(KAY THOMPSON)
(FRED ASTAIRE)
(AUDREY HEPBURN)
WE'RE STRICTLY TOURIST, BUT WE COULDN'T CARE LESS, WHEN THEY PARLEZ-VOUS ME, THEN I GOTTA CONFESS, THAT'S FOR ME!
Bonjour, Paris!!

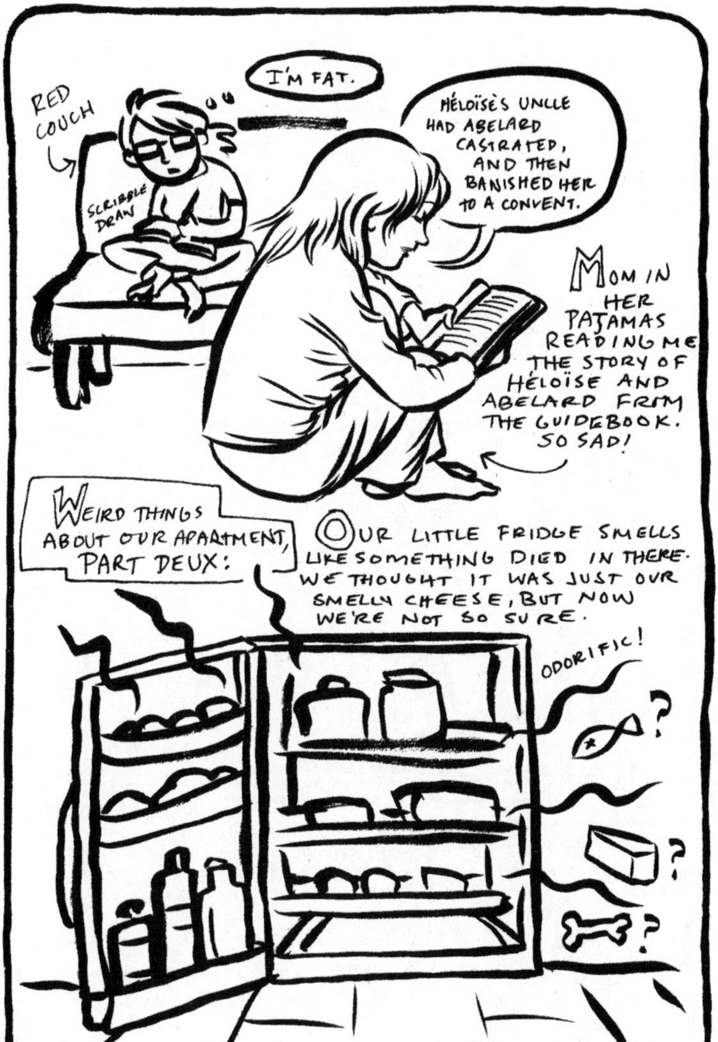
I'M FAT.
RED COUCH
SCRIBBLE DRAW
HÉLOÏSE'S UNCLE HAD ABELARD CASTRATED, AND THEN BANISHED HER TO A CONVENT.
MOM IN HER PAJAMAS READING ME THE STORY OF HÉLOÏSE AND ABELARD FROM THE GUIDEBOOK. SO SAD!
WEIRD THINGS ABOUT OUR APARTMENT, PART DEUX:
OUR LITTLE FRIDGE SMELLS LIKE SOMETHING DIED IN THERE. WE THOUGHT IT WAS JUST OUR SMELLY CHEESE, BUT NOW WE'RE NOT SO SURE.
ODORIFIC!
?
?
?

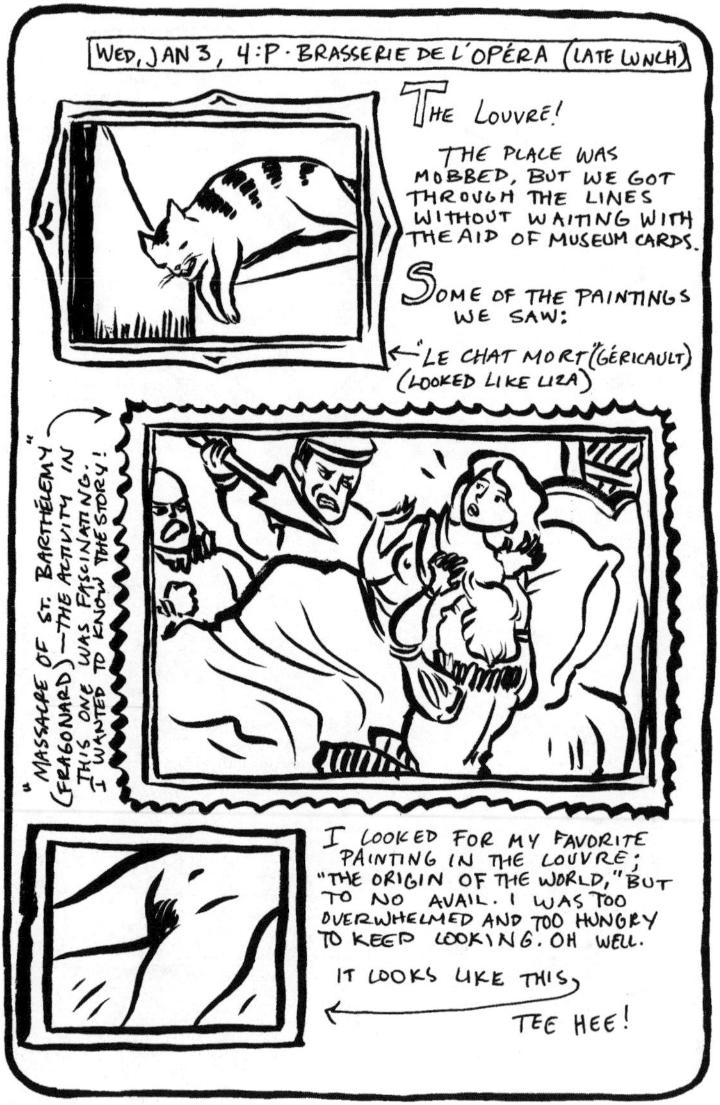
WED, JAN 3, 4:P · BRASSERIE DE L'OPÉRA (LATE LUNCH)
THE LOUVRE!
THE PLACE WAS MOBBED, BUT WE GOT THROUGH THE LINES WITHOUT WAITING WITH THE AID OF MUSEUM CARDS.
SOME OF THE PAINTINGS WE SAW:
"LE CHAT MORT" (GÉRICAULT) (LOOKED LIKE LIZA)
"MASSACRE OF ST. BARTHÉLEMY" (FRAGONARD)—THE ACTIVITY IN THIS ONE WAS FASCINATING. I WANTED TO KNOW THE STORY!
I LOOKED FOR MY FAVORITE PAINTING IN THE LOUVRE; "THE ORIGIN OF THE WORLD," BUT TO NO AVAIL. I WAS TOO OVERWHELMED AND TOO HUNGRY TO KEEP LOOKING. OH WELL.
IT LOOKS LIKE THIS,
TEE HEE!

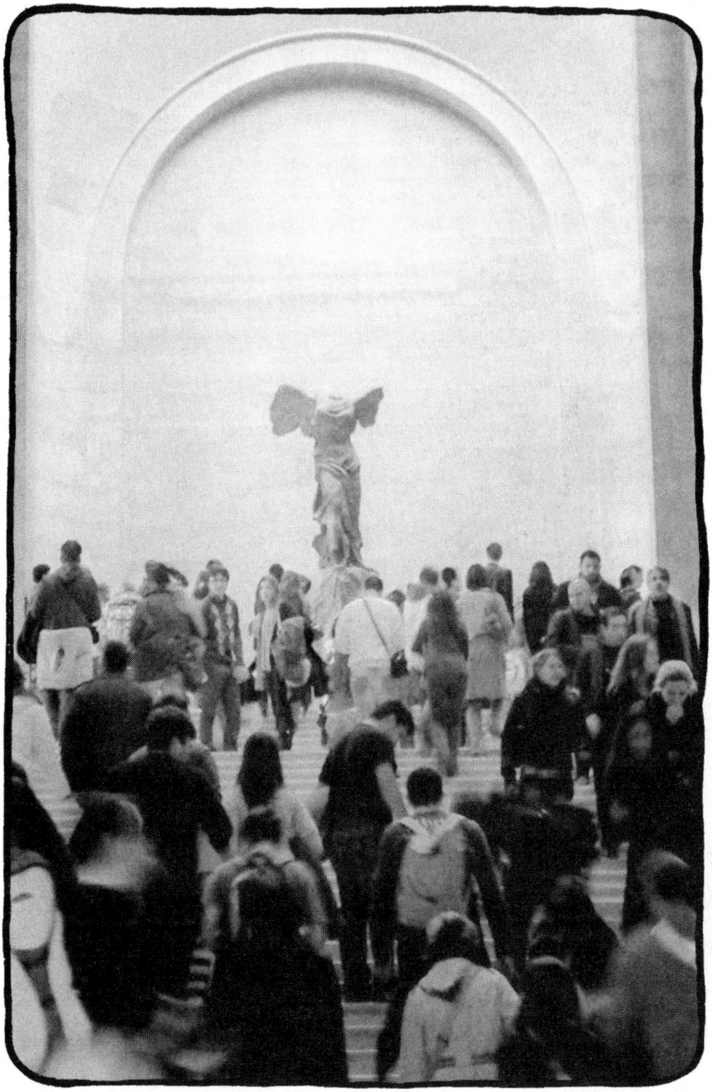

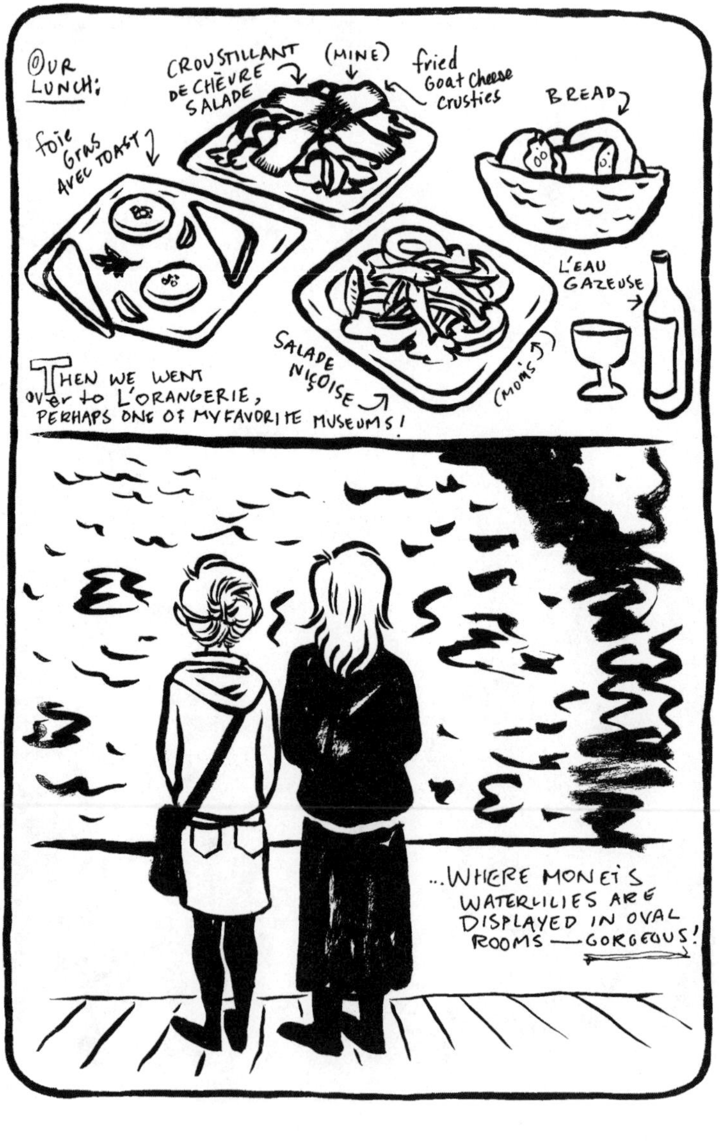

OUR LUNCH:
CROUSTILLANT DE CHÈVRE SALADE
(MINE)
fried Goat Cheese Crusties
BREAD
foie Gras AVEC TOAST
L'EAU GAZEUSE
SALADE NIÇOISE
(MOM'S)
THEN WE WENT over to L'ORANGERIE, PERHAPS ONE OF MY FAVORITE MUSEUMS!
...WHERE MONET'S WATERLILIES ARE DISPLAYED IN OVAL ROOMS—GORGEOUS!

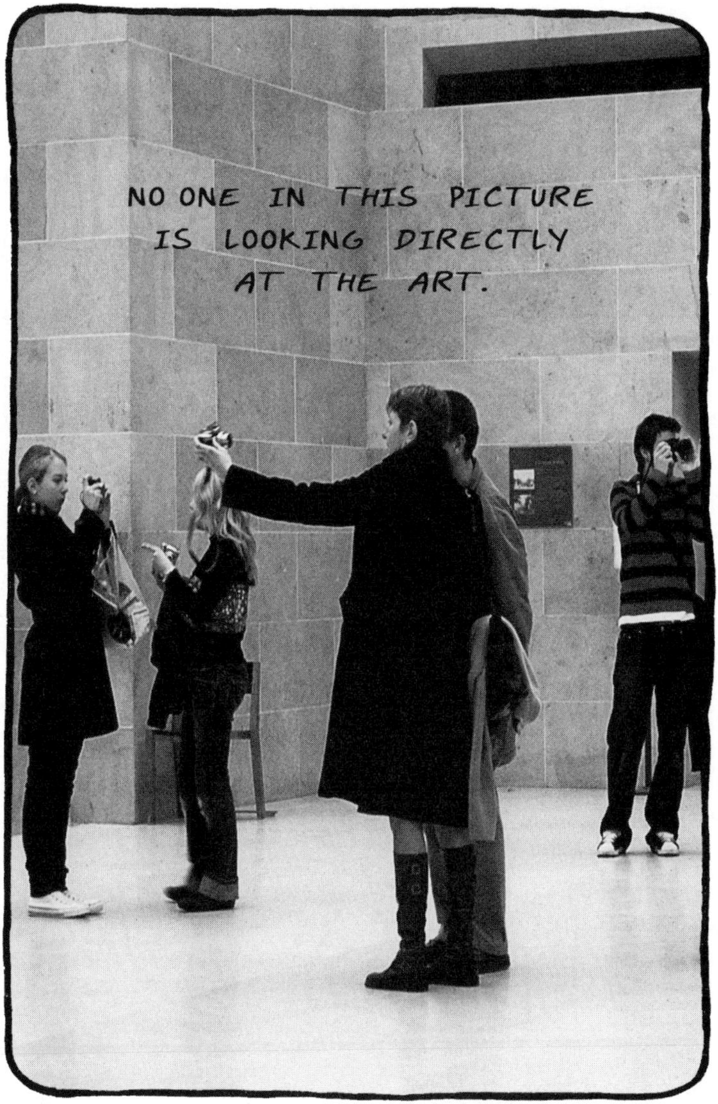
NO ONE IN THIS PICTURE
IS LOOKING DIRECTLY
AT THE ART.

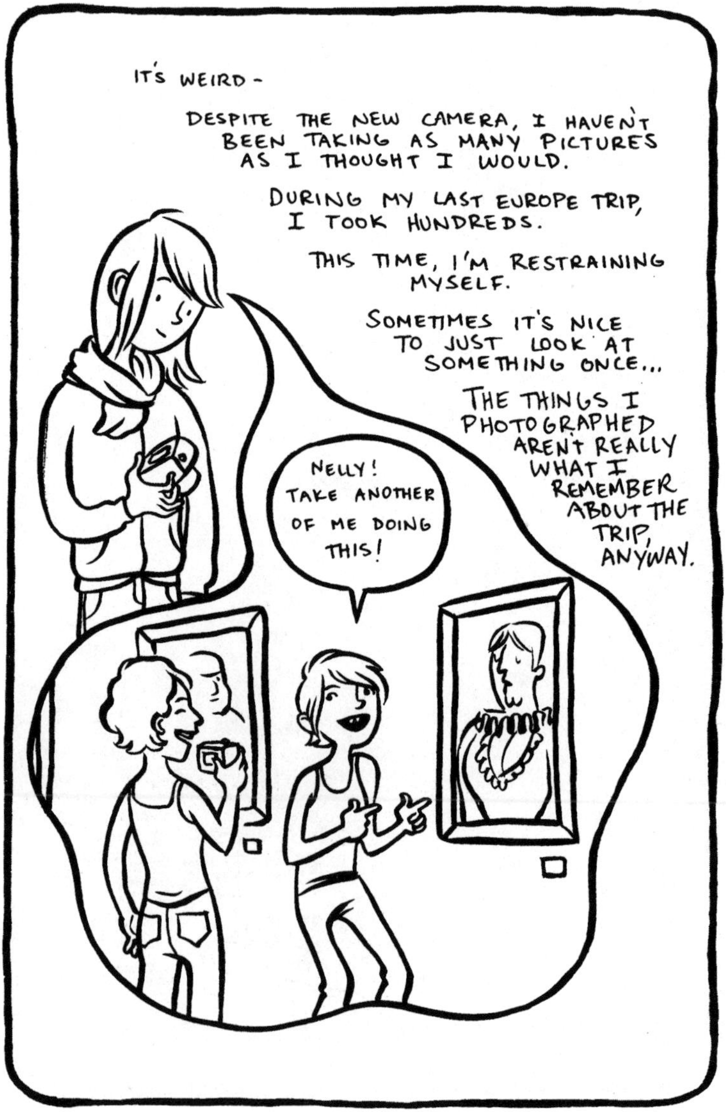

IT'S WEIRD -
DESPITE THE NEW CAMERA, I HAVEN'T BEEN TAKING AS MANY PICTURES AS I THOUGHT I WOULD.
DURING MY LAST EUROPE TRIP, I TOOK HUNDREDS.
THIS TIME, I'M RESTRAINING MYSELF.
SOMETIMES IT'S NICE TO JUST LOOK AT SOMETHING ONCE...
THE THINGS I PHOTOGRAPHED AREN'T REALLY WHAT I REMEMBER ABOUT THE TRIP, ANYWAY.
NELLY! TAKE ANOTHER OF ME DOING THIS!

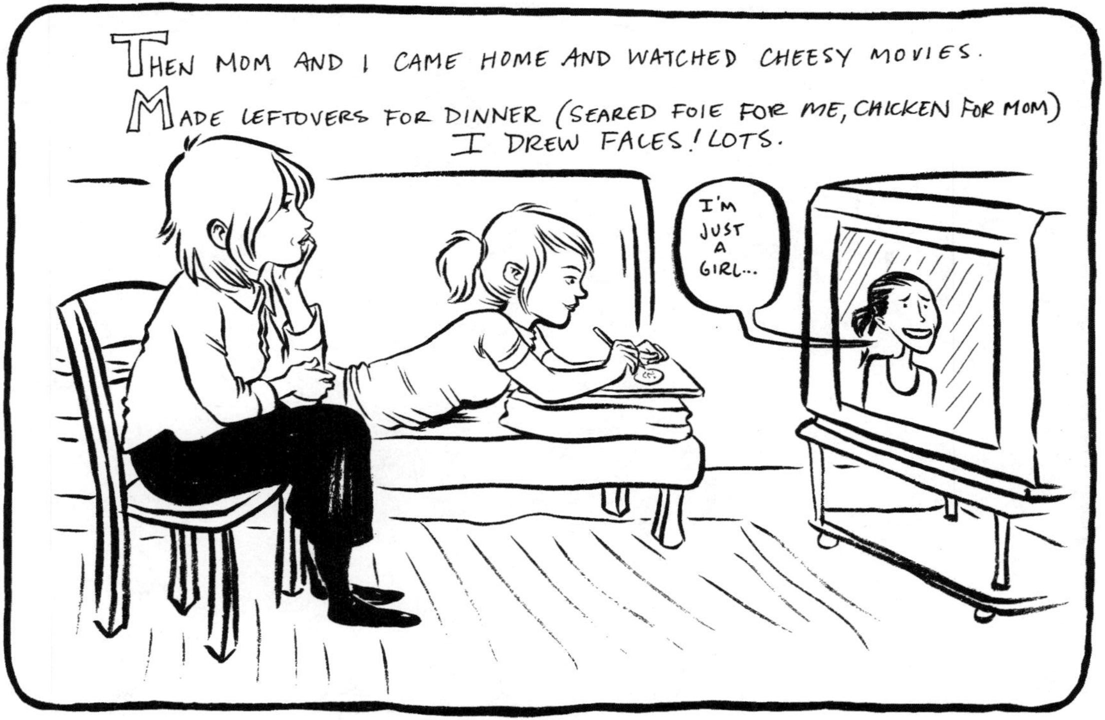
THEN MOM AND I CAME HOME AND WATCHED CHEESY MOVIES.
MADE LEFTOVERS FOR DINNER (SEARED FOIE FOR ME, CHICKEN FOR MOM)
I DREW FACES! LOTS.
I'M JUST A GIRL...

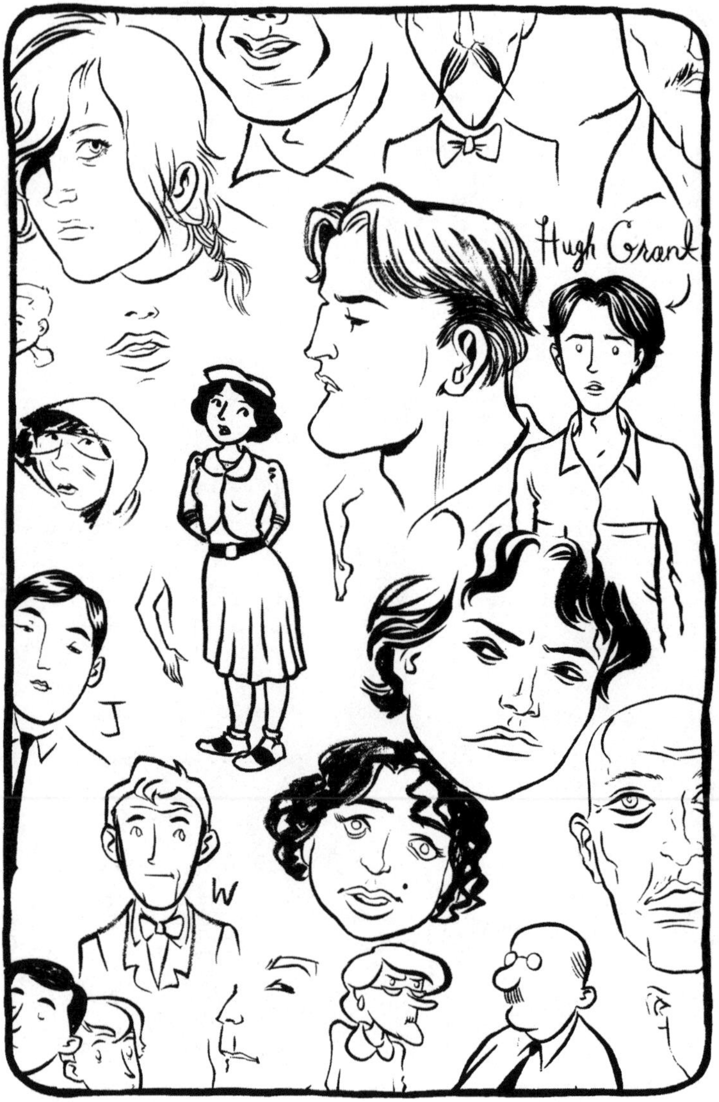
Hugh Grant
J
W

THURS, JAN 4, '07, CAFÉ ANGELINA   11:30 A.

CAFÉ ANGELINA →

A CAFÉ AU LAIT FOR MOM, WITH A BRIOCHE FOR ME; A CROISSANT AND HOT CHOCOLATE SO THICK IT'S BASICALLY A SAUCE!

THE PLACE IS GORGEOUS—ALL GOLD LEAF WITH CREAM AND ROBIN'S-EGG BLUE. OLD-FASHIONED BATHROOM, COMFORTABLE CHAIRS, MIRRORS AND MURALS AND MARBLE TABLES. LOVELY.

WHIPPED CREAM

MY HOT CHOCOLATE REMINDED ME OF THOSE DESIGNED ADS FOR CHOCOLATE FROM THE 20S WITH THE CHILDREN AND THE YELLOW BACKGROUND...

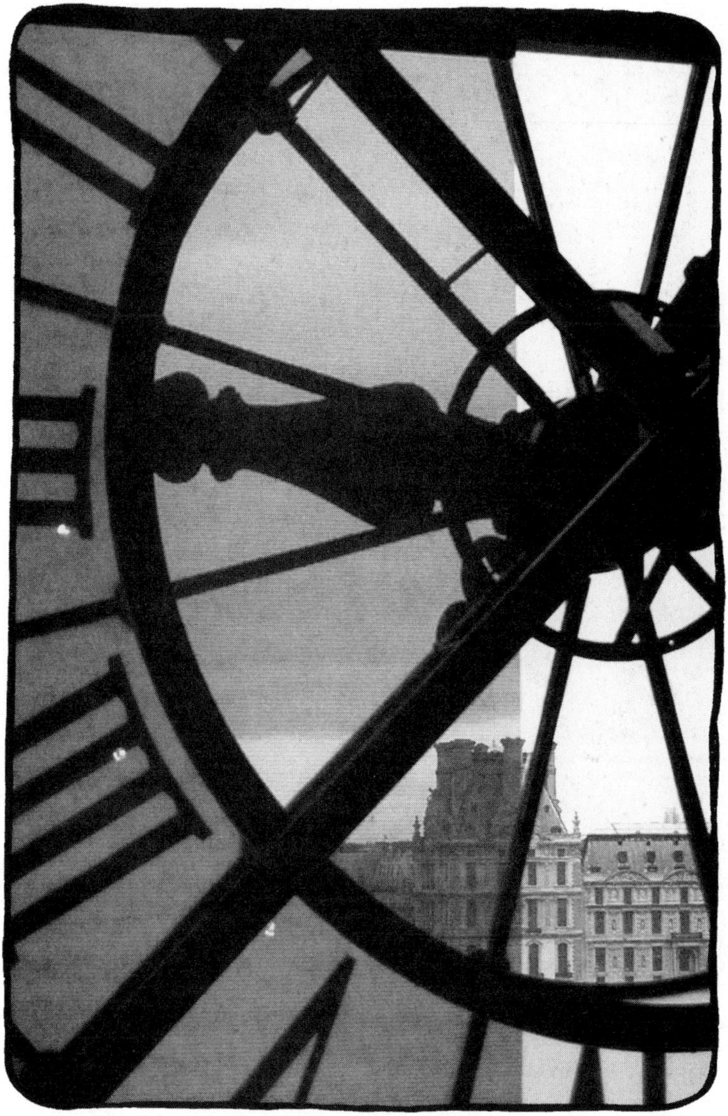

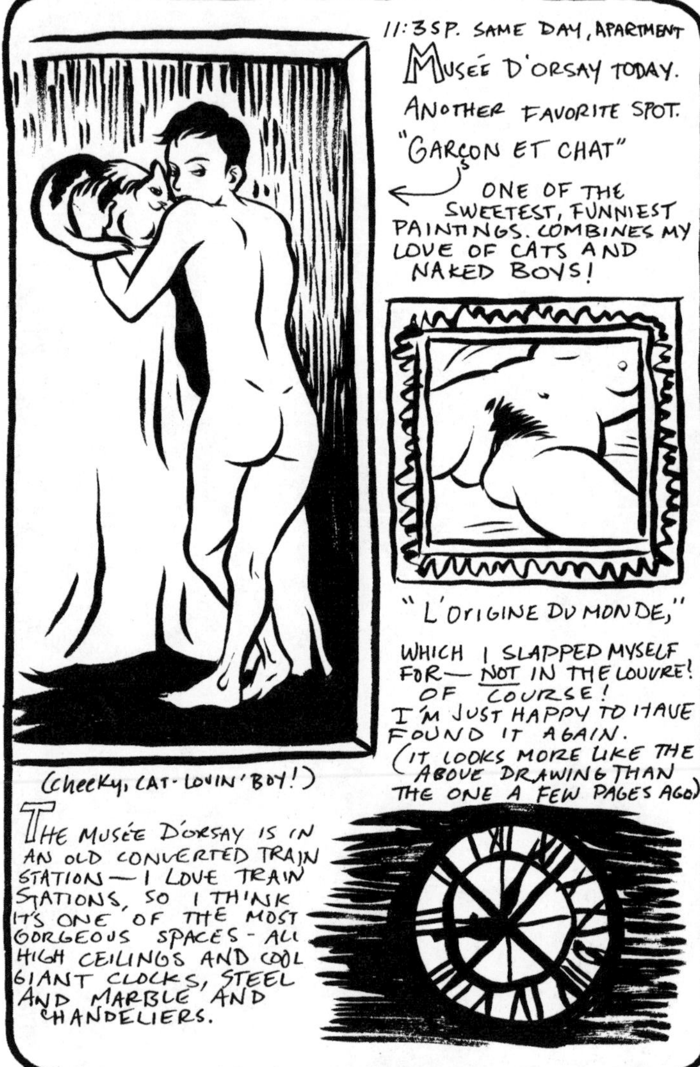
11:35P. SAME DAY, APARTMENT
MUSÉE D'ORSAY TODAY.
ANOTHER FAVORITE SPOT.
"GARÇON ET CHAT"
ONE OF THE SWEETEST, FUNNIEST PAINTINGS. COMBINES MY LOVE OF CATS AND NAKED BOYS!
"L'ORIGINE DU MONDE,"
WHICH I SLAPPED MYSELF FOR— NOT IN THE LOUVRE! OF COURSE!
I'M JUST HAPPY TO HAVE FOUND IT AGAIN.
(IT LOOKS MORE LIKE THE ABOVE DRAWING THAN THE ONE A FEW PAGES AGO)
(cheeky, CAT-LOVIN' BOY!)
THE MUSÉE D'ORSAY IS IN AN OLD CONVERTED TRAIN STATION— I LOVE TRAIN STATIONS, SO I THINK IT'S ONE OF THE MOST GORGEOUS SPACES- ALL HIGH CEILINGS AND COOL GIANT CLOCKS, STEEL AND MARBLE AND CHANDELIERS.

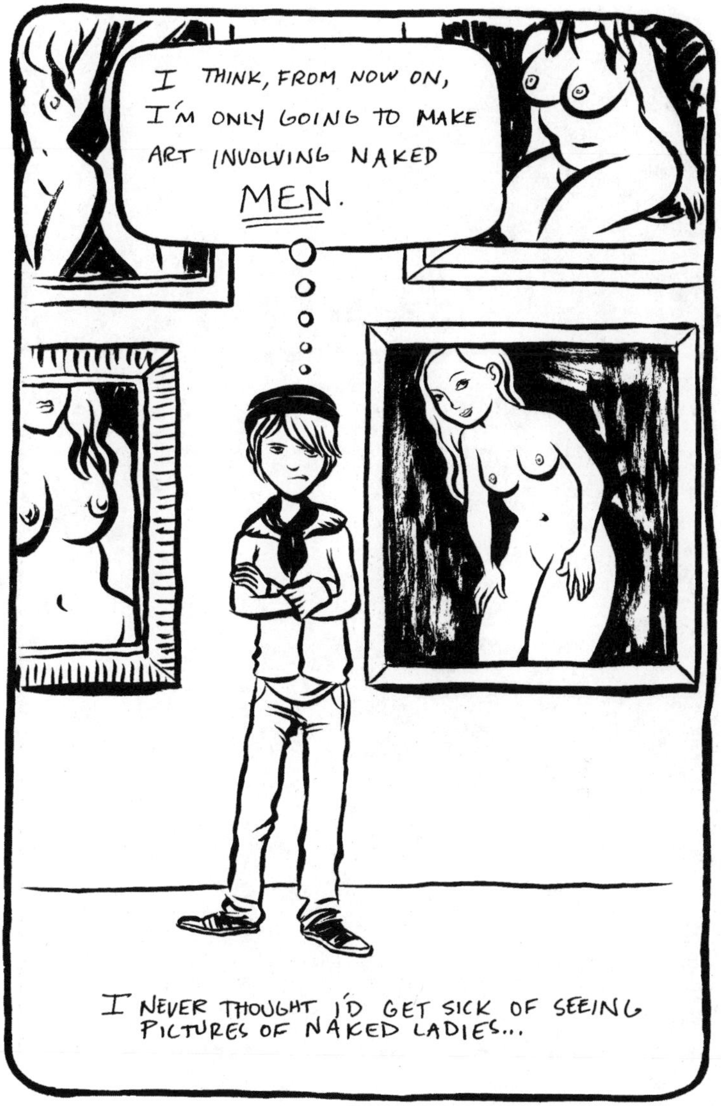
I THINK, FROM NOW ON, I'M ONLY GOING TO MAKE ART INVOLVING NAKED MEN.
I NEVER THOUGHT I'D GET SICK OF SEEING PICTURES OF NAKED LADIES...

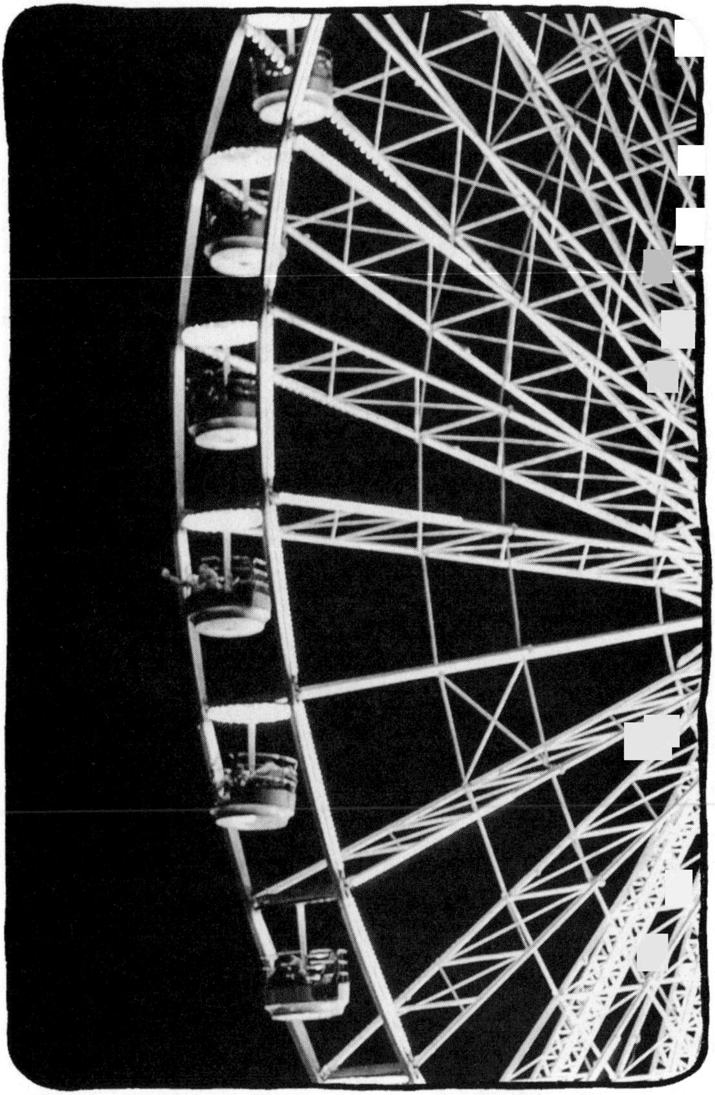

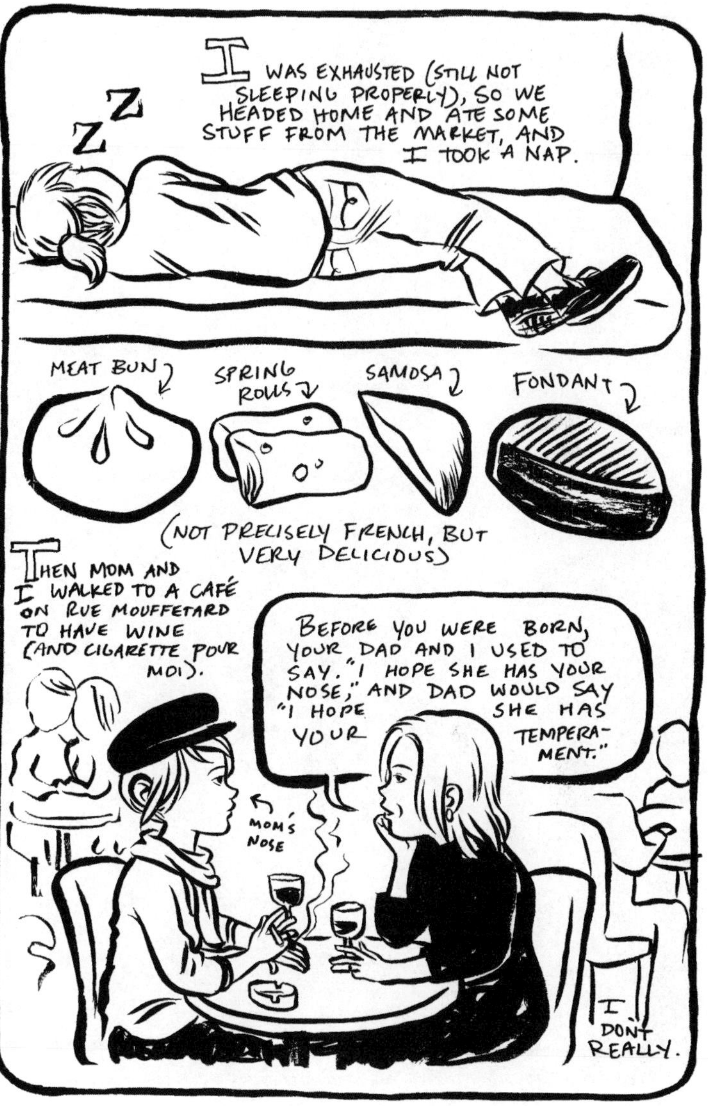
I WAS EXHAUSTED (STILL NOT SLEEPING PROPERLY), SO WE HEADED HOME AND ATE SOME STUFF FROM THE MARKET, AND I TOOK A NAP.
Z Z Z
MEAT BUN
SPRING ROLLS
SAMOSA
FONDANT
(NOT PRECISELY FRENCH, BUT VERY DELICIOUS)
THEN MOM AND I WALKED TO A CAFÉ ON RUE MOUFFETARD TO HAVE WINE (AND CIGARETTE POUR MOI).
BEFORE YOU WERE BORN, YOUR DAD AND I USED TO SAY, "I HOPE SHE HAS YOUR NOSE," AND DAD WOULD SAY "I HOPE SHE HAS YOUR TEMPERAMENT."
MOM'S NOSE
I DON'T REALLY.

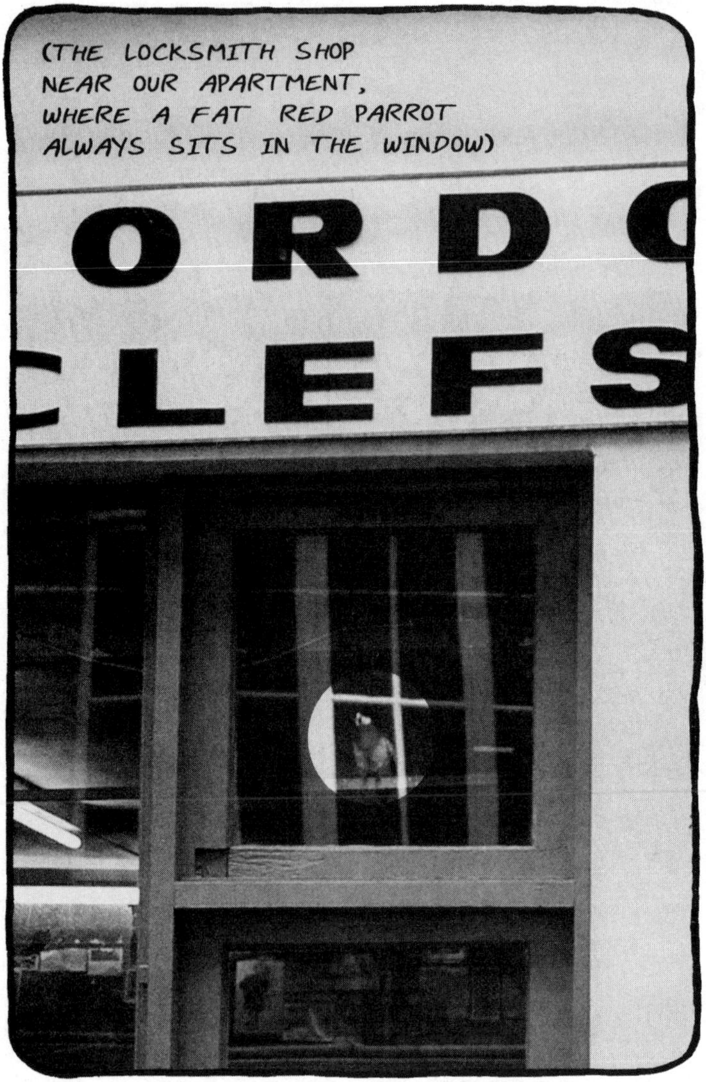
(THE LOCKSMITH SHOP
NEAR OUR APARTMENT,
WHERE A FAT RED PARROT
ALWAYS SITS IN THE WINDOW)
ORDO
CLEFS

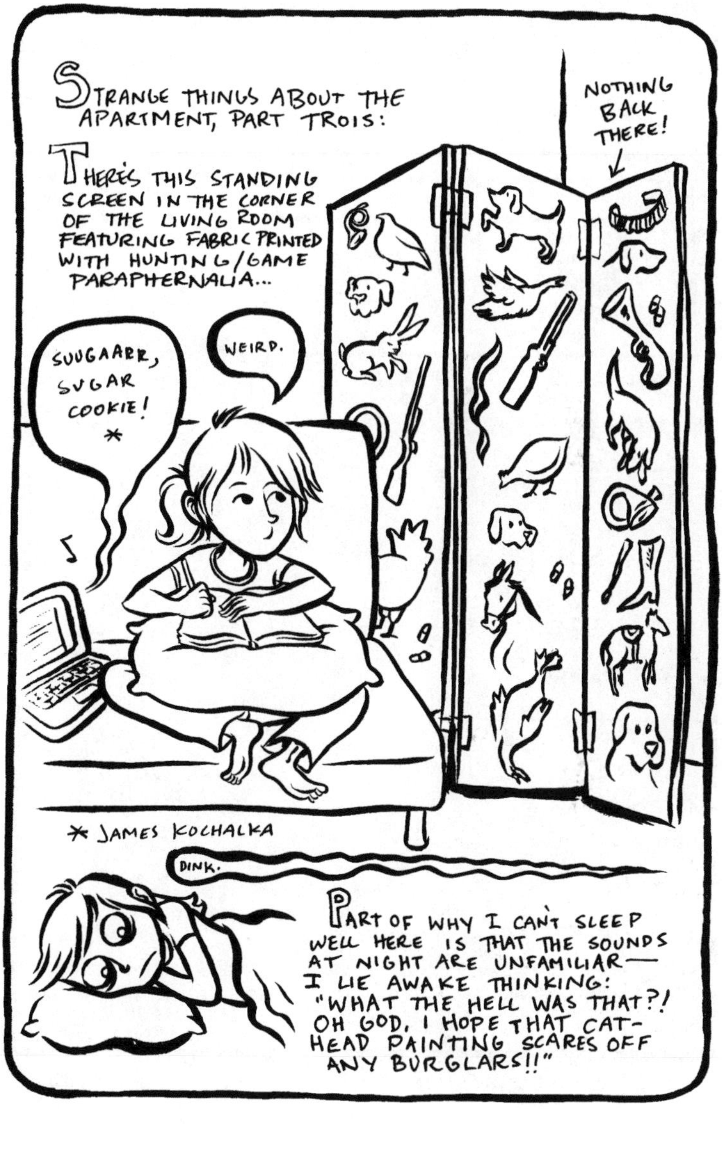
STRANGE THINGS ABOUT THE APARTMENT, PART TROIS:
THERE'S THIS STANDING SCREEN IN THE CORNER OF THE LIVING ROOM FEATURING FABRIC PRINTED WITH HUNTING/GAME PARAPHERNALIA...
NOTHING BACK THERE!
SUUGAARR, SUGAR COOKIE! *
WEIRD.
* JAMES KOCHALKA
DINK.
PART OF WHY I CAN'T SLEEP WELL HERE IS THAT THE SOUNDS AT NIGHT ARE UNFAMILIAR— I LIE AWAKE THINKING: "WHAT THE HELL WAS THAT?! OH GOD, I HOPE THAT CAT-HEAD PAINTING SCARES OFF ANY BURGLARS!!"

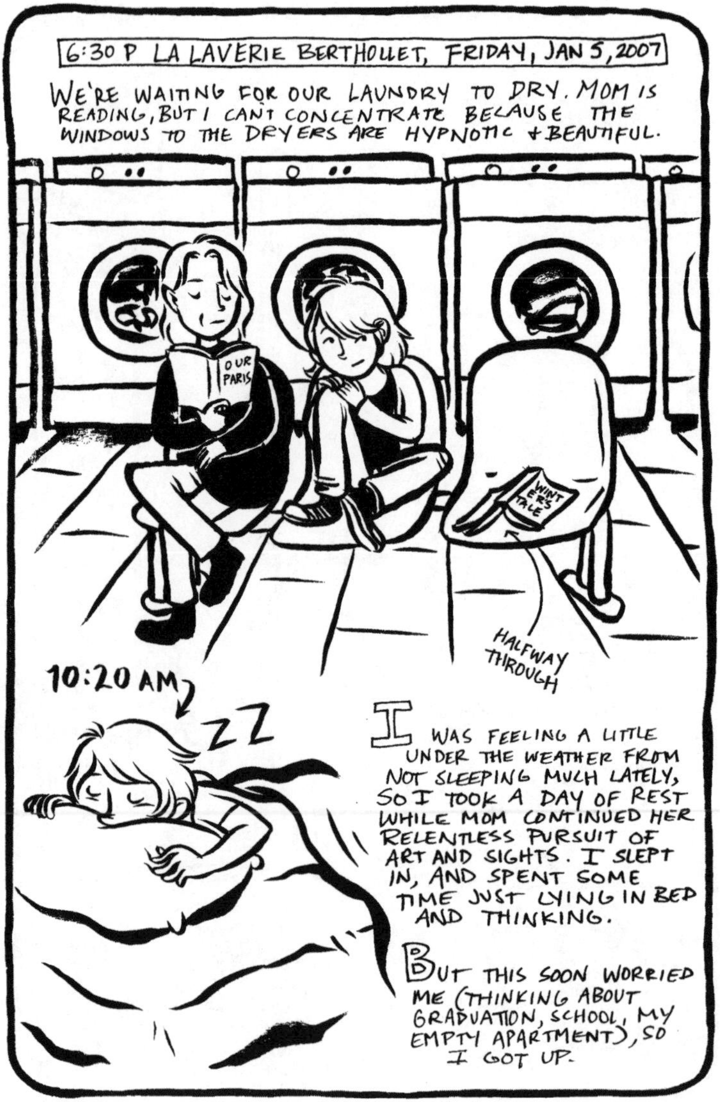
6:30 P LA LAVERIE BERTHOLLET, FRIDAY, JAN 5, 2007
WE'RE WAITING FOR OUR LAUNDRY TO DRY. MOM IS READING, BUT I CAN'T CONCENTRATE BECAUSE THE WINDOWS TO THE DRYERS ARE HYPNOTIC & BEAUTIFUL.
OUR PARIS
WINTERS TALE
HALFWAY THROUGH
10:20 AM
ZZ
I WAS FEELING A LITTLE UNDER THE WEATHER FROM NOT SLEEPING MUCH LATELY, SO I TOOK A DAY OF REST WHILE MOM CONTINUED HER RELENTLESS PURSUIT OF ART AND SIGHTS. I SLEPT IN, AND SPENT SOME TIME JUST LYING IN BED AND THINKING.
BUT THIS SOON WORRIED ME (THINKING ABOUT GRADUATION, SCHOOL, MY EMPTY APARTMENT), SO I GOT UP.

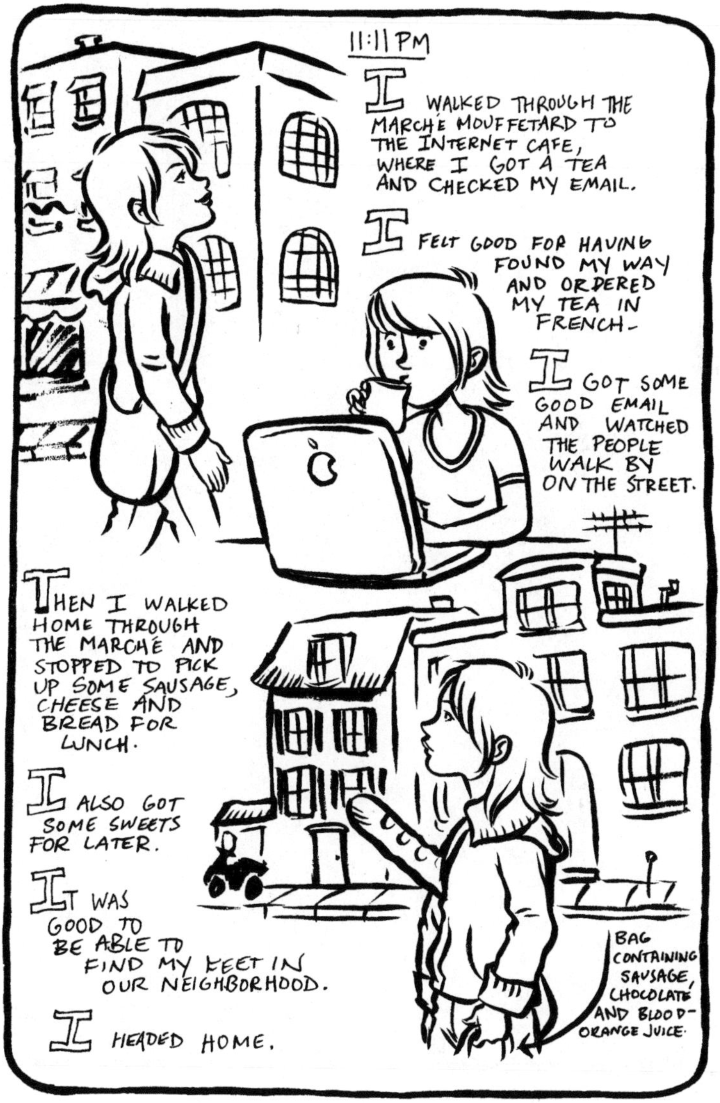
11:11 PM
I WALKED THROUGH THE MARCHÉ MOUFFETARD TO THE INTERNET CAFE, WHERE I GOT A TEA AND CHECKED MY EMAIL.
I FELT GOOD FOR HAVING FOUND MY WAY AND ORDERED MY TEA IN FRENCH.
I GOT SOME GOOD EMAIL AND WATCHED THE PEOPLE WALK BY ON THE STREET.
THEN I WALKED HOME THROUGH THE MARCHÉ AND STOPPED TO PICK UP SOME SAUSAGE, CHEESE AND BREAD FOR LUNCH.
I ALSO GOT SOME SWEETS FOR LATER.
IT WAS GOOD TO BE ABLE TO FIND MY FEET IN OUR NEIGHBORHOOD.
I HEADED HOME.
BAG CONTAINING SAUSAGE, CHOCOLATE AND BLOOD-ORANGE JUICE.

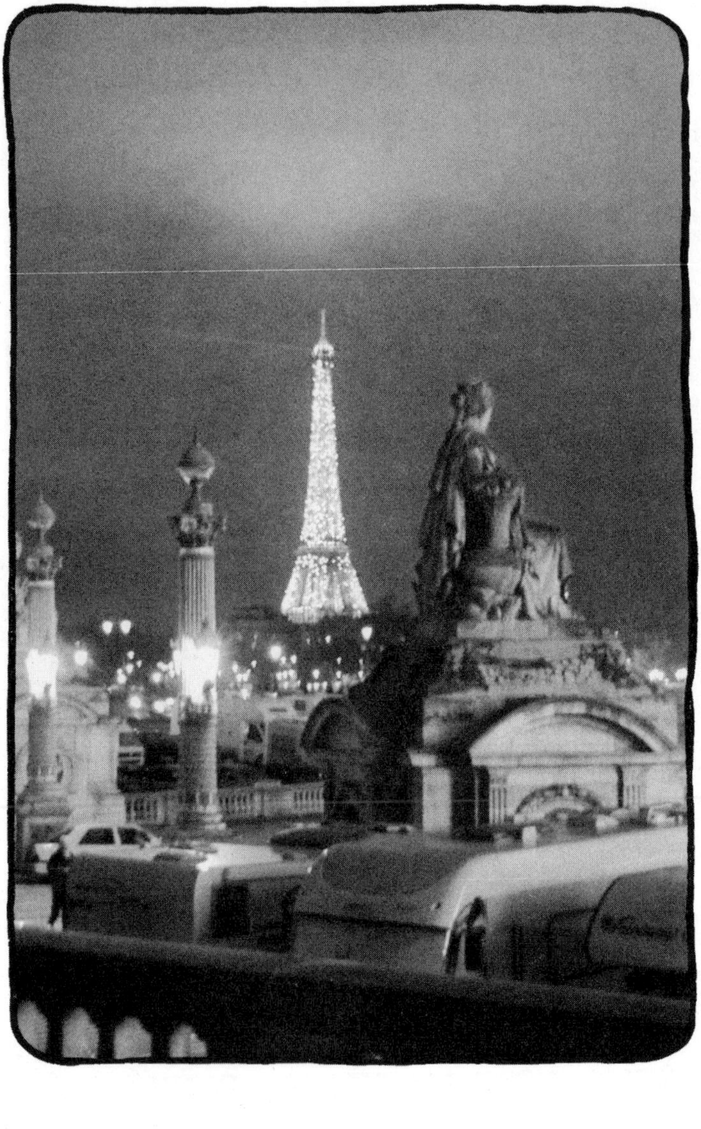

MOM AND I HAD AN "ETHEL-AND-LUCY EXPERIENCE" AT THE LAUNDROMAT AFTER WE COULDN'T READ THE FRENCH INSTRUCTIONS FOR THE MACHINES.

WE NEARLY BROKE ONE MACHINE AND NEVER FIGURED OUT THE SOAP DISPENSER THING. OH WELL—EVERYTHING WAS CLEAN EVENTUALLY.

MOM HAD SPENT THE DAY SEEING THE MAISON ROUGE (A MODERN ART MUSEUM) AND SOME GALLERY SHOWS, AS WELL AS STOPPING IN AT A FEW TEASHOPS.

IN ONE, AN OLD-FASHIONED PLACE, THEY PULLED BIG CANNISTERS OF DRY TEA DOWN FROM SHELVES TO LET HER SMELL IT.

SNIFF

Ginger

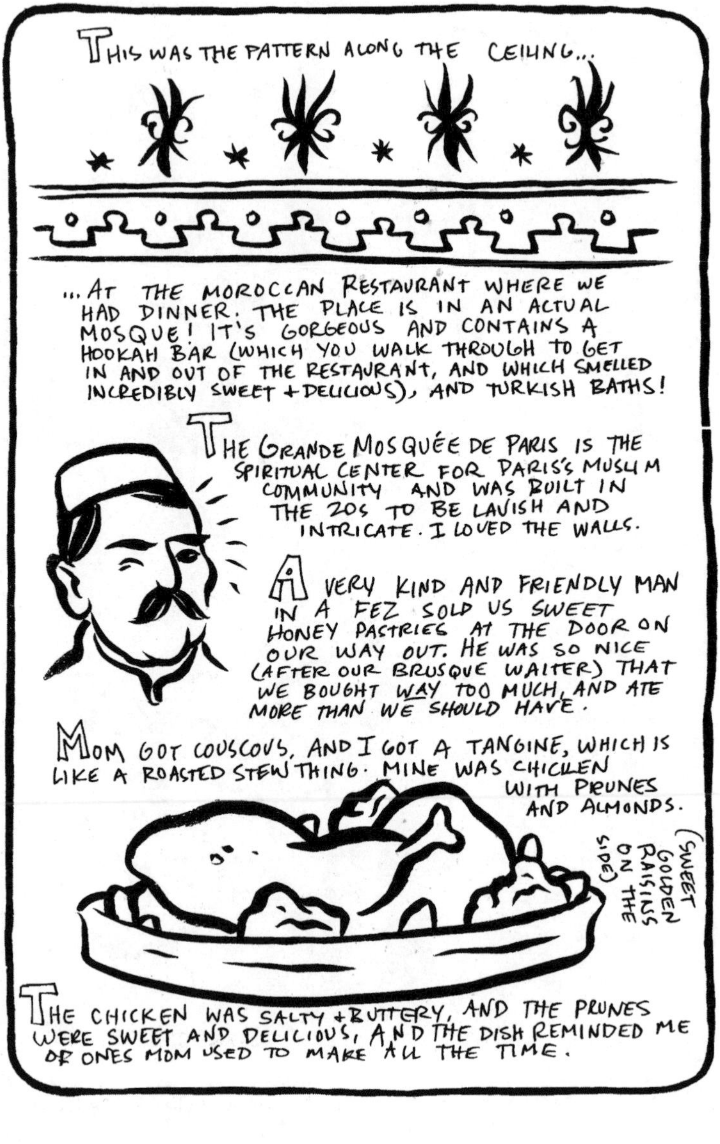
THIS WAS THE PATTERN ALONG THE CEILING...
...AT THE MOROCCAN RESTAURANT WHERE WE HAD DINNER. THE PLACE IS IN AN ACTUAL MOSQUE! IT'S GORGEOUS AND CONTAINS A HOOKAH BAR (WHICH YOU WALK THROUGH TO GET IN AND OUT OF THE RESTAURANT, AND WHICH SMELLED INCREDIBLY SWEET + DELICIOUS), AND TURKISH BATHS!
THE GRANDE MOSQUÉE DE PARIS IS THE SPIRITUAL CENTER FOR PARIS'S MUSLIM COMMUNITY AND WAS BUILT IN THE 20s TO BE LAVISH AND INTRICATE. I LOVED THE WALLS.
A VERY KIND AND FRIENDLY MAN IN A FEZ SOLD US SWEET HONEY PASTRIES AT THE DOOR ON OUR WAY OUT. HE WAS SO NICE (AFTER OUR BRUSQUE WAITER) THAT WE BOUGHT WAY TOO MUCH, AND ATE MORE THAN WE SHOULD HAVE.
MOM GOT COUSCOUS, AND I GOT A TANGINE, WHICH IS LIKE A ROASTED STEW THING. MINE WAS CHICKEN WITH PRUNES AND ALMONDS.
(SWEET GOLDEN RAISINS ON THE SIDE)
THE CHICKEN WAS SALTY + BUTTERY, AND THE PRUNES WERE SWEET AND DELICIOUS, AND THE DISH REMINDED ME OF ONES MOM USED TO MAKE ALL THE TIME.

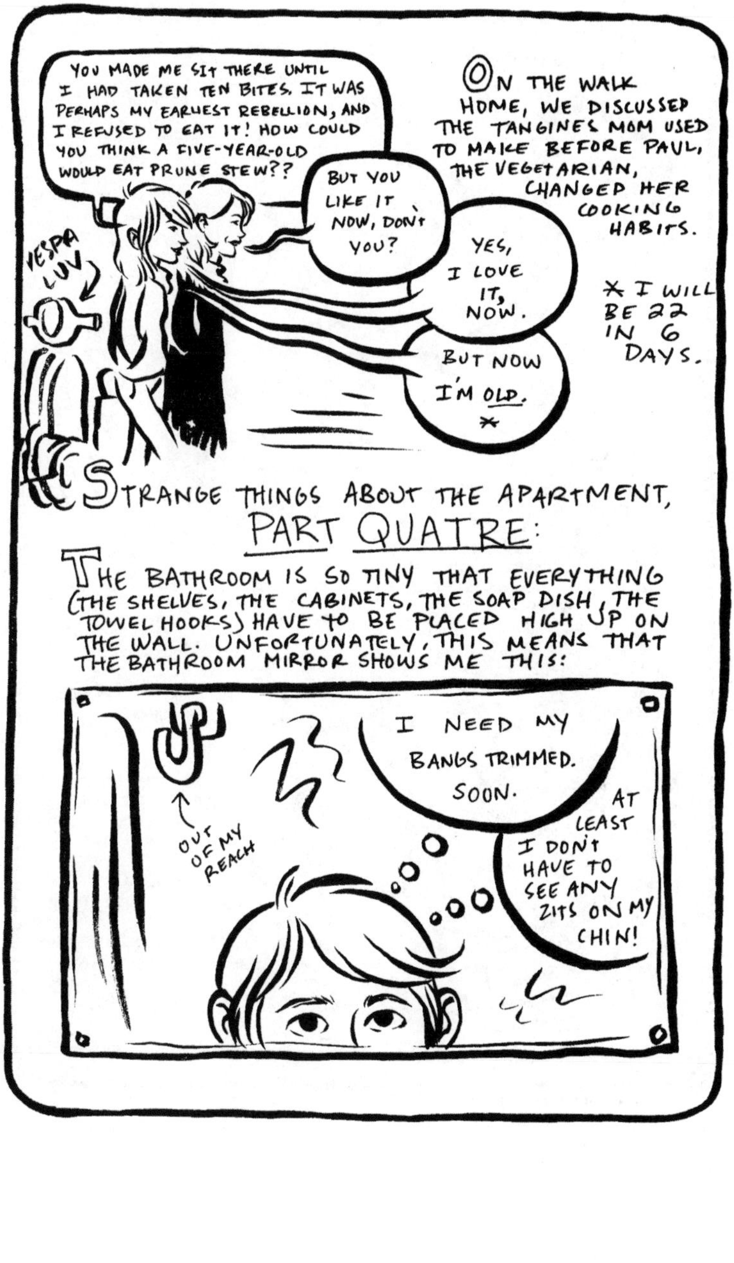
YOU MADE ME SIT THERE UNTIL I HAD TAKEN TEN BITES. IT WAS PERHAPS MY EARLIEST REBELLION, AND I REFUSED TO EAT IT! HOW COULD YOU THINK A FIVE-YEAR-OLD WOULD EAT PRUNE STEW??
BUT YOU LIKE IT NOW, DON'T YOU?
YES, I LOVE IT, NOW.
BUT NOW I'M OLD. *
ON THE WALK HOME, WE DISCUSSED THE TANGINES MOM USED TO MAKE BEFORE PAUL, THE VEGETARIAN, CHANGED HER COOKING HABITS.
* I WILL BE 22 IN 6 DAYS.
VESPA LUV
STRANGE THINGS ABOUT THE APARTMENT, PART QUATRE:
THE BATHROOM IS SO TINY THAT EVERYTHING (THE SHELVES, THE CABINETS, THE SOAP DISH, THE TOWEL HOOKS) HAVE TO BE PLACED HIGH UP ON THE WALL. UNFORTUNATELY, THIS MEANS THAT THE BATHROOM MIRROR SHOWS ME THIS:
OUT OF MY REACH
I NEED MY BANGS TRIMMED. SOON.
AT LEAST I DON'T HAVE TO SEE ANY ZITS ON MY CHIN!

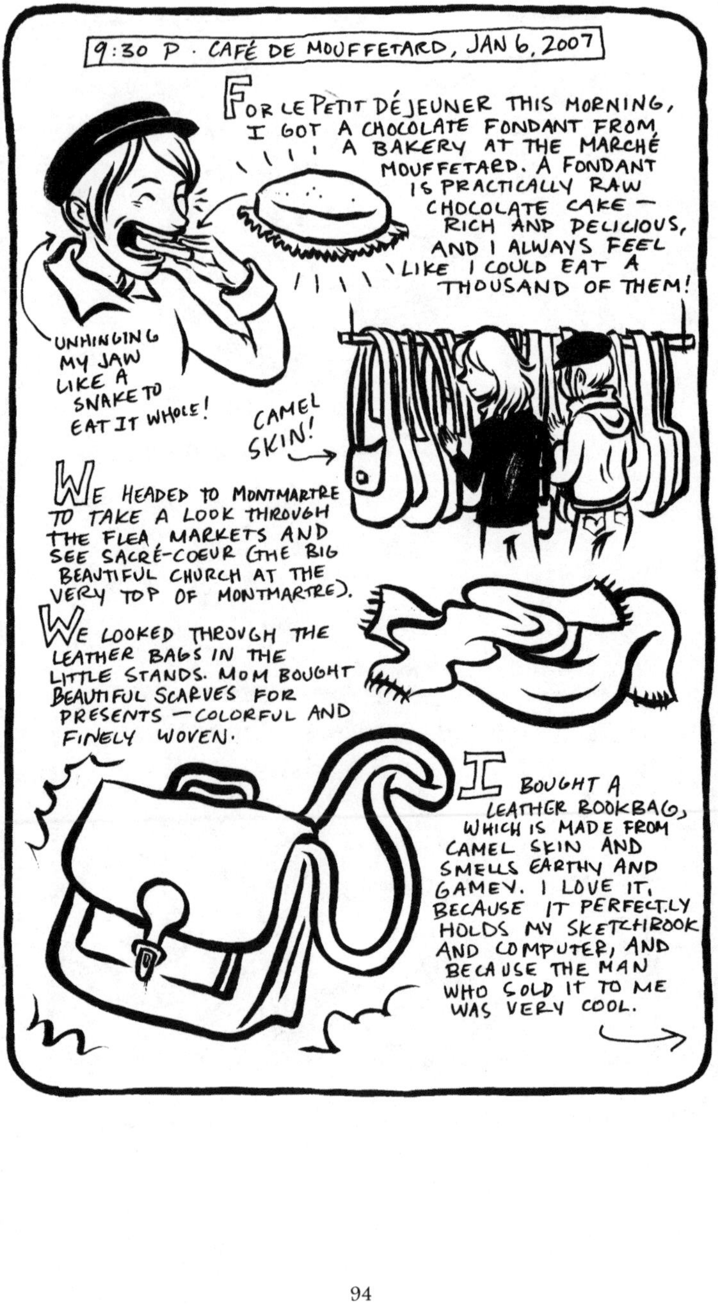
9:30 P · CAFÉ DE MOUFFETARD, JAN 6, 2007
FOR LE PETIT DÉJEUNER THIS MORNING, I GOT A CHOCOLATE FONDANT FROM A BAKERY AT THE MARCHÉ MOUFFETARD. A FONDANT IS PRACTICALLY RAW CHOCOLATE CAKE — RICH AND DELICIOUS, AND I ALWAYS FEEL LIKE I COULD EAT A THOUSAND OF THEM!
UNHINGING MY JAW LIKE A SNAKE TO EAT IT WHOLE!
CAMEL SKIN!
WE HEADED TO MONTMARTRE TO TAKE A LOOK THROUGH THE FLEA MARKETS AND SEE SACRÉ-COEUR (THE BIG BEAUTIFUL CHURCH AT THE VERY TOP OF MONTMARTRE).
WE LOOKED THROUGH THE LEATHER BAGS IN THE LITTLE STANDS. MOM BOUGHT BEAUTIFUL SCARVES FOR PRESENTS — COLORFUL AND FINELY WOVEN.
I BOUGHT A LEATHER BOOKBAG, WHICH IS MADE FROM CAMEL SKIN AND SMELLS EARTHY AND GAMEY. I LOVE IT, BECAUSE IT PERFECTLY HOLDS MY SKETCHBOOK AND COMPUTER, AND BECAUSE THE MAN WHO SOLD IT TO ME WAS VERY COOL.

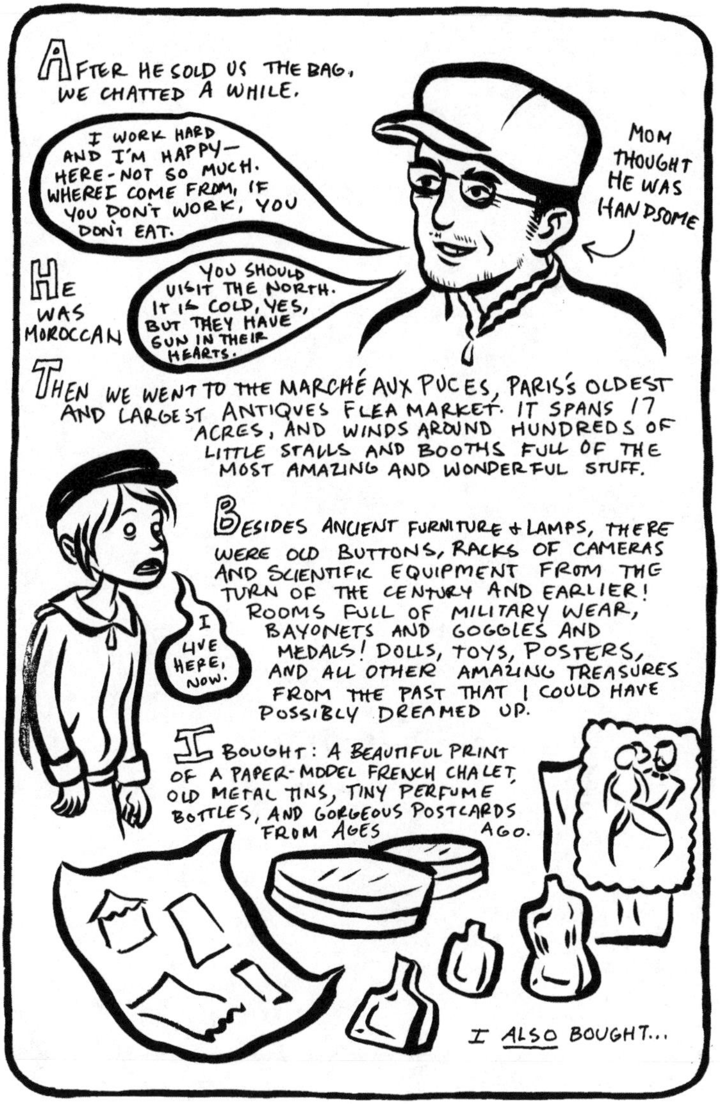
AFTER HE SOLD US THE BAG, WE CHATTED A WHILE.
I WORK HARD AND I'M HAPPY— HERE-NOT SO MUCH. WHERE I COME FROM, IF YOU DON'T WORK, YOU DON'T EAT.
MOM THOUGHT HE WAS HANDSOME
HE WAS MOROCCAN
YOU SHOULD VISIT THE NORTH. IT IS COLD, YES, BUT THEY HAVE SUN IN THEIR HEARTS.
THEN WE WENT TO THE MARCHÉ AUX PUCES, PARIS'S OLDEST AND LARGEST ANTIQUES FLEA MARKET. IT SPANS 17 ACRES, AND WINDS AROUND HUNDREDS OF LITTLE STALLS AND BOOTHS FULL OF THE MOST AMAZING AND WONDERFUL STUFF.
BESIDES ANCIENT FURNITURE & LAMPS, THERE WERE OLD BUTTONS, RACKS OF CAMERAS AND SCIENTIFIC EQUIPMENT FROM THE TURN OF THE CENTURY AND EARLIER! ROOMS FULL OF MILITARY WEAR, BAYONETS AND GOGGLES AND MEDALS! DOLLS, TOYS, POSTERS, AND ALL OTHER AMAZING TREASURES FROM THE PAST THAT I COULD HAVE POSSIBLY DREAMED UP.
I LIVE HERE, NOW.
I BOUGHT: A BEAUTIFUL PRINT OF A PAPER-MODEL FRENCH CHALET, OLD METAL TINS, TINY PERFUME BOTTLES, AND GORGEOUS POSTCARDS FROM AGES AGO.
I ALSO BOUGHT...

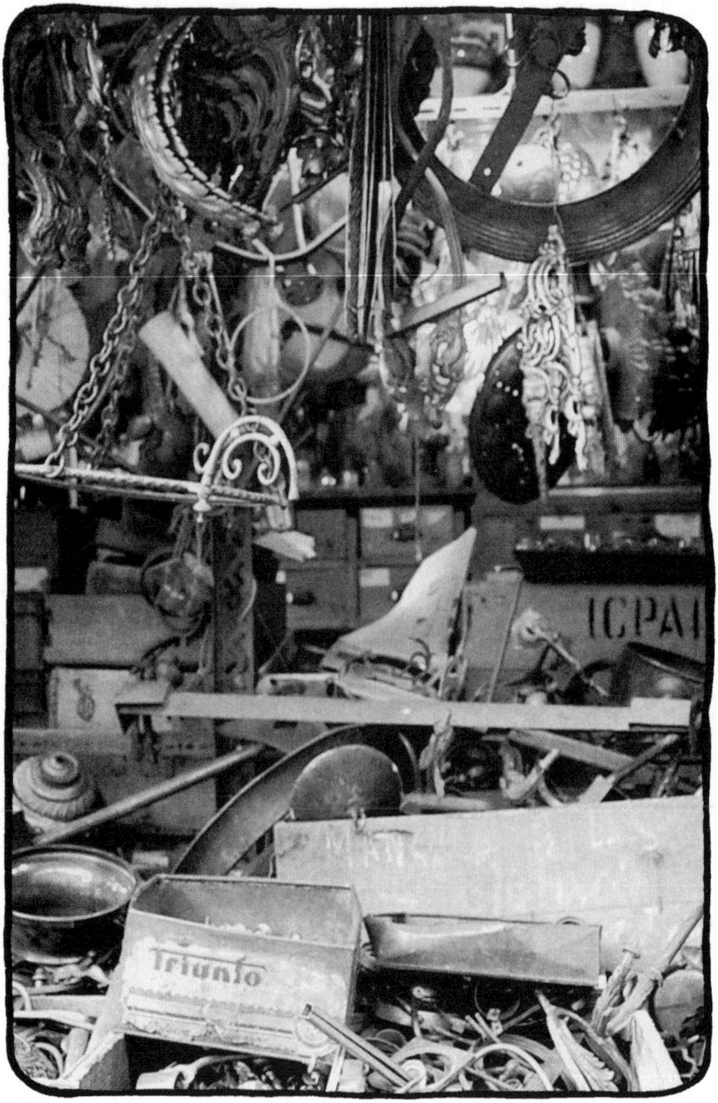
Triunfo

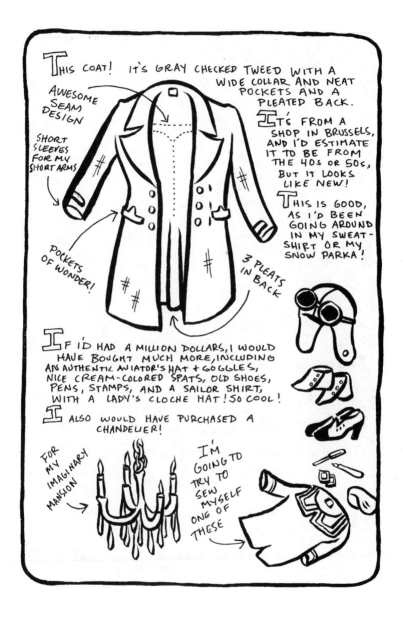

THIS COAT! IT'S GRAY CHECKED TWEED WITH A WIDE COLLAR AND NEAT POCKETS AND A PLEATED BACK.

AWESOME SEAM DESIGN

SHORT SLEEVES FOR MY SHORT ARMS

IT'S FROM A SHOP IN BRUSSELS, AND I'D ESTIMATE IT TO BE FROM THE 40S OR 50S, BUT IT LOOKS LIKE NEW!

THIS IS GOOD, AS I'D BEEN GOING AROUND IN MY SWEAT-SHIRT OR MY SNOW PARKA!

POCKETS OF WONDER!

3 PLEATS IN BACK

IF I'D HAD A MILLION DOLLARS, I WOULD HAVE BOUGHT MUCH MORE, INCLUDING AN AUTHENTIC AVIATOR'S HAT + GOGGLES, NICE CREAM-COLORED SPATS, OLD SHOES, PENS, STAMPS, AND A SAILOR SHIRT, WITH A LADY'S CLOCHE HAT! SO COOL!

I ALSO WOULD HAVE PURCHASED A CHANDELIER!

FOR MY IMAGINARY MANSION

I'M GOING TO TRY TO SEW MYSELF ONE OF THESE

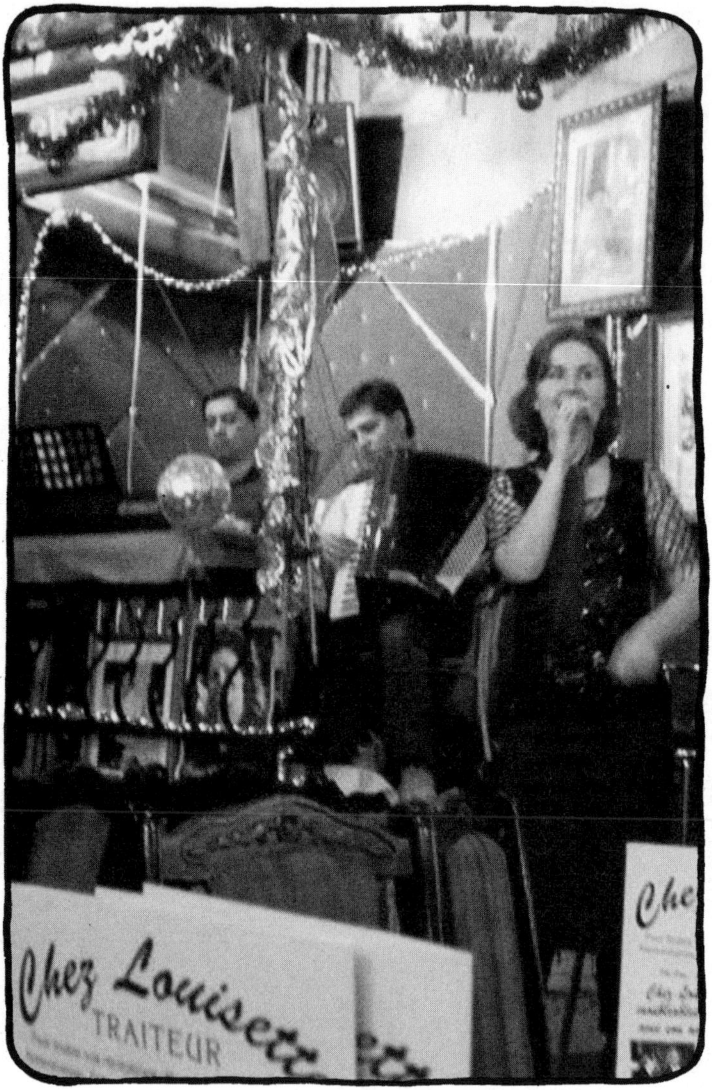
Chez Louisette
TRAITEUR
Che

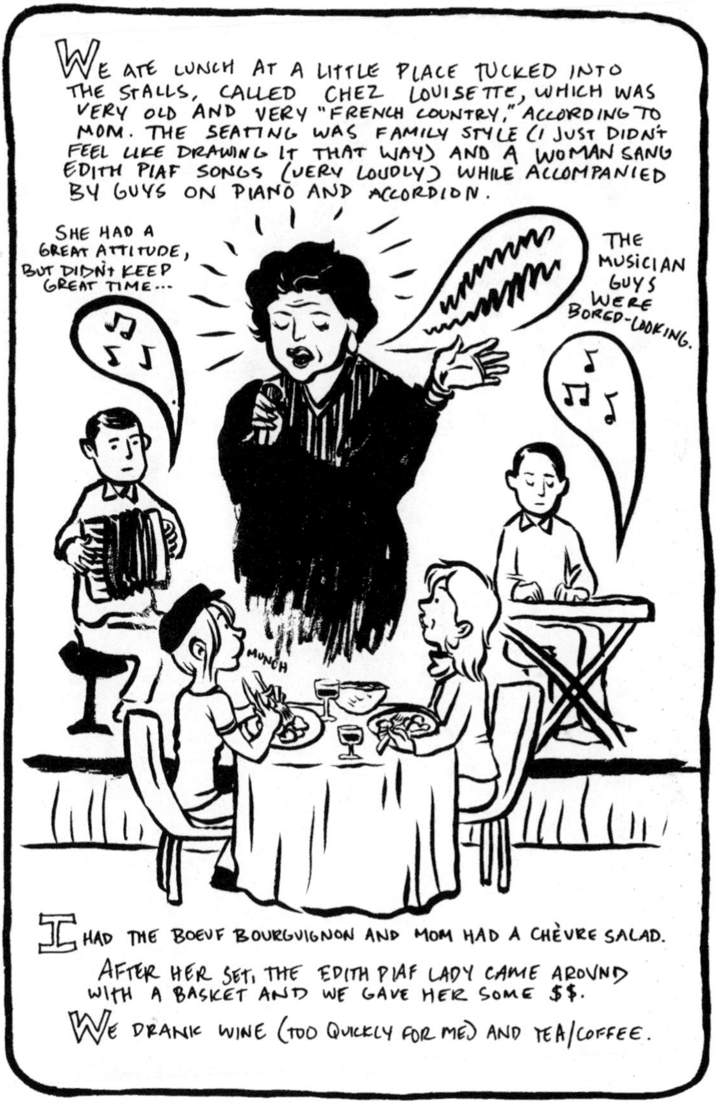

WE ATE LUNCH AT A LITTLE PLACE TUCKED INTO THE STALLS, CALLED CHEZ LOUISETTE, WHICH WAS VERY OLD AND VERY "FRENCH COUNTRY," ACCORDING TO MOM. THE SEATING WAS FAMILY STYLE (I JUST DIDN'T FEEL LIKE DRAWING IT THAT WAY) AND A WOMAN SANG EDITH PIAF SONGS (VERY LOUDLY) WHILE ACCOMPANIED BY GUYS ON PIANO AND ACCORDION.
SHE HAD A GREAT ATTITUDE, BUT DIDN'T KEEP GREAT TIME...
THE MUSICIAN GUYS WERE BORED-LOOKING.
MUNCH
I HAD THE BOEUF BOURGUIGNON AND MOM HAD A CHÈVRE SALAD.
AFTER HER SET, THE EDITH PIAF LADY CAME AROUND WITH A BASKET AND WE GAVE HER SOME $$.
WE DRANK WINE (TOO QUICKLY FOR ME) AND TEA/COFFEE.

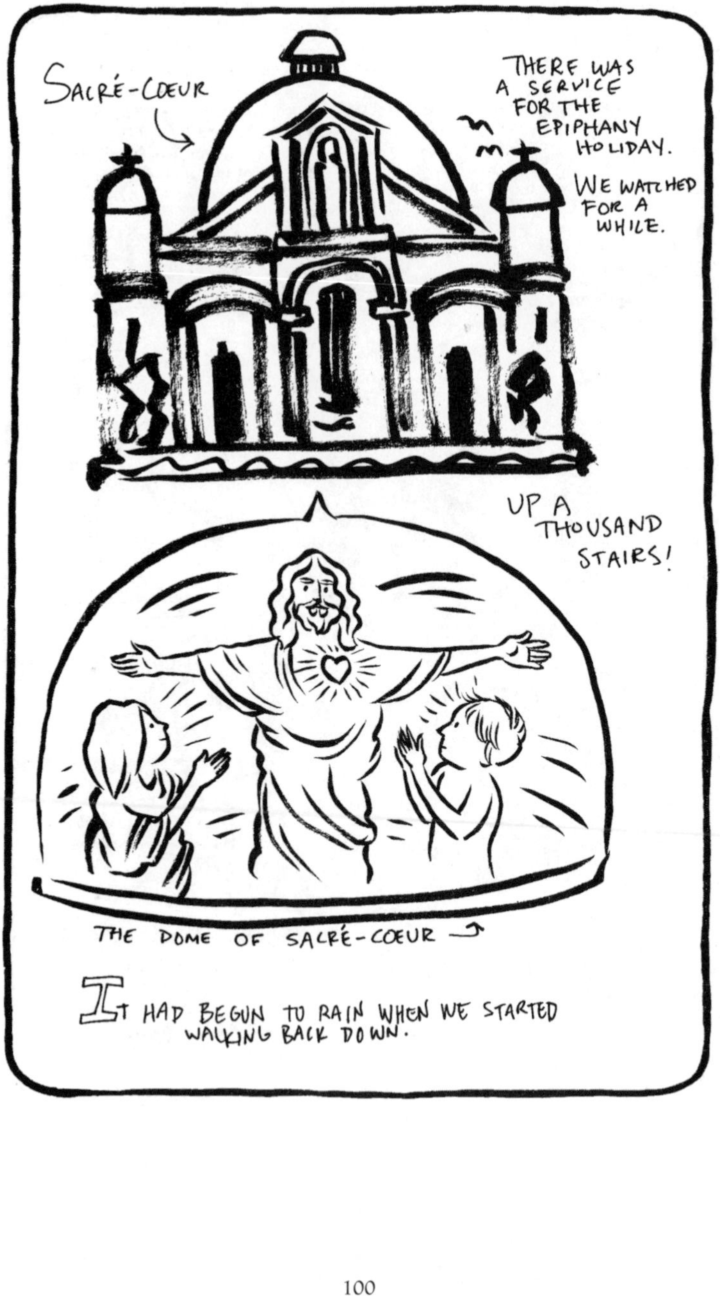
SACRÉ-COEUR
THERE WAS A SERVICE FOR THE EPIPHANY HOLIDAY.
WE WATCHED FOR A WHILE.
UP A THOUSAND STAIRS!
THE DOME OF SACRÉ-COEUR
IT HAD BEGUN TO RAIN WHEN WE STARTED WALKING BACK DOWN.

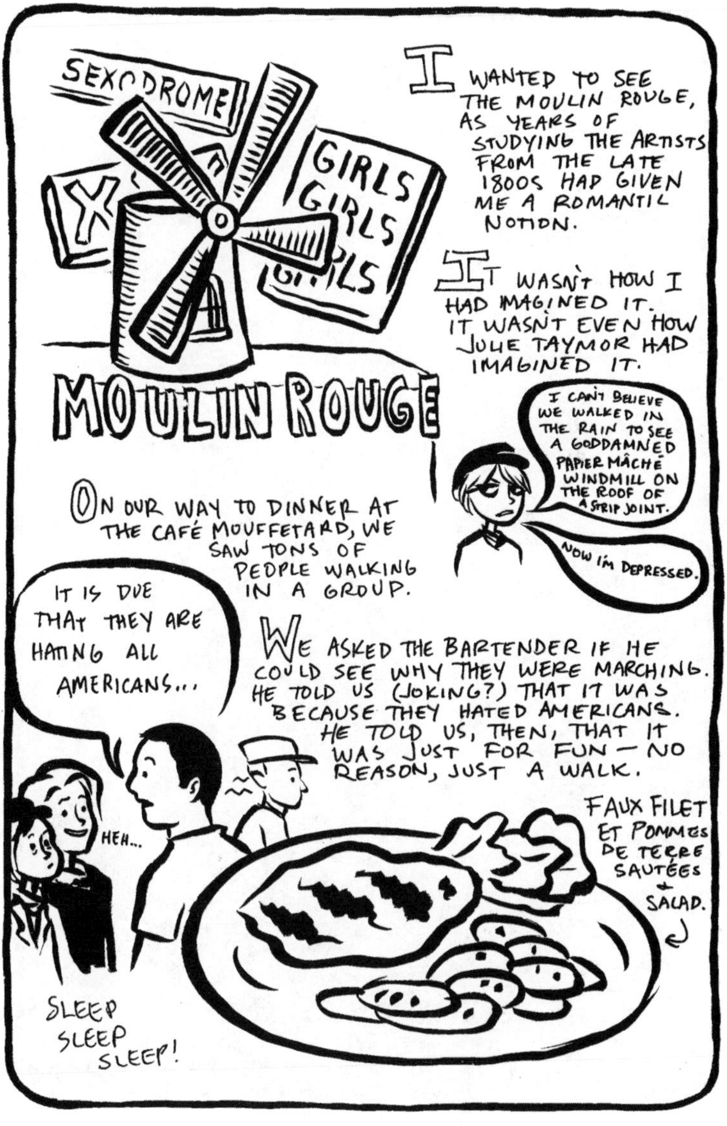
SEXODROME
GIRLS GIRLS GIRLS GIRLS
MOULIN ROUGE
I WANTED TO SEE THE MOULIN ROUGE, AS YEARS OF STUDYING THE ARTISTS FROM THE LATE 1800S HAD GIVEN ME A ROMANTIC NOTION.
IT WASN'T HOW I HAD IMAGINED IT. IT WASN'T EVEN HOW JULIE TAYMOR HAD IMAGINED IT.
I CAN'T BELIEVE WE WALKED IN THE RAIN TO SEE A GODDAMNED PAPIER MÂCHÉ WINDMILL ON THE ROOF OF A STRIP JOINT.
NOW I'M DEPRESSED.
ON OUR WAY TO DINNER AT THE CAFÉ MOUFFETARD, WE SAW TONS OF PEOPLE WALKING IN A GROUP.
IT IS DUE THAT THEY ARE HATING ALL AMERICANS...
WE ASKED THE BARTENDER IF HE COULD SEE WHY THEY WERE MARCHING. HE TOLD US (JOKING?) THAT IT WAS BECAUSE THEY HATED AMERICANS. HE TOLD US, THEN, THAT IT WAS JUST FOR FUN — NO REASON, JUST A WALK.
HEH...
FAUX FILET ET POMMES DE TERRE SAUTÉES + SALAD.
SLEEP SLEEP SLEEP!

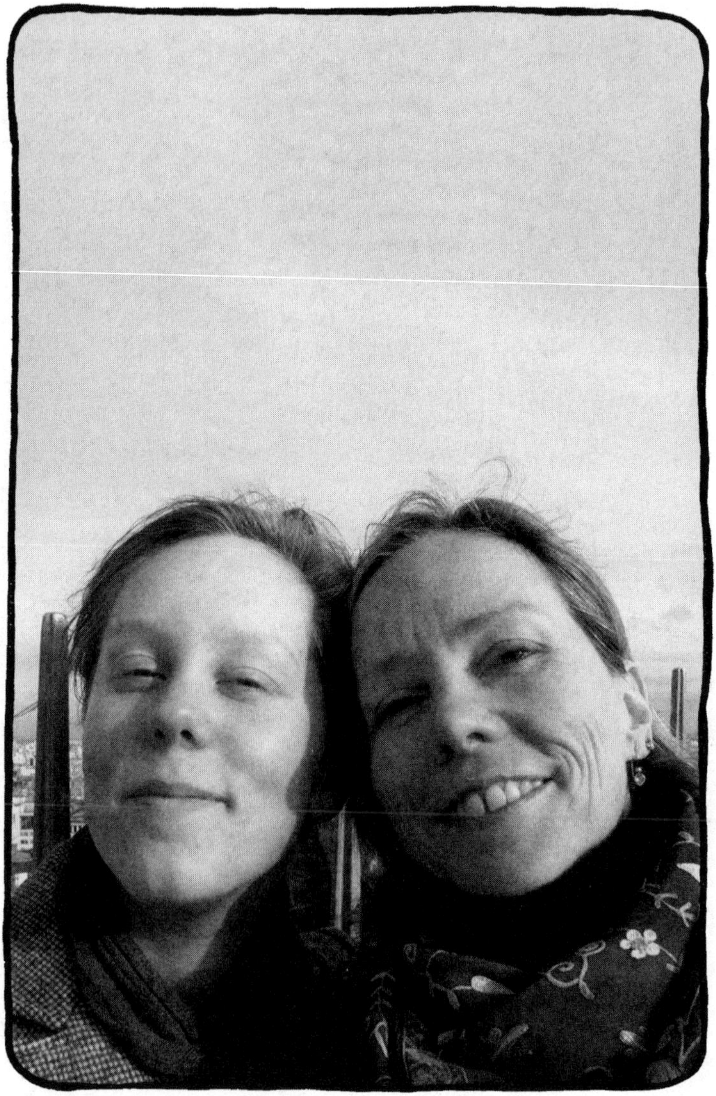

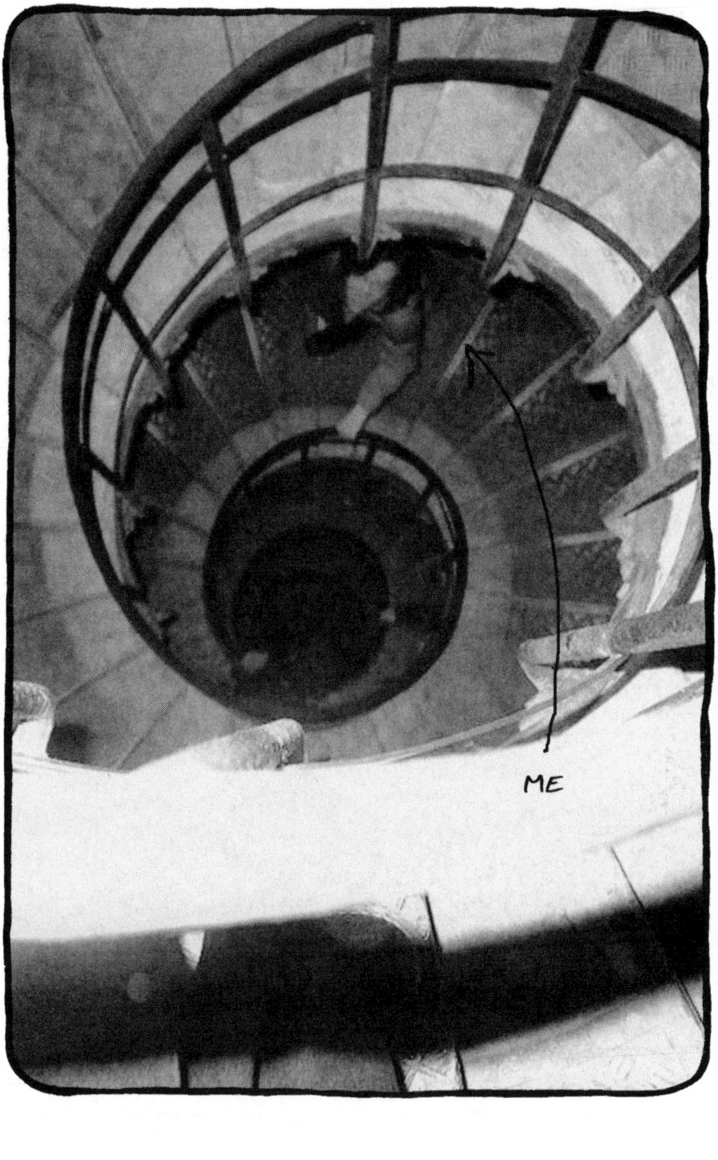
ME

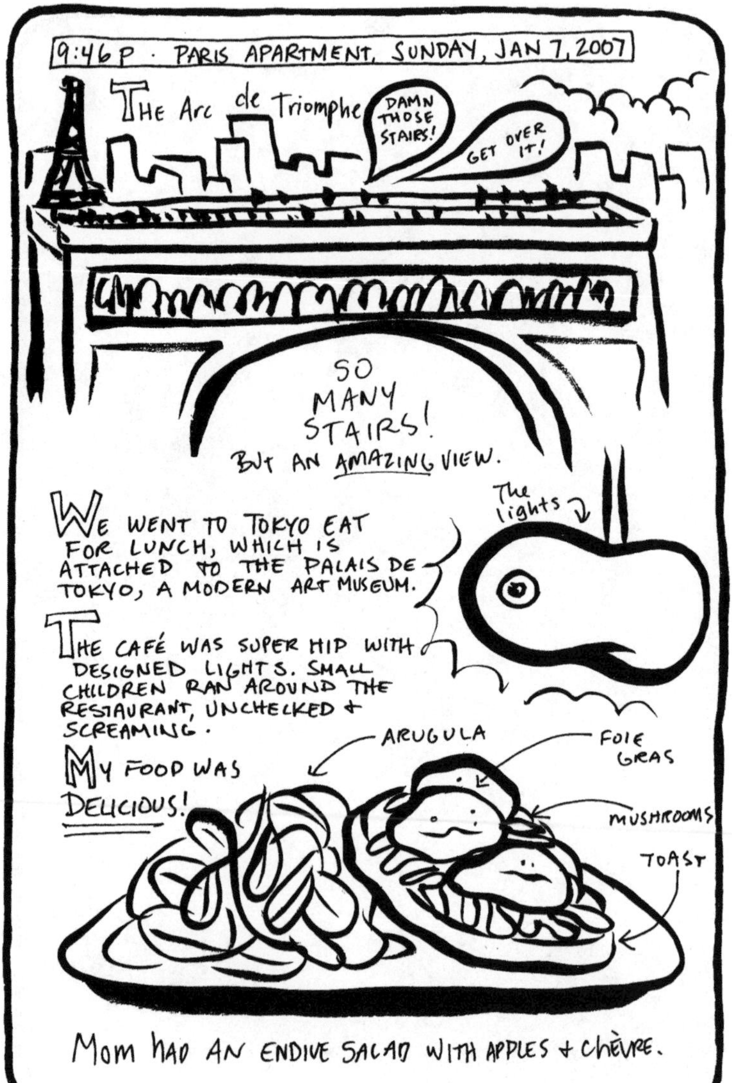

9:46P · PARIS APARTMENT, SUNDAY, JAN 7, 2007
THE Arc de Triomphe
DAMN THOSE STAIRS!
GET OVER IT!
SO MANY STAIRS!
BUT AN AMAZING VIEW.
WE WENT TO TOKYO EAT FOR LUNCH, WHICH IS ATTACHED TO THE PALAIS DE TOKYO, A MODERN ART MUSEUM.
THE CAFÉ WAS SUPER HIP WITH DESIGNED LIGHTS. SMALL CHILDREN RAN AROUND THE RESTAURANT, UNCHECKED & SCREAMING.
The lights
MY FOOD WAS DELICIOUS!
ARUGULA
FOIE GRAS
MUSHROOMS
TOAST
Mom HAD AN ENDIVE SALAD WITH APPLES & Chèvre.

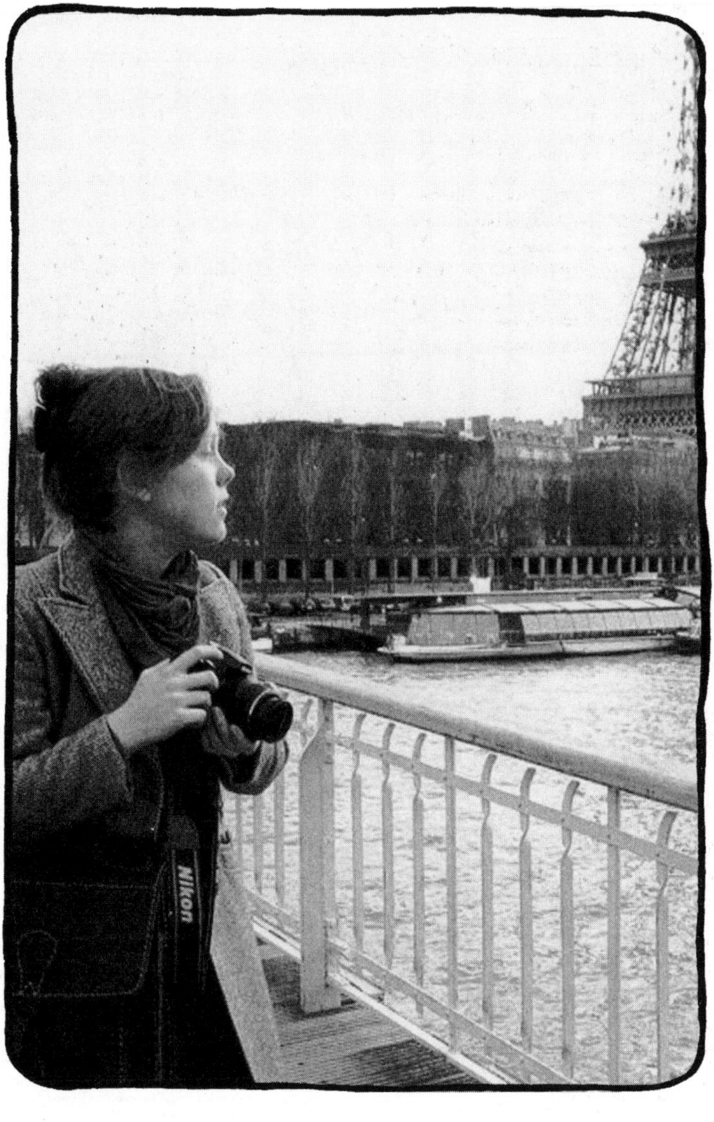
Nikon

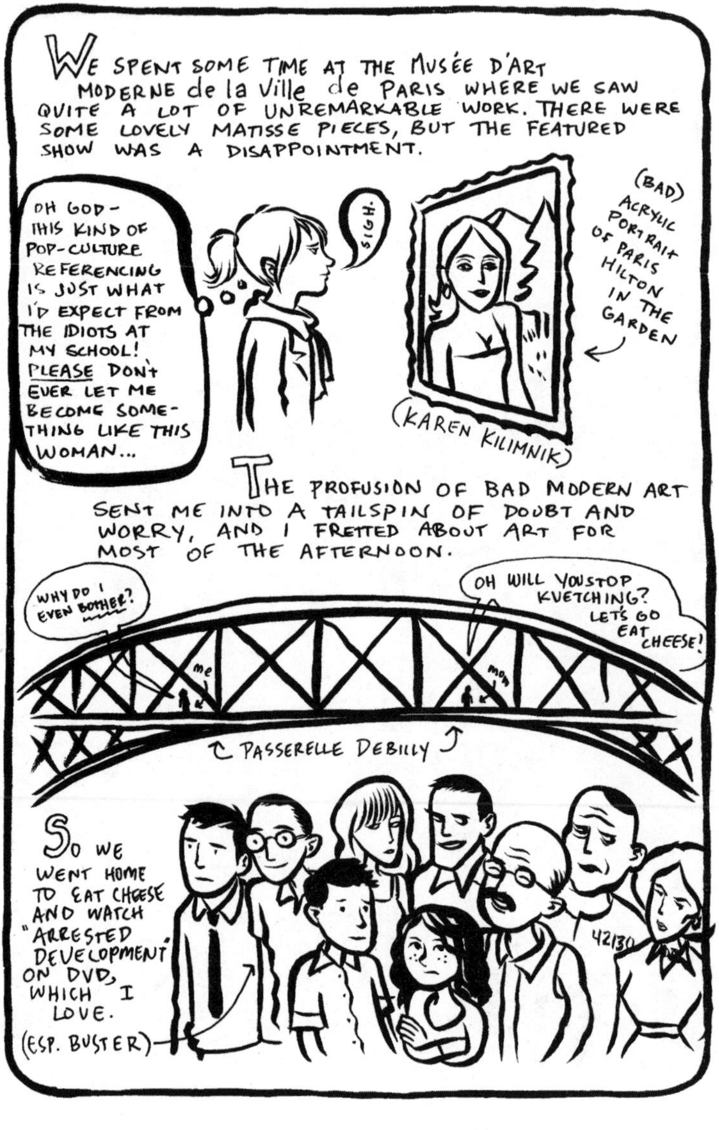
WE SPENT SOME TIME AT THE MUSÉE D'ART MODERNE de la Ville de PARIS WHERE WE SAW QUITE A LOT OF UNREMARKABLE WORK. THERE WERE SOME LOVELY MATISSE PIECES, BUT THE FEATURED SHOW WAS A DISAPPOINTMENT.
OH GOD- THIS KIND OF POP-CULTURE REFERENCING IS JUST WHAT I'D EXPECT FROM THE IDIOTS AT MY SCHOOL! PLEASE DON'T EVER LET ME BECOME SOMETHING LIKE THIS WOMAN...
SIGH.
(BAD) ACRYLIC PORTRAIT OF PARIS HILTON IN THE GARDEN
(KAREN KILIMNIK)
THE PROFUSION OF BAD MODERN ART SENT ME INTO A TAILSPIN OF DOUBT AND WORRY, AND I FRETTED ABOUT ART FOR MOST OF THE AFTERNOON.
WHY DO I EVEN BOTHER?
OH WILL YOU STOP KVETCHING? LET'S GO EAT CHEESE!
me
mom
PASSERELLE DEBILLY
SO WE WENT HOME TO EAT CHEESE AND WATCH "ARRESTED DEVELOPMENT" ON DVD, WHICH I LOVE.
(ESP. BUSTER)
42130

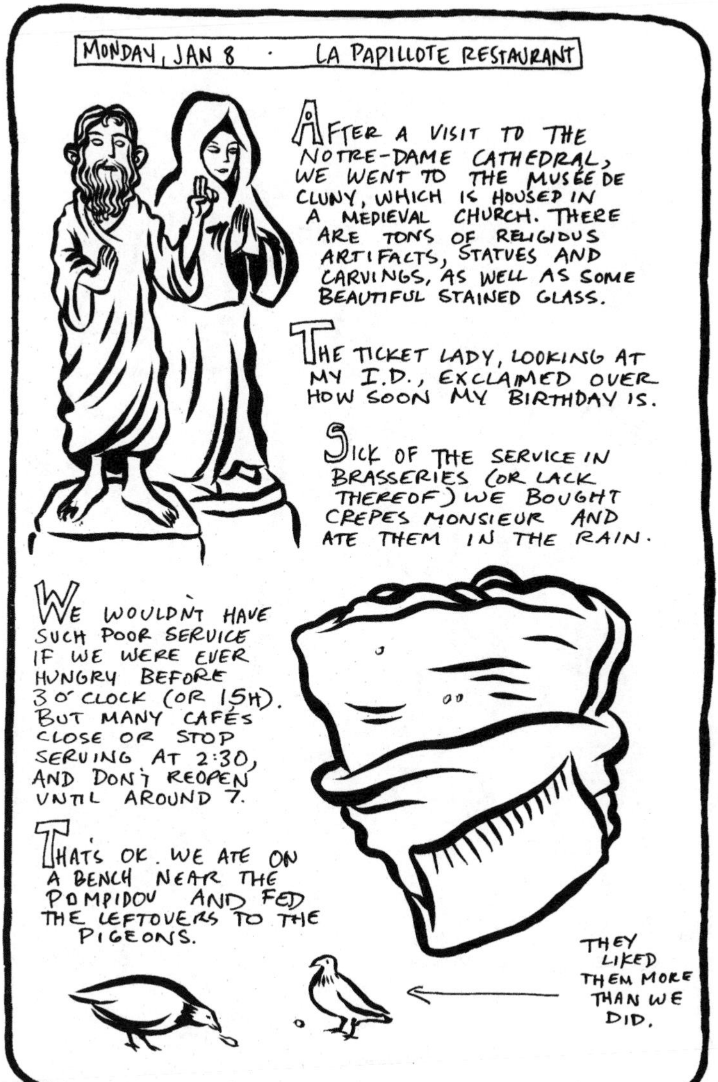
MONDAY, JAN 8 · LA PAPILLOTE RESTAURANT
AFTER A VISIT TO THE NOTRE-DAME CATHEDRAL, WE WENT TO THE MUSÉE DE CLUNY, WHICH IS HOUSED IN A MEDIEVAL CHURCH. THERE ARE TONS OF RELIGIOUS ARTIFACTS, STATUES AND CARVINGS, AS WELL AS SOME BEAUTIFUL STAINED GLASS.
THE TICKET LADY, LOOKING AT MY I.D., EXCLAIMED OVER HOW SOON MY BIRTHDAY IS.
SICK OF THE SERVICE IN BRASSERIES (OR LACK THEREOF) WE BOUGHT CREPES MONSIEUR AND ATE THEM IN THE RAIN.
WE WOULDN'T HAVE SUCH POOR SERVICE IF WE WERE EVER HUNGRY BEFORE 3 O'CLOCK (OR 15H). BUT MANY CAFÉS CLOSE OR STOP SERVING AT 2:30, AND DON'T REOPEN UNTIL AROUND 7.
THAT'S OK. WE ATE ON A BENCH NEAR THE POMPIDOU AND FED THE LEFTOVERS TO THE PIGEONS.
THEY LIKED THEM MORE THAN WE DID.

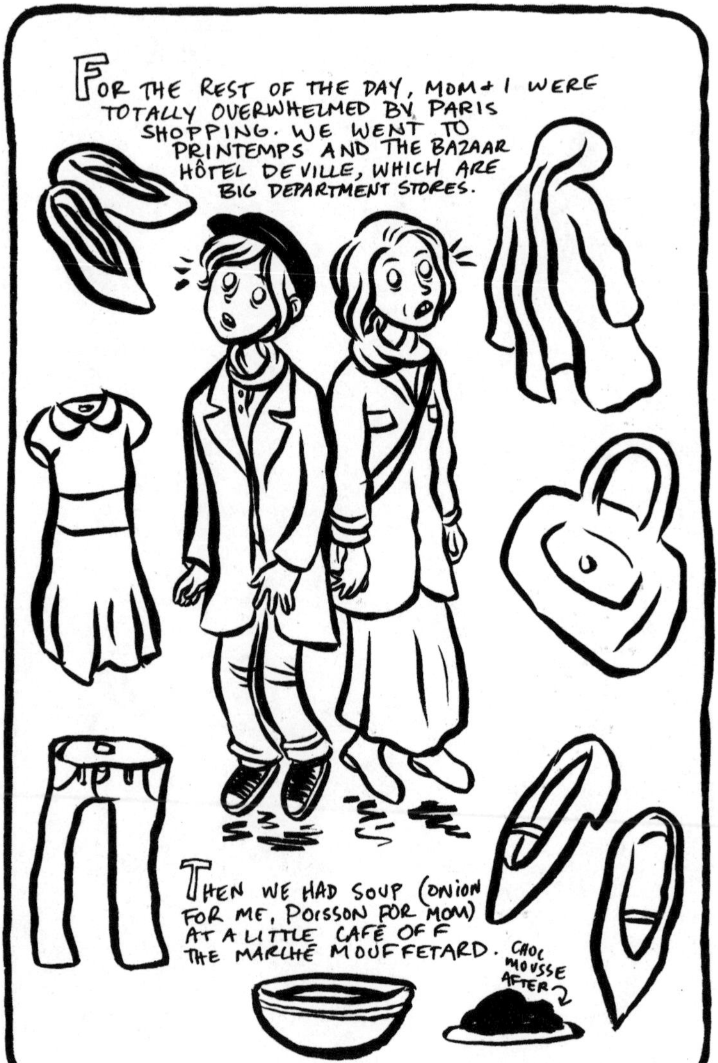
FOR THE REST OF THE DAY, MOM + I WERE TOTALLY OVERWHELMED BY PARIS SHOPPING. WE WENT TO PRINTEMPS AND THE BAZAAR HÔTEL DE VILLE, WHICH ARE BIG DEPARTMENT STORES.
THEN WE HAD SOUP (ONION FOR ME, POISSON FOR MOM) AT A LITTLE CAFÉ OFF THE MARCHÉ MOUFFETARD.
CHOC MOUSSE AFTER

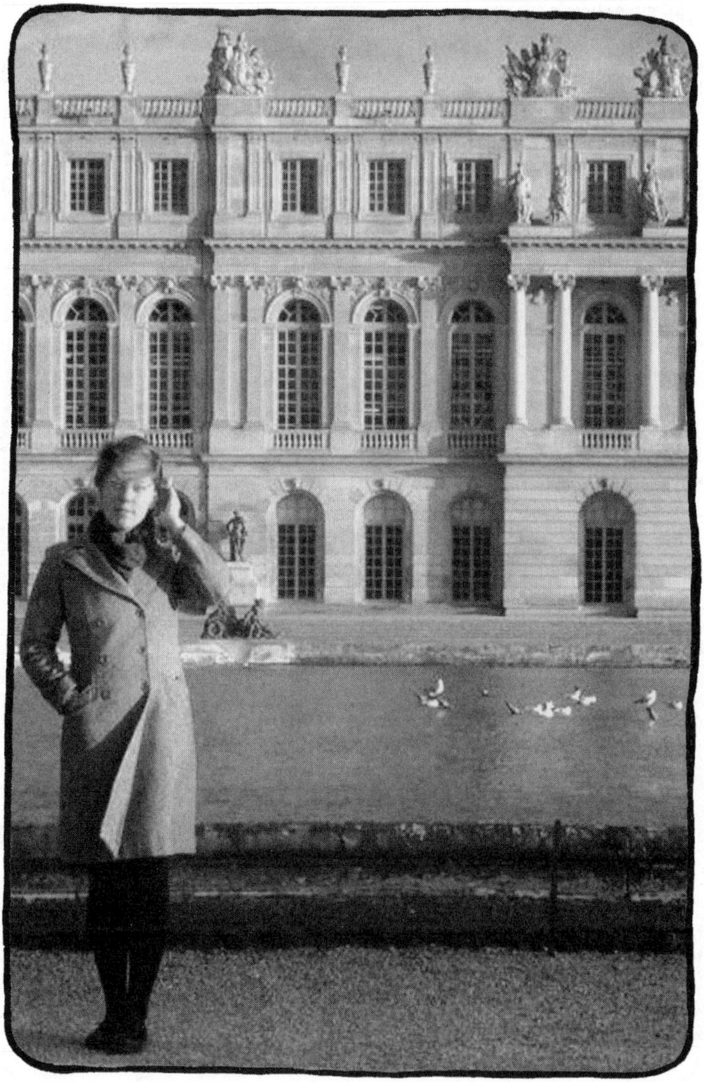

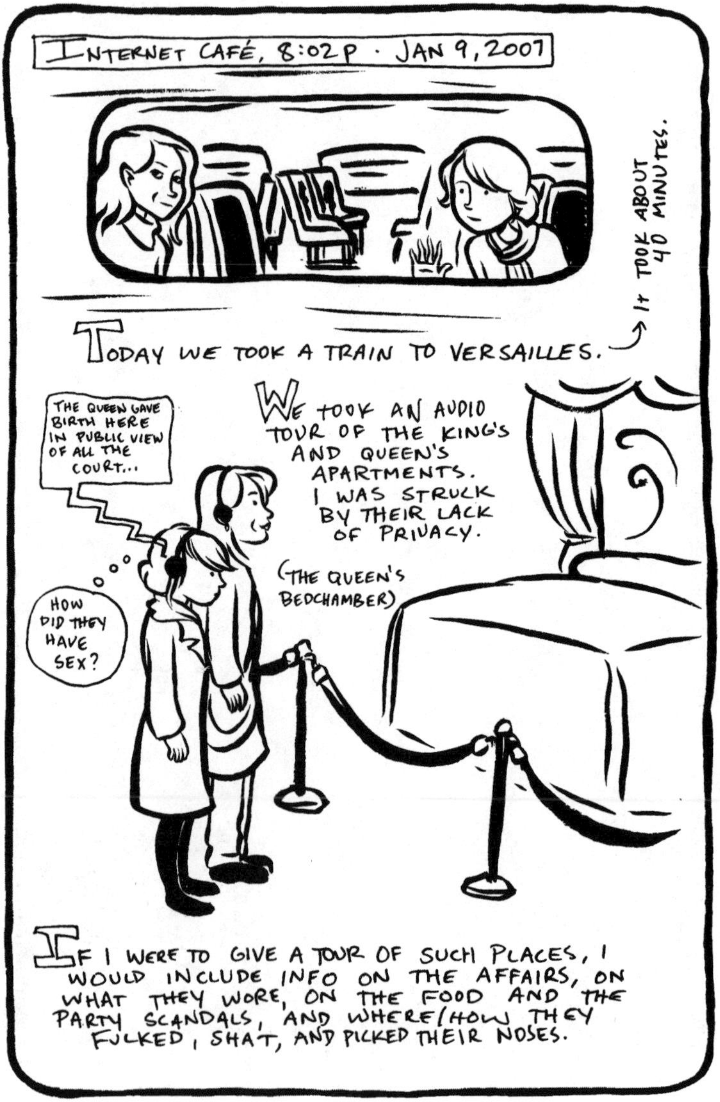
INTERNET CAFÉ, 8:02P · JAN 9, 2007
IT TOOK ABOUT 40 MINUTES.
TODAY WE TOOK A TRAIN TO VERSAILLES.
THE QUEEN GAVE BIRTH HERE IN PUBLIC VIEW OF ALL THE COURT...
WE TOOK AN AUDIO TOUR OF THE KING'S AND QUEEN'S APARTMENTS. I WAS STRUCK BY THEIR LACK OF PRIVACY.
HOW DID THEY HAVE SEX?
(THE QUEEN'S BEDCHAMBER)
IF I WERE TO GIVE A TOUR OF SUCH PLACES, I WOULD INCLUDE INFO ON THE AFFAIRS, ON WHAT THEY WORE, ON THE FOOD AND THE PARTY SCANDALS, AND WHERE/HOW THEY FUCKED, SHAT, AND PICKED THEIR NOSES.

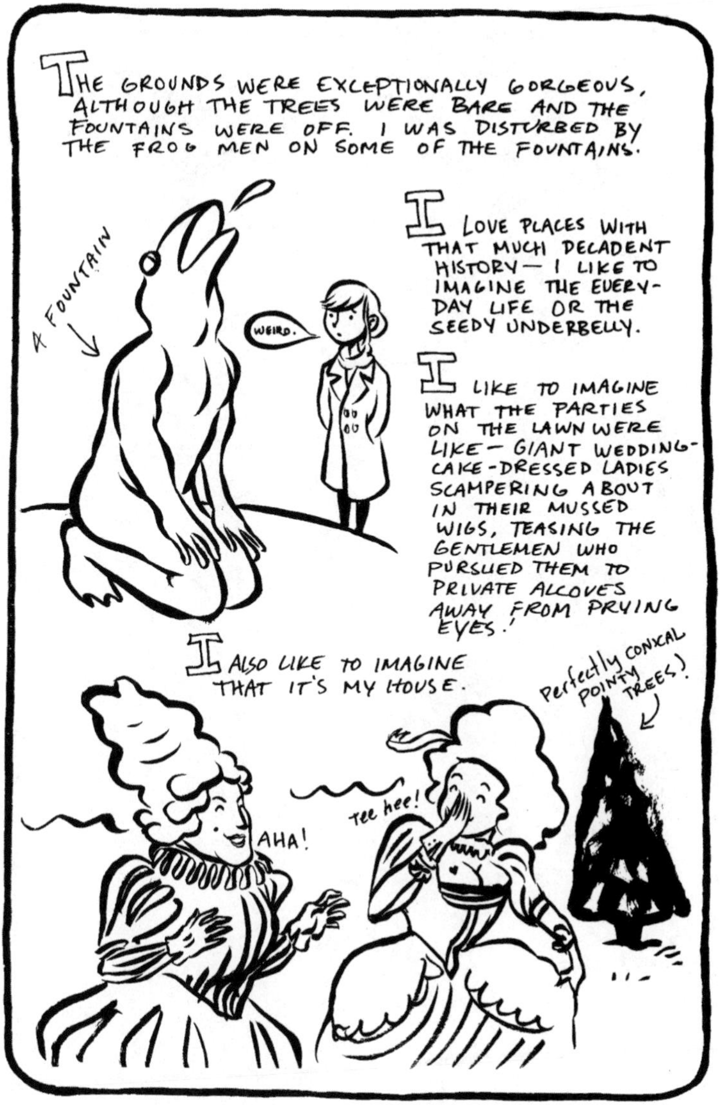
THE GROUNDS WERE EXCEPTIONALLY GORGEOUS, ALTHOUGH THE TREES WERE BARE AND THE FOUNTAINS WERE OFF. I WAS DISTURBED BY THE FROG MEN ON SOME OF THE FOUNTAINS.
A FOUNTAIN
WEIRD.
I LOVE PLACES WITH THAT MUCH DECADENT HISTORY— I LIKE TO IMAGINE THE EVERY-DAY LIFE OR THE SEEDY UNDERBELLY.
I LIKE TO IMAGINE WHAT THE PARTIES ON THE LAWN WERE LIKE— GIANT WEDDING-CAKE-DRESSED LADIES SCAMPERING ABOUT IN THEIR MUSSED WIGS, TEASING THE GENTLEMEN WHO PURSUED THEM TO PRIVATE ALCOVES AWAY FROM PRYING EYES.
I ALSO LIKE TO IMAGINE THAT IT'S MY HOUSE.
Perfectly CONICAL POINTY TREES!
AHA!
tee hee!

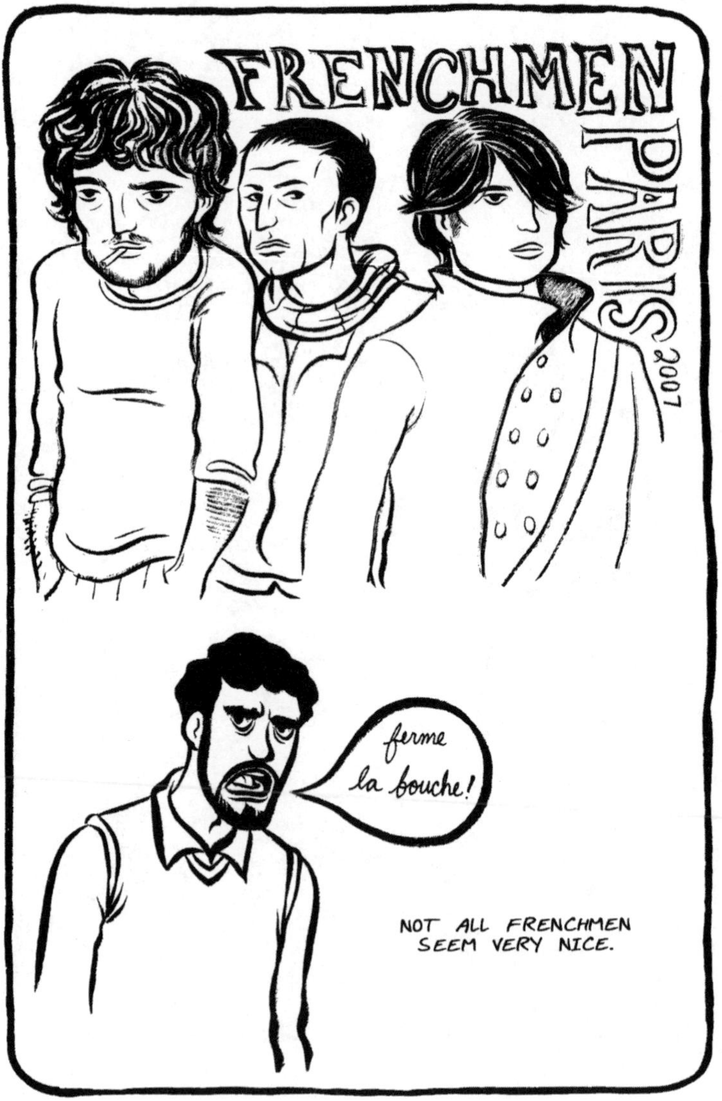
FRENCHMEN
PARIS
2007
ferme la bouche!
NOT ALL FRENCHMEN SEEM VERY NICE.

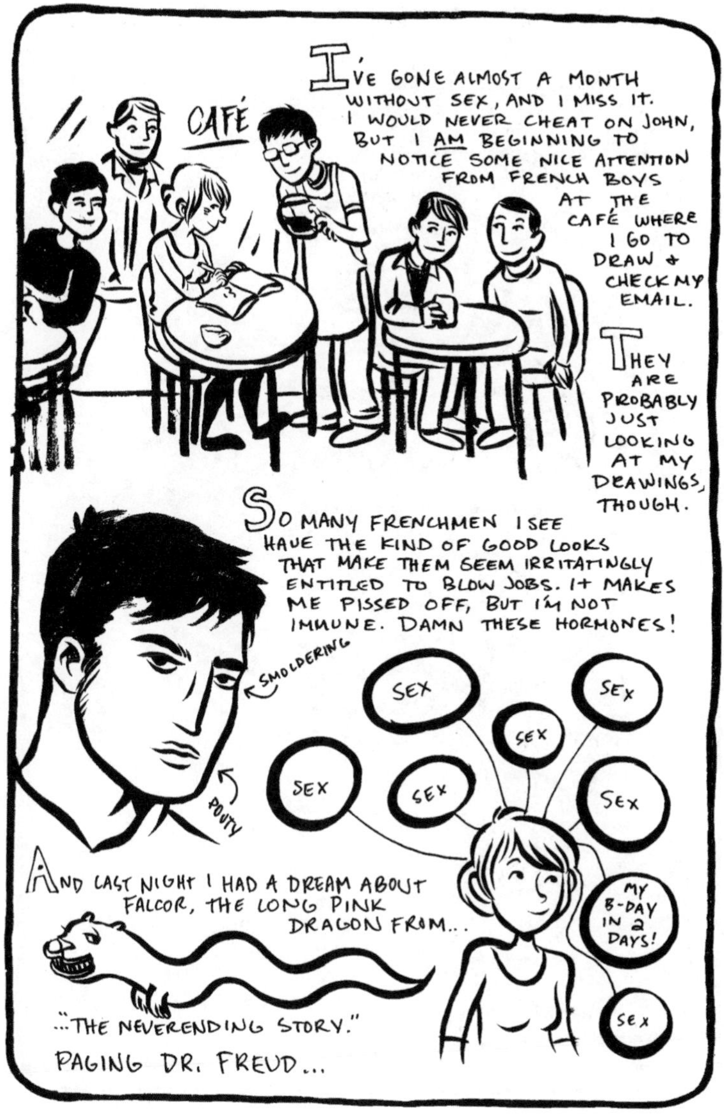
I'VE GONE ALMOST A MONTH WITHOUT SEX, AND I MISS IT. I WOULD NEVER CHEAT ON JOHN, BUT I AM BEGINNING TO NOTICE SOME NICE ATTENTION FROM FRENCH BOYS AT THE CAFÉ WHERE I GO TO DRAW & CHECK MY EMAIL.
CAFÉ
THEY ARE PROBABLY JUST LOOKING AT MY DRAWINGS, THOUGH.
SO MANY FRENCHMEN I SEE HAVE THE KIND OF GOOD LOOKS THAT MAKE THEM SEEM IRRITATINGLY ENTITLED TO BLOW JOBS. IT MAKES ME PISSED OFF, BUT I'M NOT IMMUNE. DAMN THESE HORMONES!
SMOLDERING
POUTY
SEX
SEX
SEX
SEX
SEX
SEX
SEX
MY B-DAY IN 2 DAYS!
SEX
AND LAST NIGHT I HAD A DREAM ABOUT FALCOR, THE LONG PINK DRAGON FROM...
..."THE NEVERENDING STORY."
PAGING DR. FREUD...

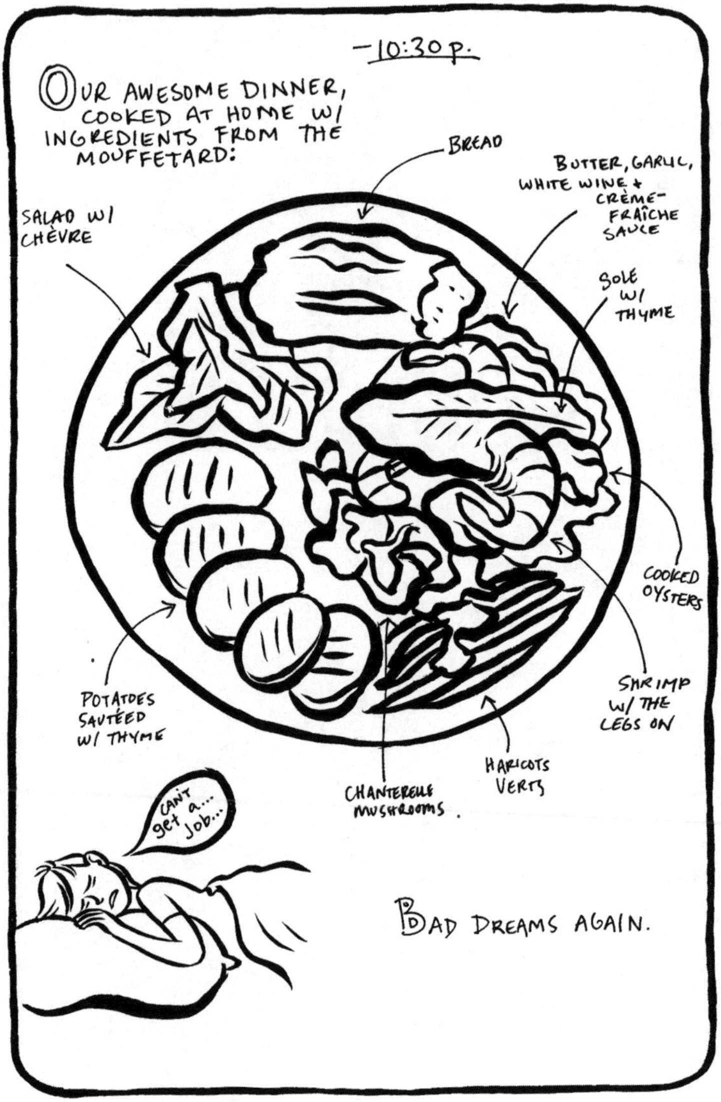

-10:30 p.
OUR AWESOME DINNER, COOKED AT HOME W/ INGREDIENTS FROM THE MOUFFETARD:
BREAD
BUTTER, GARLIC, WHITE WINE + CRÈME-FRAÎCHE SAUCE
SALAD W/ CHÈVRE
SOLE W/ THYME
COOKED OYSTERS
SHRIMP W/ THE LEGS ON
POTATOES SAUTÉED W/ THYME
HARICOTS VERTS
CHANTERELLE MUSHROOMS
CAN'T get a... job...
BAD DREAMS AGAIN.

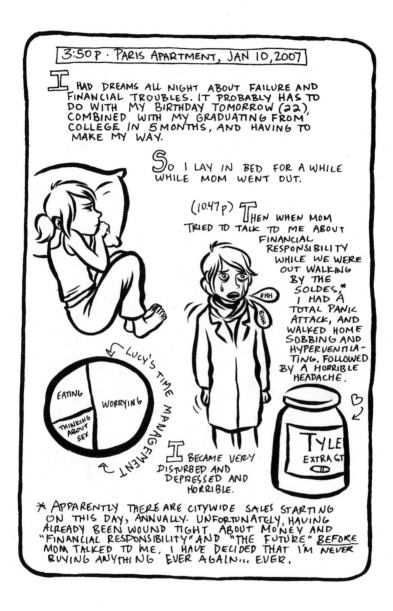

3:50p · PARIS APARTMENT, JAN 10, 2007

I HAD DREAMS ALL NIGHT ABOUT FAILURE AND FINANCIAL TROUBLES. IT PROBABLY HAS TO DO WITH MY BIRTHDAY TOMORROW (22), COMBINED WITH MY GRADUATING FROM COLLEGE IN 5 MONTHS, AND HAVING TO MAKE MY WAY.

So I LAY IN BED FOR A WHILE WHILE MOM WENT OUT.

(10.47p) THEN WHEN MOM TRIED TO TALK TO ME ABOUT FINANCIAL RESPONSIBILITY WHILE WE WERE OUT WALKING BY THE SOLDES,* I HAD A TOTAL PANIC ATTACK, AND WALKED HOME SOBBING AND HYPERVENTILA-TING. FOLLOWED BY A HORRIBLE HEADACHE.

EHH
EHH

LUCY'S TIME MANAGEMENT

EATING
WORRYING
THINKING ABOUT SEX

I BECAME VERY DISTURBED AND DEPRESSED AND HORRIBLE.

TYLE
EXTRA GT

* APPARENTLY THERE ARE CITYWIDE SALES STARTING ON THIS DAY, ANNUALLY. UNFORTUNATELY, HAVING ALREADY BEEN WOUND TIGHT ABOUT MONEY AND "FINANCIAL RESPONSIBILITY" AND "THE FUTURE" BEFORE MOM TALKED TO ME, I HAVE DECIDED THAT I'M NEVER BUYING ANYTHING EVER AGAIN... EVER.

115

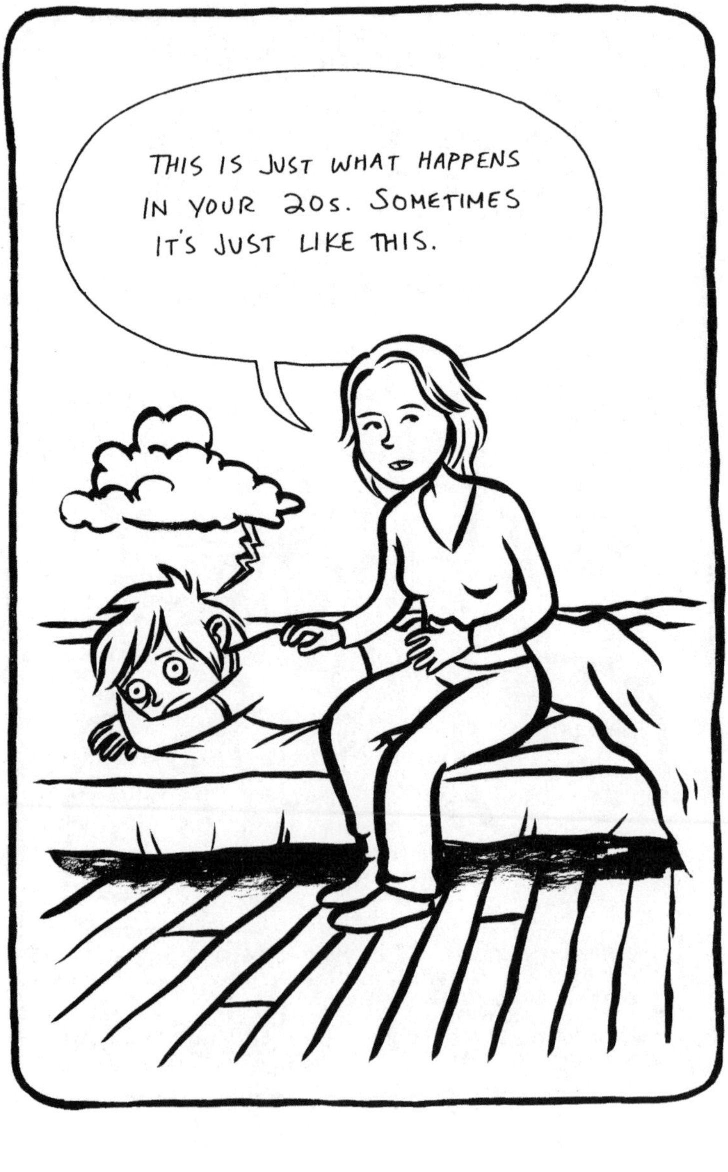
THIS IS JUST WHAT HAPPENS IN YOUR 20S. SOMETIMES IT'S JUST LIKE THIS.

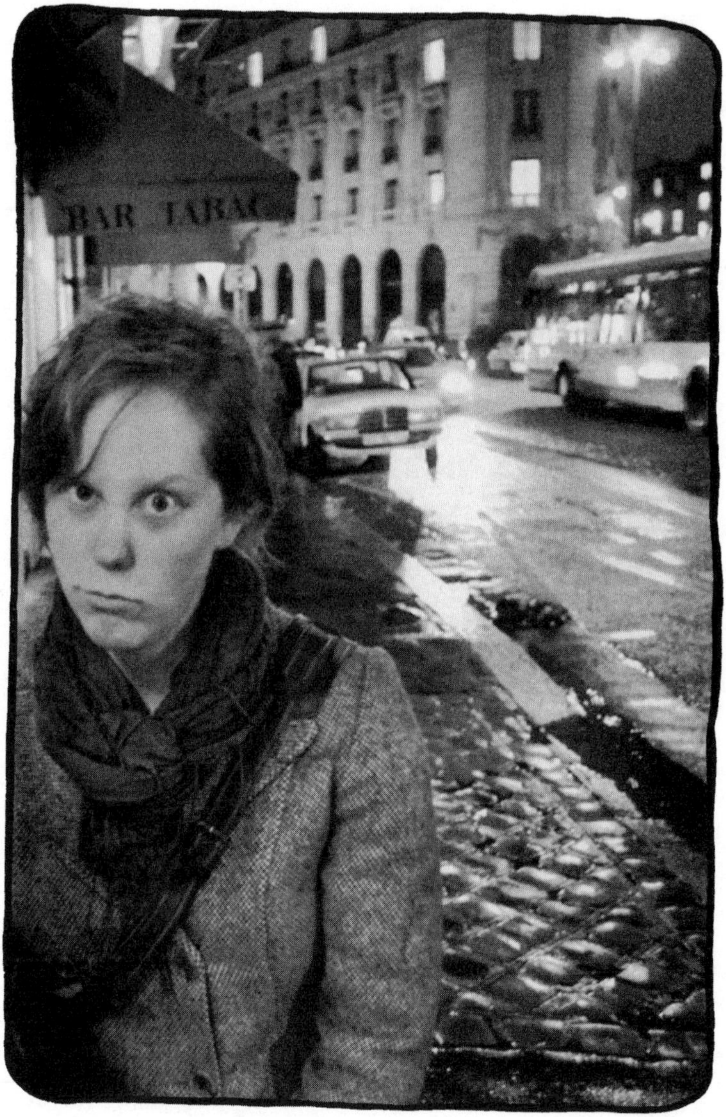
BAR TABAC

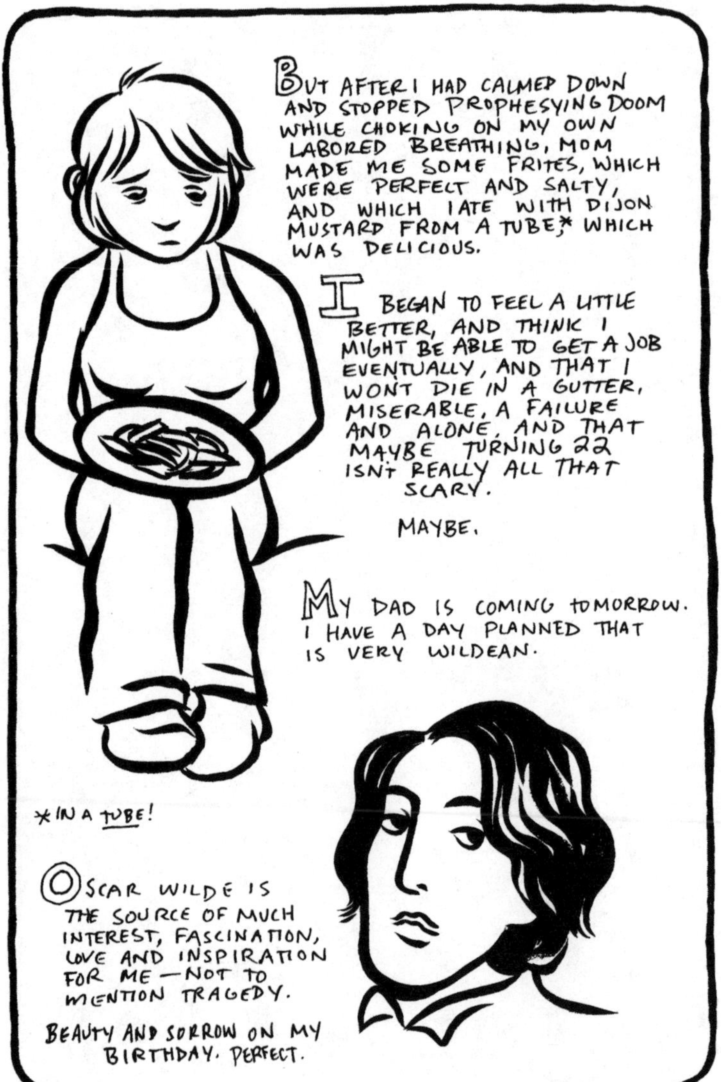

BUT AFTER I HAD CALMED DOWN AND STOPPED PROPHESYING DOOM WHILE CHOKING ON MY OWN LABORED BREATHING, MOM MADE ME SOME FRITES, WHICH WERE PERFECT AND SALTY, AND WHICH I ATE WITH DIJON MUSTARD FROM A TUBE,* WHICH WAS DELICIOUS.
I BEGAN TO FEEL A LITTLE BETTER, AND THINK I MIGHT BE ABLE TO GET A JOB EVENTUALLY, AND THAT I WON'T DIE IN A GUTTER, MISERABLE, A FAILURE AND ALONE, AND THAT MAYBE TURNING 22 ISN'T REALLY ALL THAT SCARY.
MAYBE.
MY DAD IS COMING TOMORROW. I HAVE A DAY PLANNED THAT IS VERY WILDEAN.
*IN A TUBE!
OSCAR WILDE IS THE SOURCE OF MUCH INTEREST, FASCINATION, LOVE AND INSPIRATION FOR ME—NOT TO MENTION TRAGEDY.
BEAUTY AND SORROW ON MY BIRTHDAY. PERFECT.

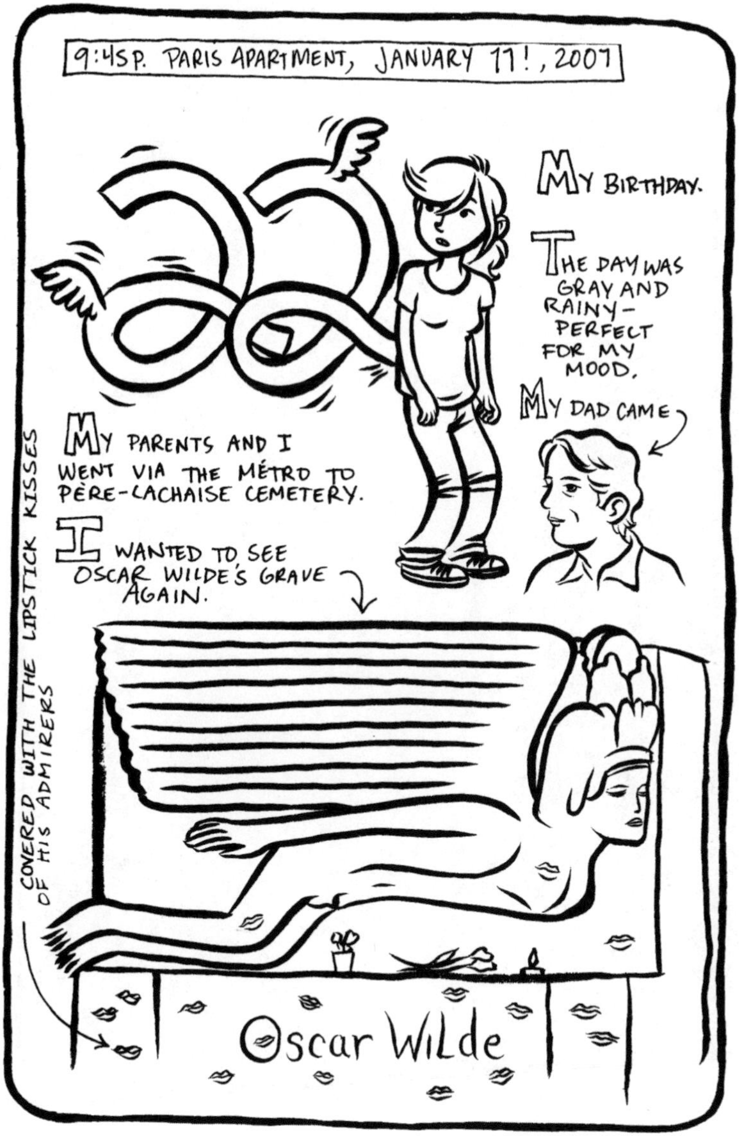
9:45P. PARIS APARTMENT, JANUARY 17!, 2007
MY BIRTHDAY.
THE DAY WAS GRAY AND RAINY—PERFECT FOR MY MOOD.
MY DAD CAME
MY PARENTS AND I WENT VIA THE MÉTRO TO PÈRE-LACHAISE CEMETERY.
I WANTED TO SEE OSCAR WILDE'S GRAVE AGAIN.
COVERED WITH THE LIPSTICK KISSES OF HIS ADMIRERS
Oscar Wilde

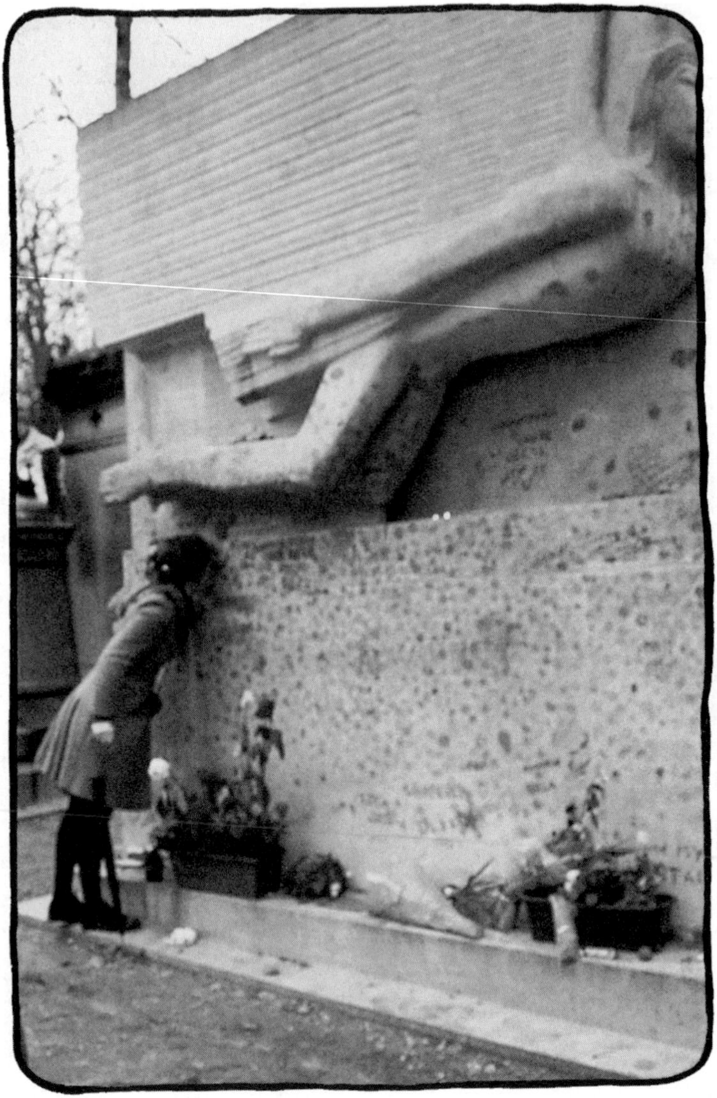

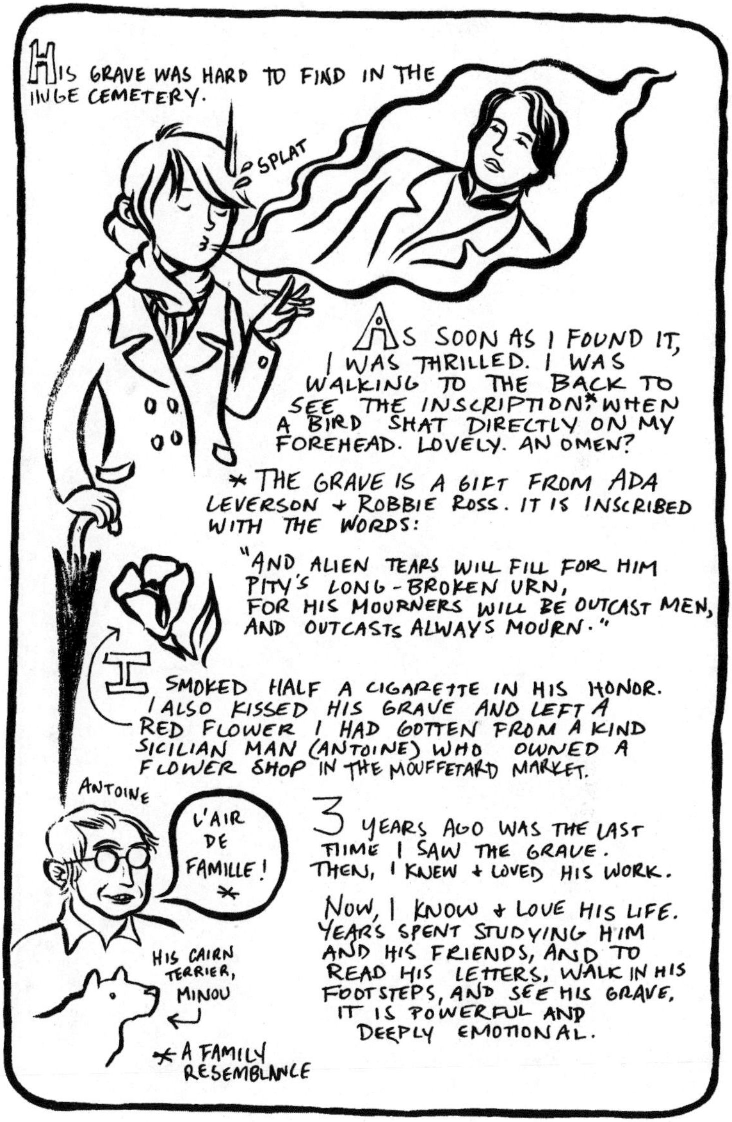
HIS GRAVE WAS HARD TO FIND IN THE HUGE CEMETERY.
SPLAT
AS SOON AS I FOUND IT, I WAS THRILLED. I WAS WALKING TO THE BACK TO SEE THE INSCRIPTION* WHEN A BIRD SHAT DIRECTLY ON MY FOREHEAD. LOVELY. AN OMEN?
* THE GRAVE IS A GIFT FROM ADA LEVERSON + ROBBIE ROSS. IT IS INSCRIBED WITH THE WORDS:
"AND ALIEN TEARS WILL FILL FOR HIM
PITY'S LONG-BROKEN URN,
FOR HIS MOURNERS WILL BE OUTCAST MEN,
AND OUTCASTS ALWAYS MOURN."
I SMOKED HALF A CIGARETTE IN HIS HONOR. I ALSO KISSED HIS GRAVE AND LEFT A RED FLOWER I HAD GOTTEN FROM A KIND SICILIAN MAN (ANTOINE) WHO OWNED A FLOWER SHOP IN THE MOUFFETARD MARKET.
ANTOINE
L'AIR DE FAMILLE! *
HIS CAIRN TERRIER, MINOU
* A FAMILY RESEMBLANCE
3 YEARS AGO WAS THE LAST TIME I SAW THE GRAVE. THEN, I KNEW + LOVED HIS WORK.
NOW, I KNOW + LOVE HIS LIFE. YEARS SPENT STUDYING HIM AND HIS FRIENDS, AND TO READ HIS LETTERS, WALK IN HIS FOOTSTEPS, AND SEE HIS GRAVE, IT IS POWERFUL AND DEEPLY EMOTIONAL.

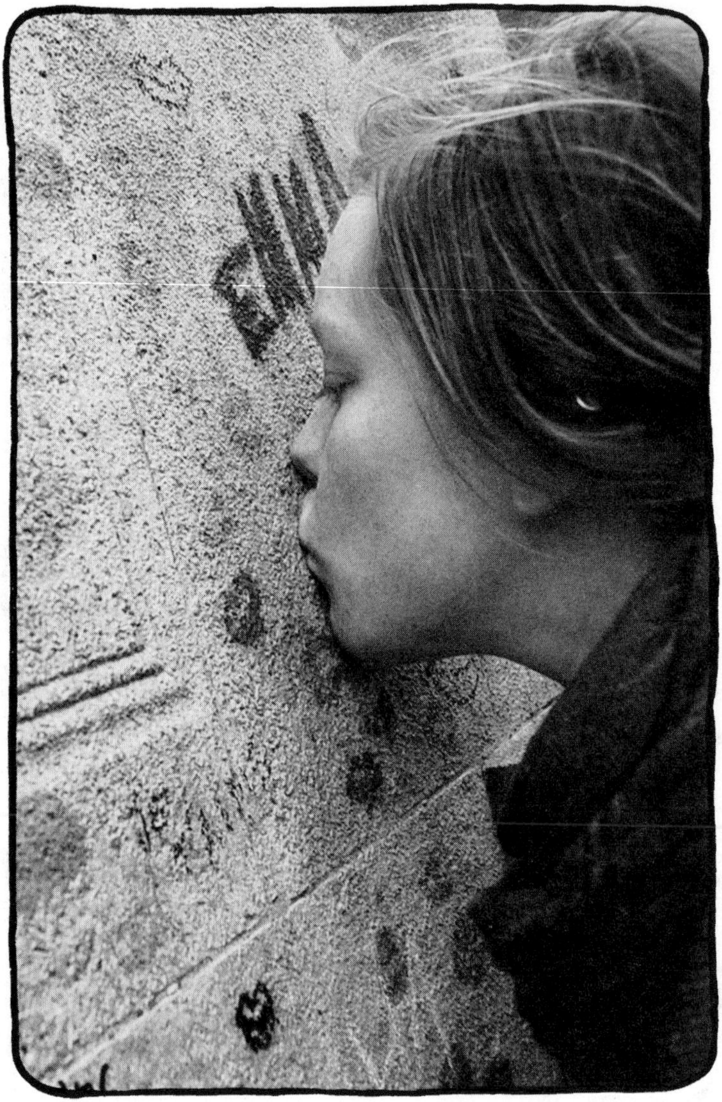

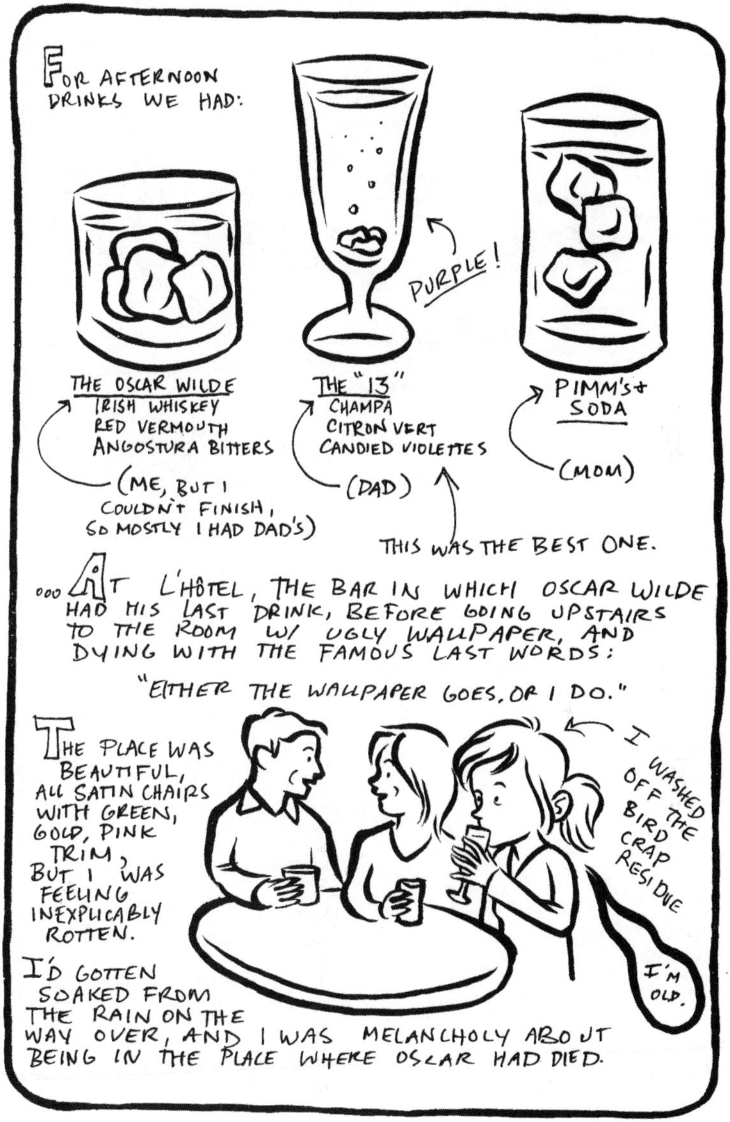
FOR AFTERNOON DRINKS WE HAD:
PURPLE!
THE OSCAR WILDE
IRISH WHISKEY
RED VERMOUTH
ANGOSTURA BITTERS
THE "13"
CHAMPA
CITRON VERT
CANDIED VIOLETTES
PIMM'S + SODA
(ME, BUT I COULDN'T FINISH, SO MOSTLY I HAD DAD'S)
(DAD)
(MOM)
THIS WAS THE BEST ONE.
...AT L'HÔTEL, THE BAR IN WHICH OSCAR WILDE HAD HIS LAST DRINK, BEFORE GOING UPSTAIRS TO THE ROOM W/ UGLY WALLPAPER, AND DYING WITH THE FAMOUS LAST WORDS:
"EITHER THE WALLPAPER GOES, OR I DO."
THE PLACE WAS BEAUTIFUL, ALL SATIN CHAIRS WITH GREEN, GOLD, PINK TRIM, BUT I WAS FEELING INEXPLICABLY ROTTEN.
I WASHED OFF THE BIRD CRAP RESIDUE
I'M OLD.
I'D GOTTEN SOAKED FROM THE RAIN ON THE WAY OVER, AND I WAS MELANCHOLY ABOUT BEING IN THE PLACE WHERE OSCAR HAD DIED.

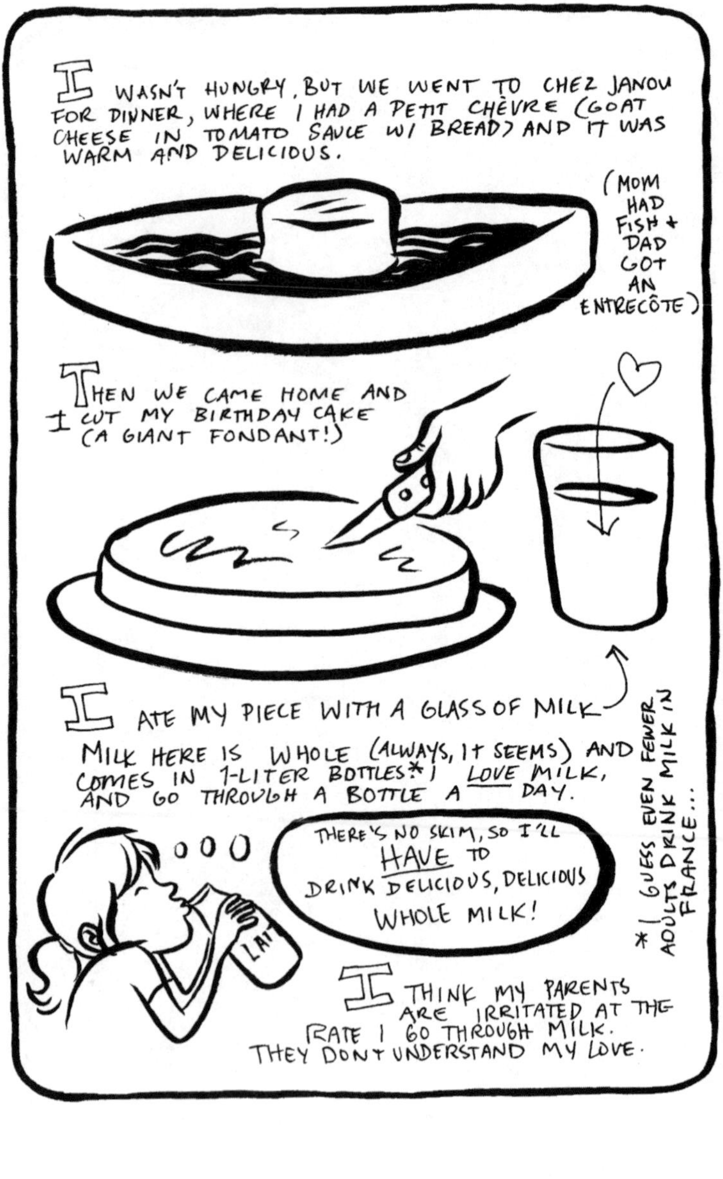
I WASN'T HUNGRY, BUT WE WENT TO CHEZ JANOU FOR DINNER, WHERE I HAD A PETIT CHÈVRE (GOAT CHEESE IN TOMATO SAUCE W/ BREAD) AND IT WAS WARM AND DELICIOUS.
(MOM HAD FISH + DAD GOT AN ENTRECÔTE)
THEN WE CAME HOME AND I CUT MY BIRTHDAY CAKE (A GIANT FONDANT!)
I ATE MY PIECE WITH A GLASS OF MILK
MILK HERE IS WHOLE (ALWAYS, IT SEEMS) AND COMES IN 1-LITER BOTTLES.* I LOVE MILK, AND GO THROUGH A BOTTLE A DAY.
*I GUESS EVEN FEWER ADULTS DRINK MILK IN FRANCE...
THERE'S NO SKIM, SO I'LL HAVE TO DRINK DELICIOUS, DELICIOUS WHOLE MILK!
LAIT
I THINK MY PARENTS ARE IRRITATED AT THE RATE I GO THROUGH MILK. THEY DONT UNDERSTAND MY LOVE.

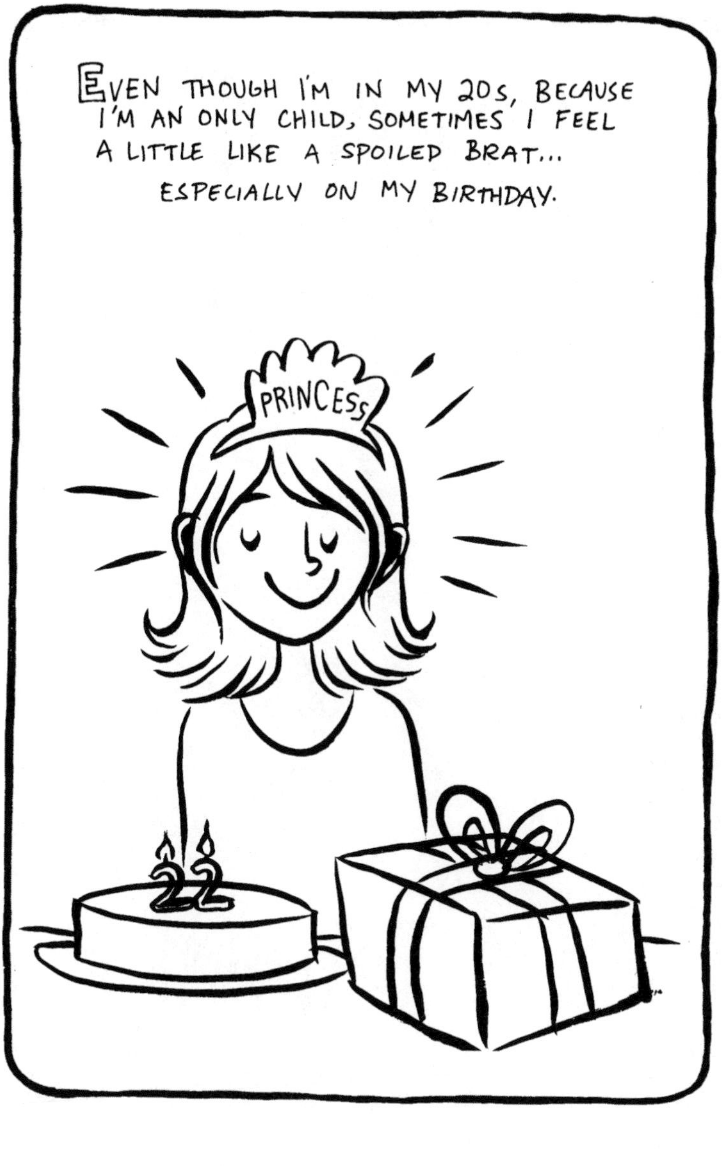
EVEN THOUGH I'M IN MY 20S, BECAUSE I'M AN ONLY CHILD, SOMETIMES I FEEL A LITTLE LIKE A SPOILED BRAT...
ESPECIALLY ON MY BIRTHDAY.
PRINCESS
22

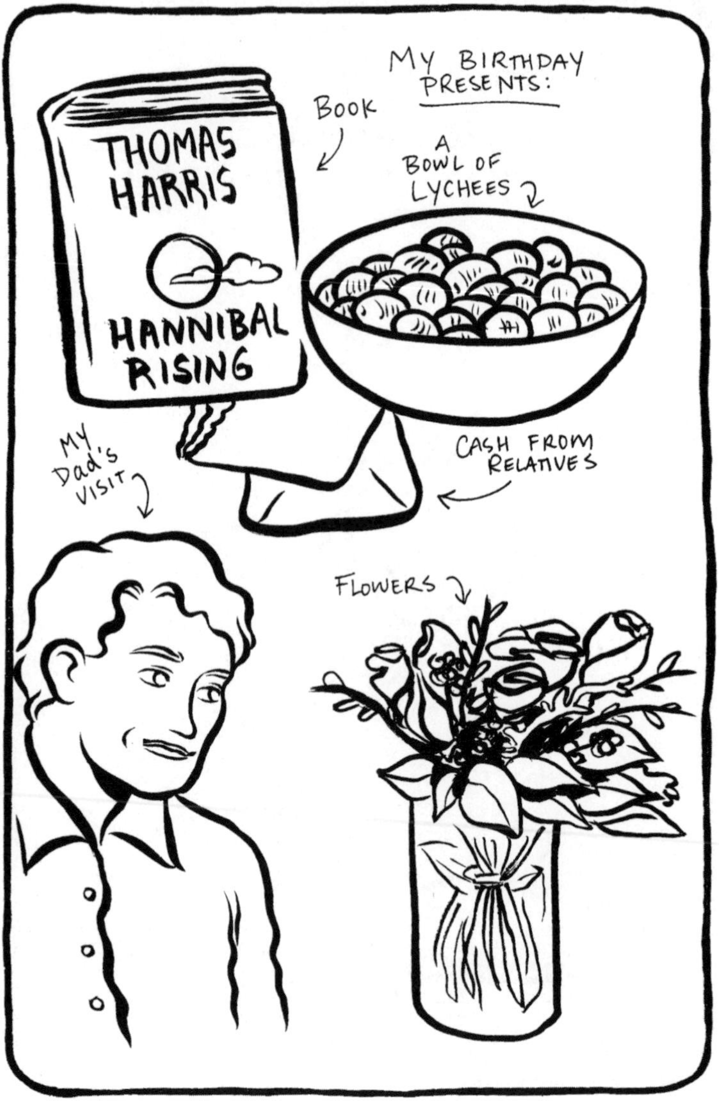

MY BIRTHDAY PRESENTS:
BOOK
THOMAS HARRIS
HANNIBAL RISING
A BOWL OF LYCHEES
MY Dad's VISIT
CASH FROM RELATIVES
FLOWERS

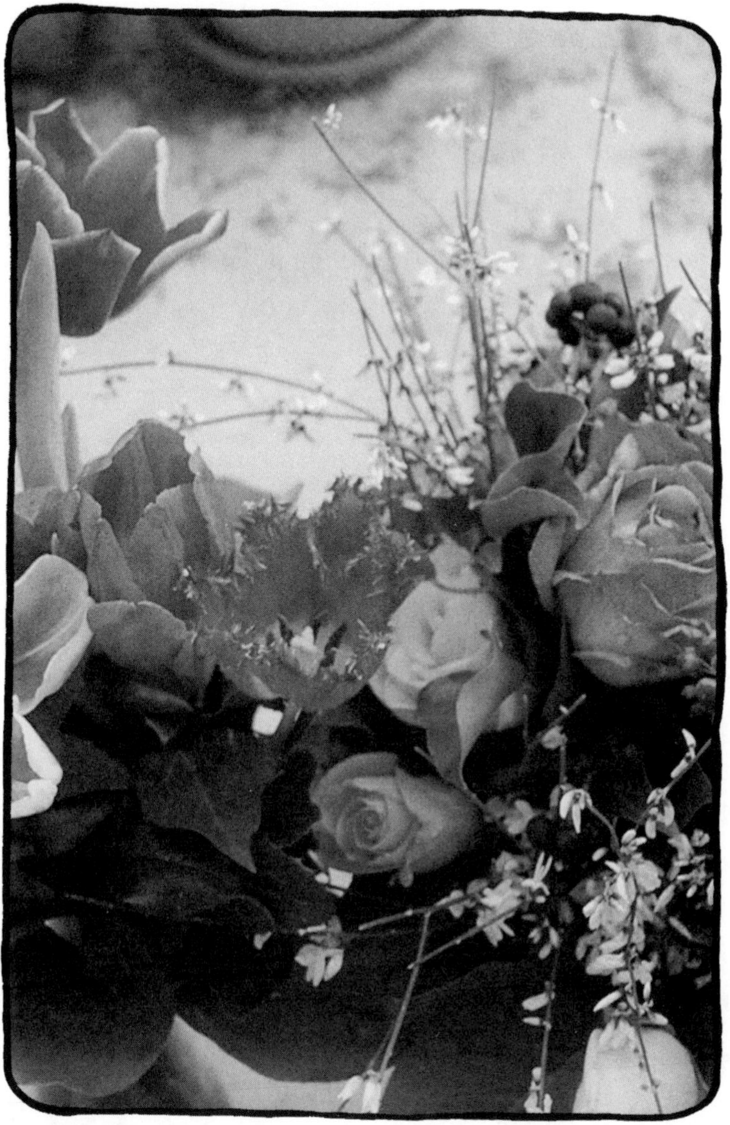

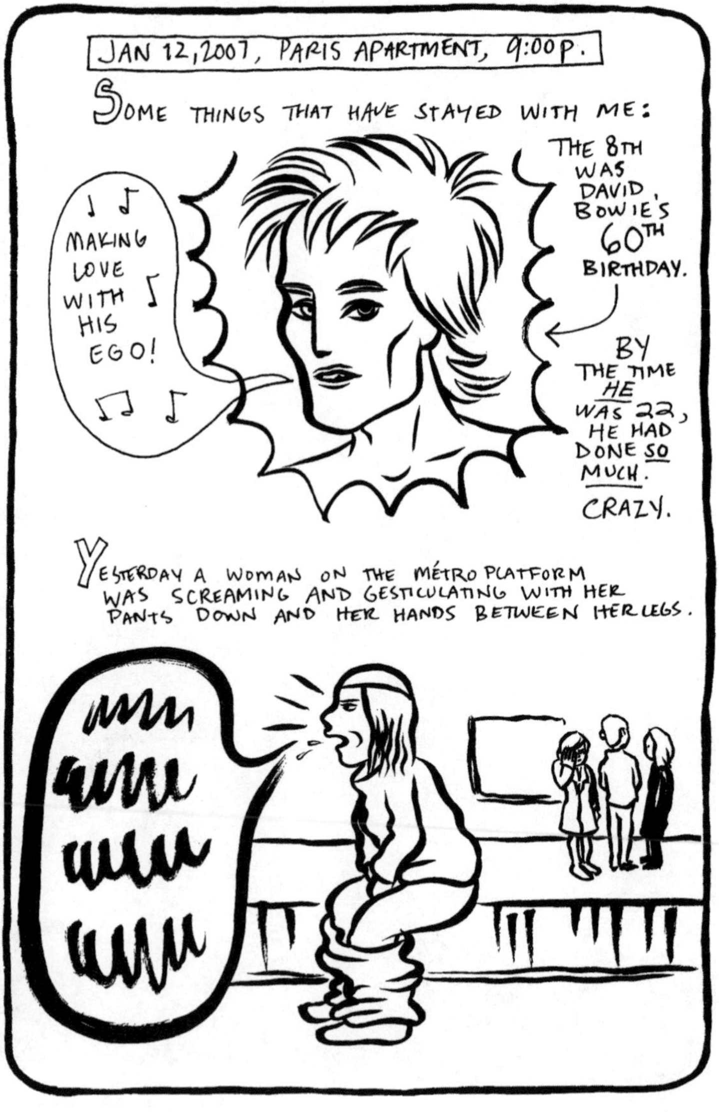
JAN 12, 2007, PARIS APARTMENT, 9:00P.
SOME THINGS THAT HAVE STAYED WITH ME:
MAKING LOVE WITH HIS EGO!
THE 8TH WAS DAVID BOWIE'S 60TH BIRTHDAY.
BY THE TIME HE WAS 22, HE HAD DONE SO MUCH.
CRAZY.
YESTERDAY A WOMAN ON THE MÉTRO PLATFORM WAS SCREAMING AND GESTICULATING WITH HER PANTS DOWN AND HER HANDS BETWEEN HER LEGS.

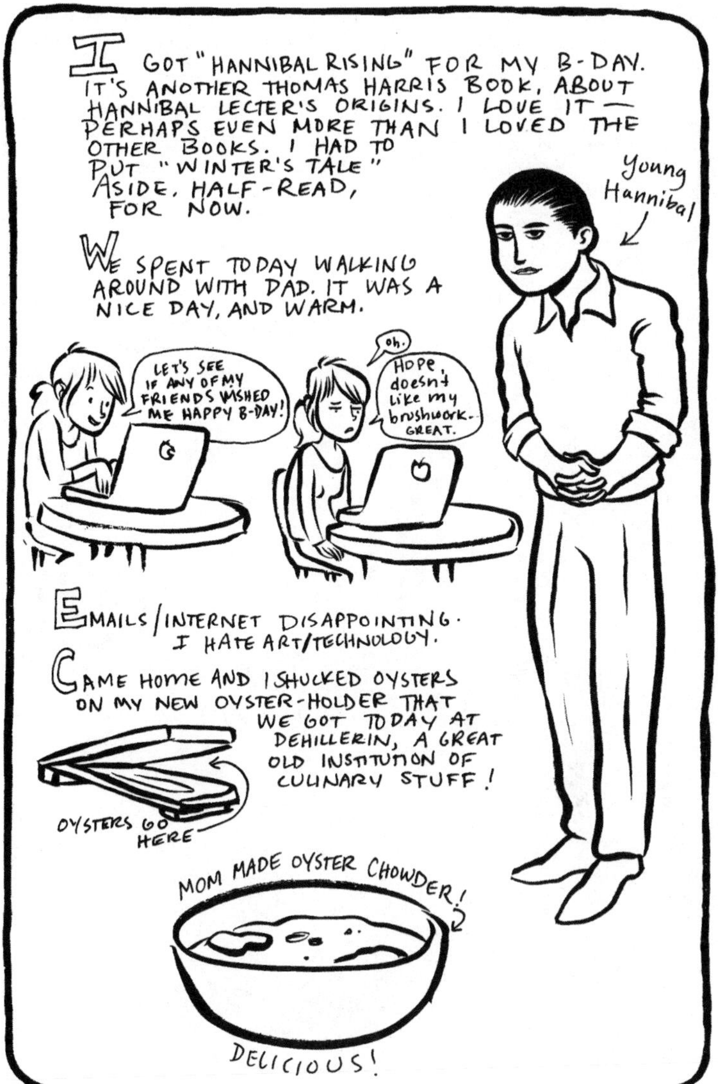
I GOT "HANNIBAL RISING" FOR MY B-DAY. IT'S ANOTHER THOMAS HARRIS BOOK, ABOUT HANNIBAL LECTER'S ORIGINS. I LOVE IT — PERHAPS EVEN MORE THAN I LOVED THE OTHER BOOKS. I HAD TO PUT "WINTER'S TALE" ASIDE, HALF-READ, FOR NOW.
Young Hannibal
WE SPENT TODAY WALKING AROUND WITH DAD. IT WAS A NICE DAY, AND WARM.
LET'S SEE IF ANY OF MY FRIENDS WISHED ME HAPPY B-DAY!
oh.
Hope doesn't like my brushwork. GREAT.
EMAILS/INTERNET DISAPPOINTING. I HATE ART/TECHNOLOGY.
CAME HOME AND I SHUCKED OYSTERS ON MY NEW OYSTER-HOLDER THAT WE GOT TODAY AT DEHILLERIN, A GREAT OLD INSTITUTION OF CULINARY STUFF!
OYSTERS GO HERE
MOM MADE OYSTER CHOWDER!
DELICIOUS!

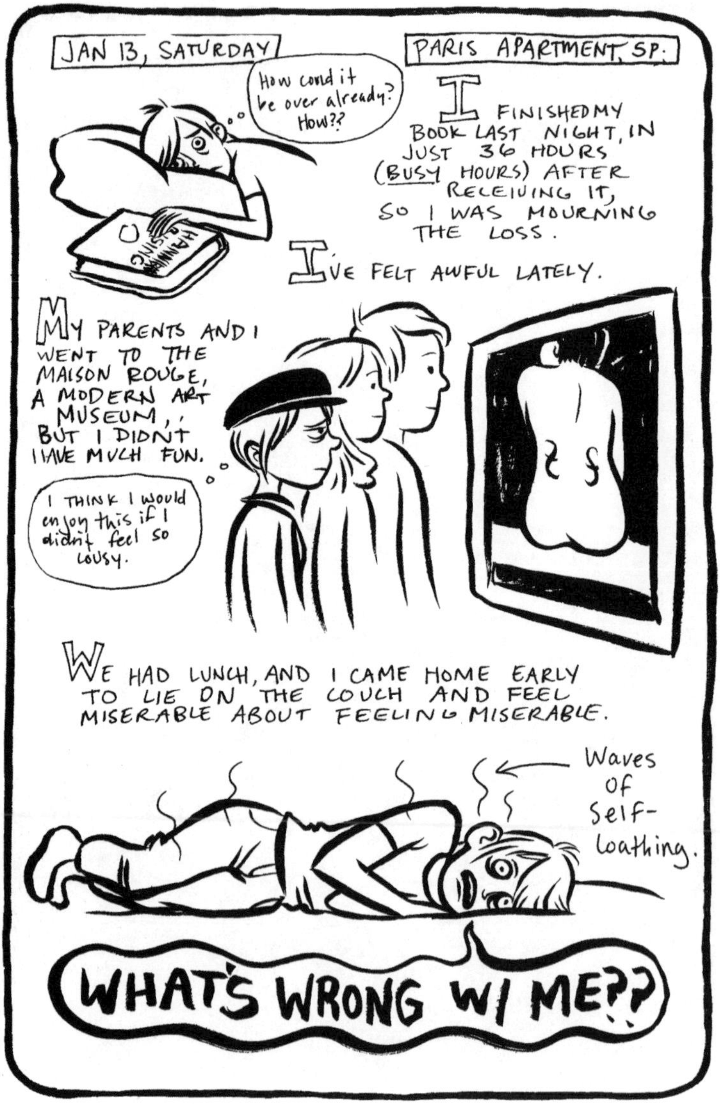
JAN 13, SATURDAY
PARIS APARTMENT, SP.
How could it be over already? How??
I FINISHED MY BOOK LAST NIGHT, IN JUST 36 HOURS (BUSY HOURS) AFTER RECEIVING IT, SO I WAS MOURNING THE LOSS.
I'VE FELT AWFUL LATELY.
MY PARENTS AND I WENT TO THE MAISON ROUGE, A MODERN ART MUSEUM, BUT I DIDN'T HAVE MUCH FUN.
I THINK I would enjoy this if I didn't feel so lousy.
WE HAD LUNCH, AND I CAME HOME EARLY TO LIE ON THE COUCH AND FEEL MISERABLE ABOUT FEELING MISERABLE.
Waves of Self-loathing.
WHAT'S WRONG W/ ME??

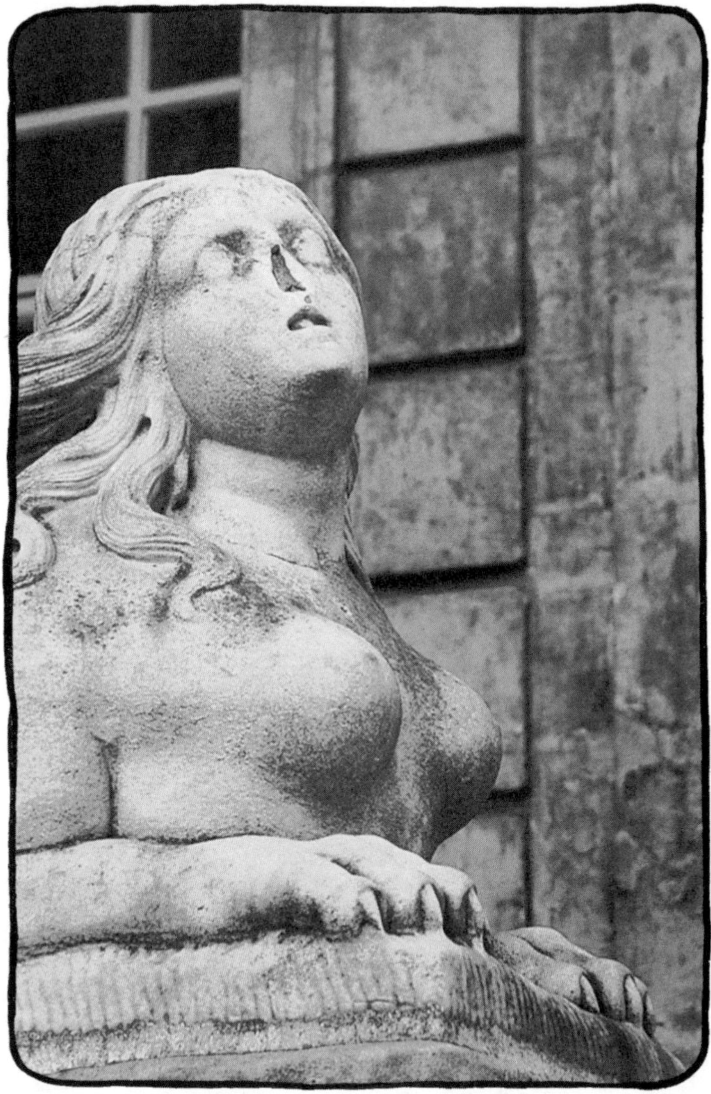

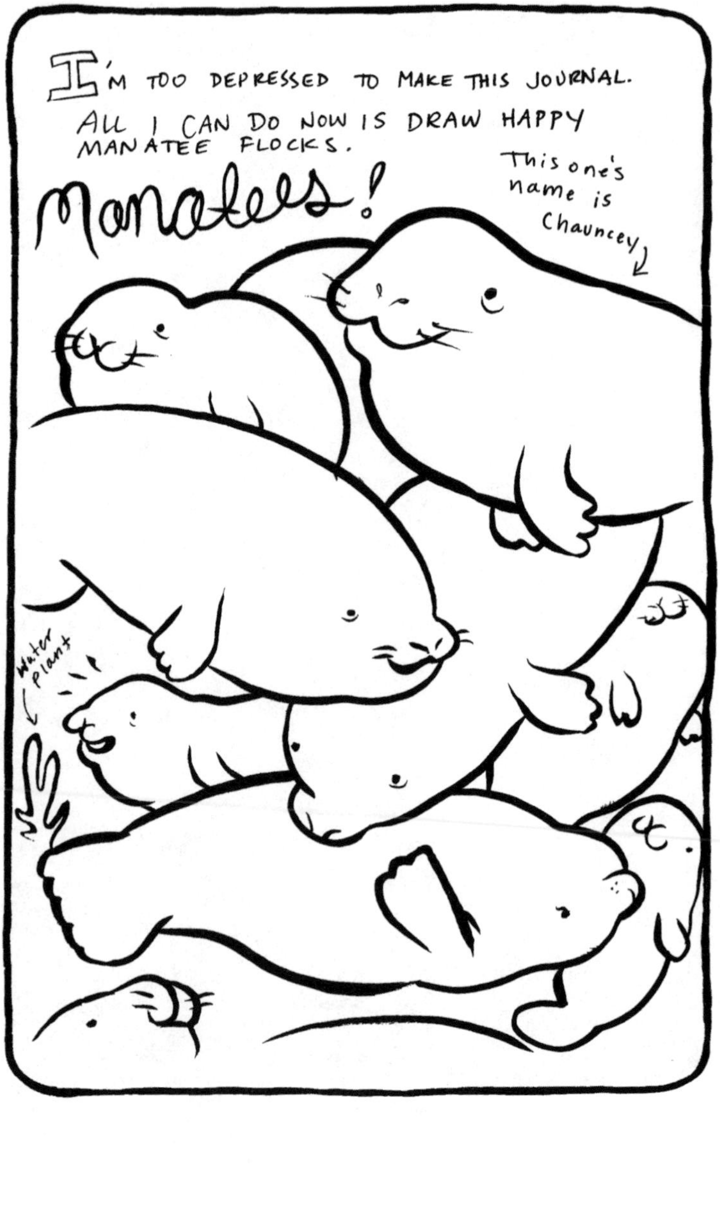
I'M TOO DEPRESSED TO MAKE THIS JOURNAL.
ALL I CAN DO NOW IS DRAW HAPPY MANATEE FLOCKS.
Manatees!
This one's name is Chauncey
Water plant

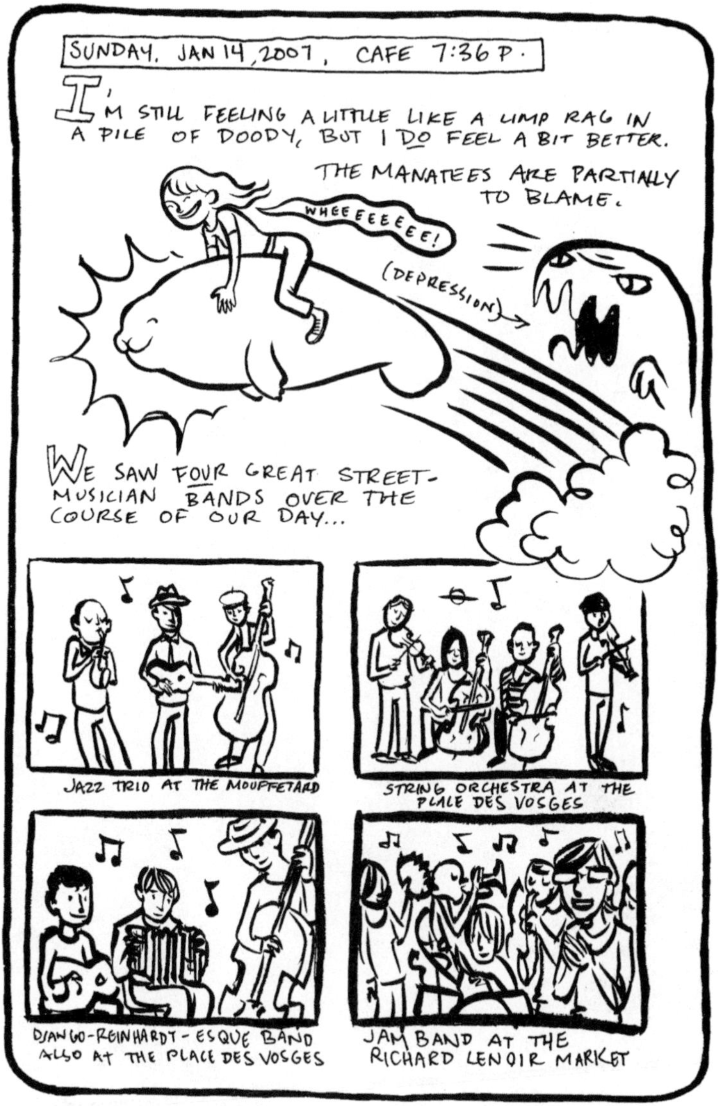
SUNDAY, JAN 14, 2007, CAFE 7:36 P.
I'M STILL FEELING A LITTLE LIKE A LIMP RAG IN A PILE OF DOODY, BUT I DO FEEL A BIT BETTER.
THE MANATEES ARE PARTIALLY TO BLAME.
WHEEEEEEEEE!
(DEPRESSION)
WE SAW FOUR GREAT STREET-MUSICIAN BANDS OVER THE COURSE OF OUR DAY...
JAZZ TRIO AT THE MOUFFETARD
STRING ORCHESTRA AT THE PLACE DES VOSGES
DJANGO-REINHARDT-ESQUE BAND ALSO AT THE PLACE DES VOSGES
JAM BAND AT THE RICHARD LENOIR MARKET

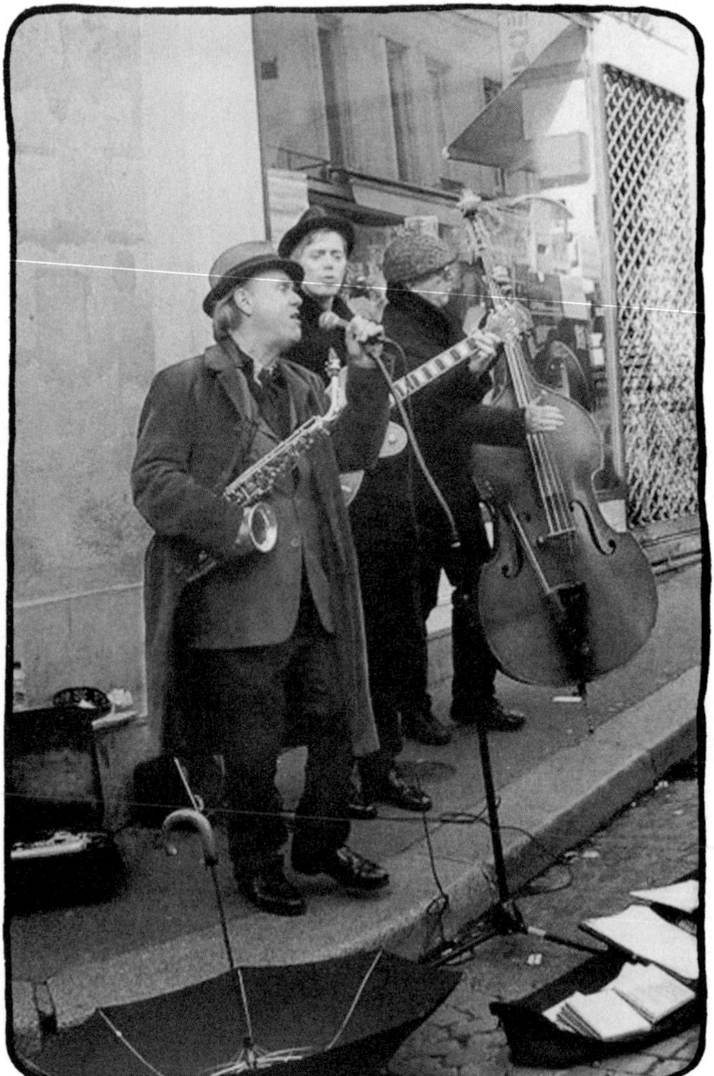

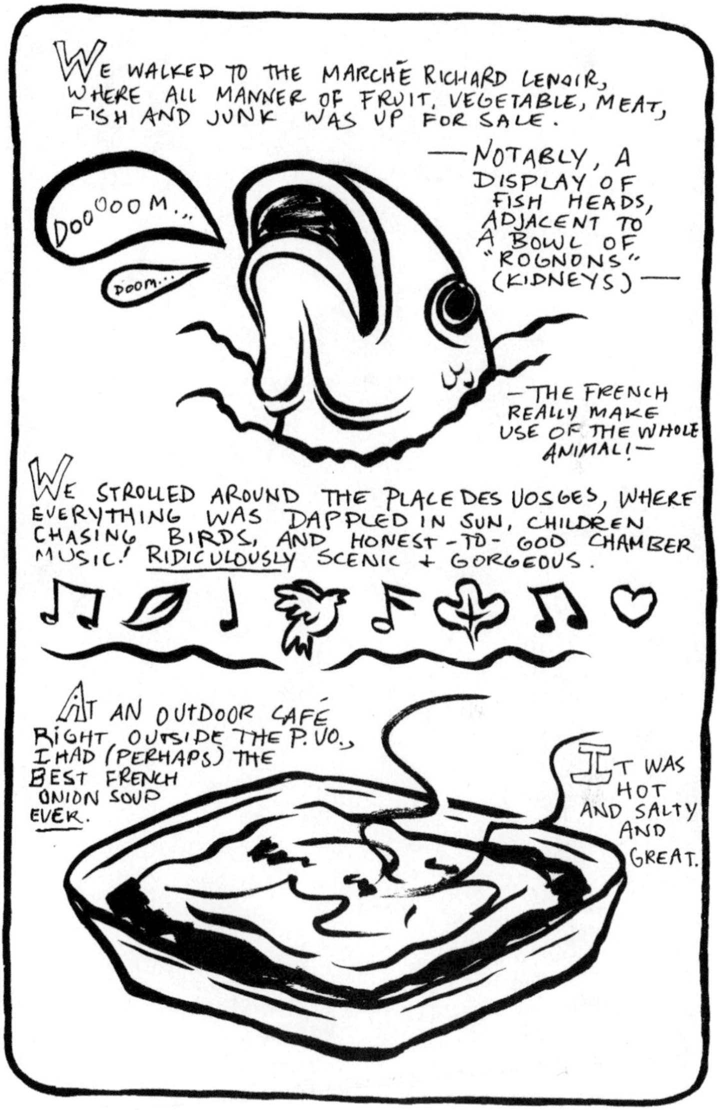
WE WALKED TO THE MARCHÉ RICHARD LENOIR, WHERE ALL MANNER OF FRUIT, VEGETABLE, MEAT, FISH AND JUNK WAS UP FOR SALE.
—NOTABLY, A DISPLAY OF FISH HEADS, ADJACENT TO A BOWL OF "ROGNONS" (KIDNEYS)—
DOOOOOM...
DOOM...
—THE FRENCH REALLY MAKE USE OF THE WHOLE ANIMAL!—
WE STROLLED AROUND THE PLACE DES VOSGES, WHERE EVERYTHING WAS DAPPLED IN SUN, CHILDREN CHASING BIRDS, AND HONEST-TO-GOD CHAMBER MUSIC! RIDICULOUSLY SCENIC + GORGEOUS.
AT AN OUTDOOR CAFÉ RIGHT OUTSIDE THE P. VO., I HAD (PERHAPS) THE BEST FRENCH ONION SOUP EVER.
IT WAS HOT AND SALTY AND GREAT.

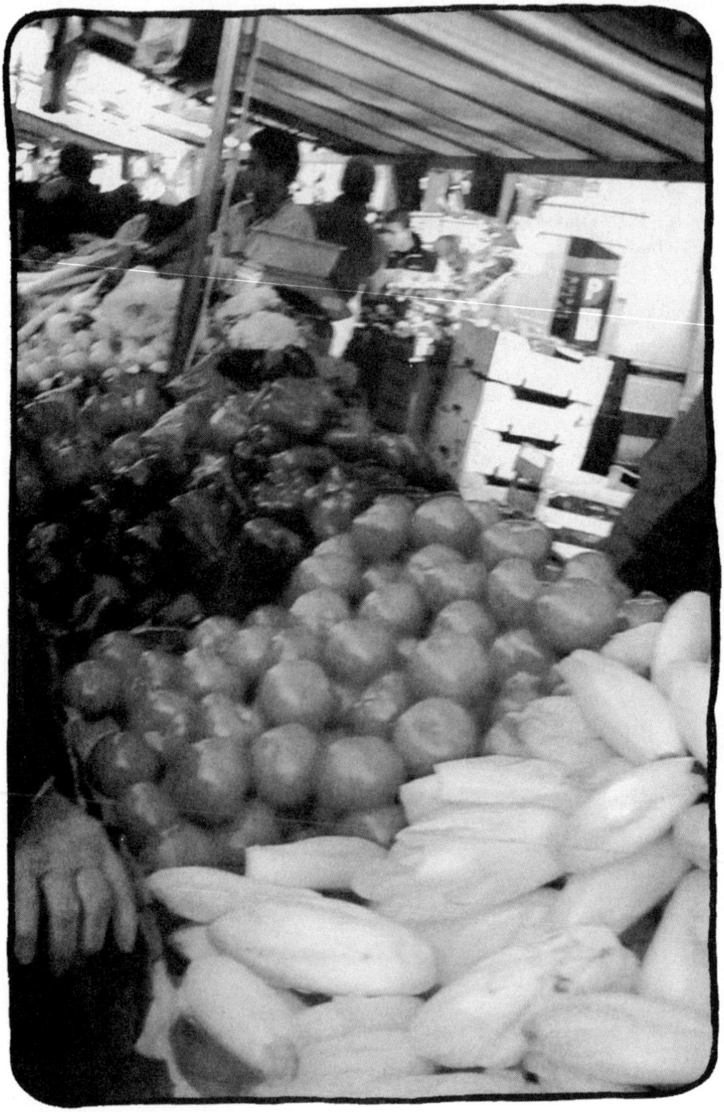
P

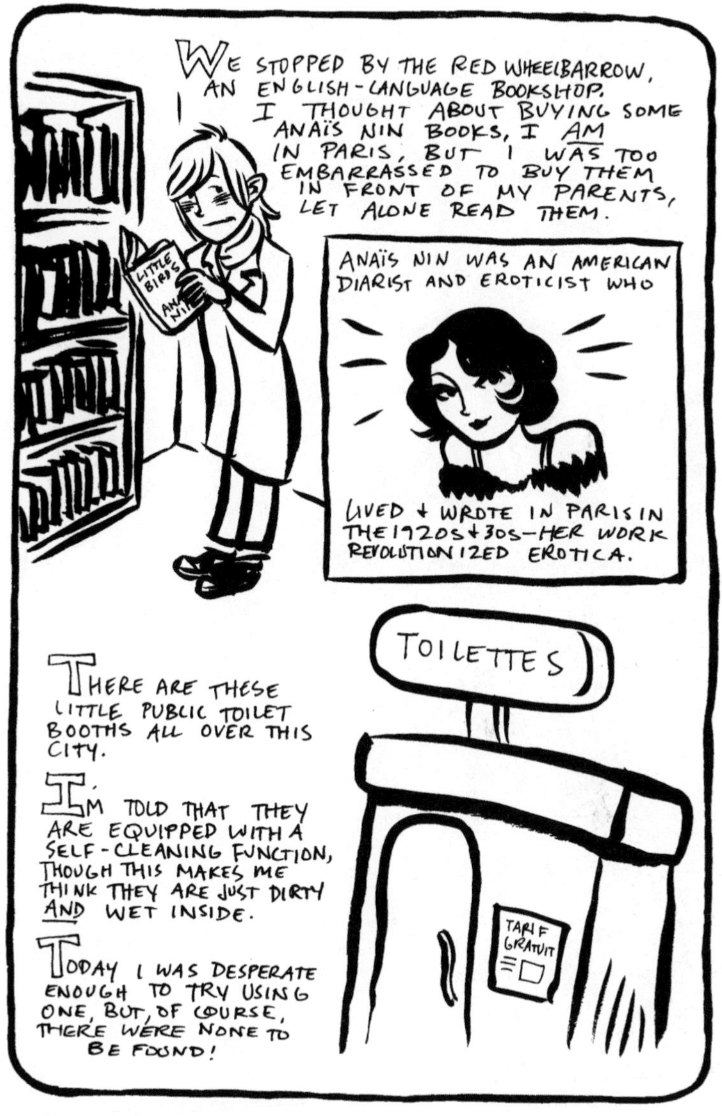
WE STOPPED BY THE RED WHEELBARROW, AN ENGLISH-LANGUAGE BOOKSHOP. I THOUGHT ABOUT BUYING SOME ANAÏS NIN BOOKS, I AM IN PARIS, BUT I WAS TOO EMBARRASSED TO BUY THEM IN FRONT OF MY PARENTS, LET ALONE READ THEM.
LITTLE BIRDS ANAÏS NIN
ANAÏS NIN WAS AN AMERICAN DIARIST AND EROTICIST WHO
LIVED + WROTE IN PARIS IN THE 1920S + 30S—HER WORK REVOLUTIONIZED EROTICA.
TOILETTES
THERE ARE THESE LITTLE PUBLIC TOILET BOOTHS ALL OVER THIS CITY.
I'M TOLD THAT THEY ARE EQUIPPED WITH A SELF-CLEANING FUNCTION, THOUGH THIS MAKES ME THINK THEY ARE JUST DIRTY AND WET INSIDE.
TARIF GRATUIT
TODAY I WAS DESPERATE ENOUGH TO TRY USING ONE, BUT, OF COURSE, THERE WERE NONE TO BE FOUND!

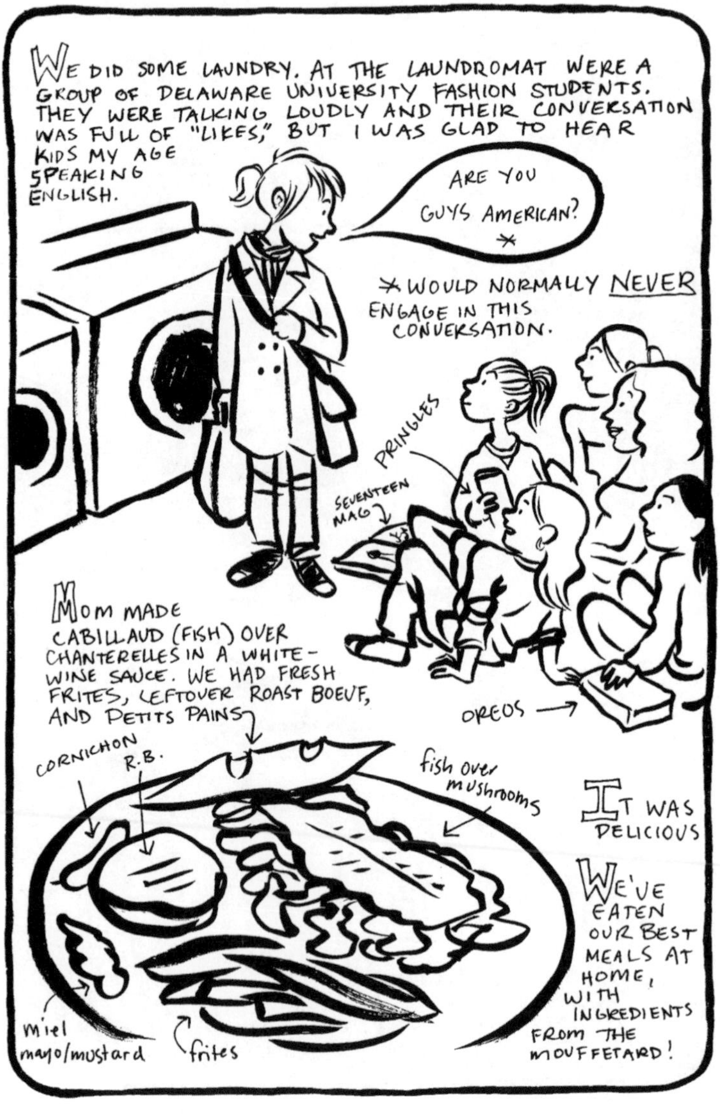

WE DID SOME LAUNDRY. AT THE LAUNDROMAT WERE A GROUP OF DELAWARE UNIVERSITY FASHION STUDENTS. THEY WERE TALKING LOUDLY AND THEIR CONVERSATION WAS FULL OF "LIKES," BUT I WAS GLAD TO HEAR KIDS MY AGE SPEAKING ENGLISH.
ARE YOU GUYS AMERICAN? *
* WOULD NORMALLY NEVER ENGAGE IN THIS CONVERSATION.
PRINGLES
SEVENTEEN MAG
OREOS
MOM MADE CABILLAUD (FISH) OVER CHANTERELLES IN A WHITE-WINE SAUCE. WE HAD FRESH FRITES, LEFTOVER ROAST BOEUF, AND PETITS PAINS
CORNICHON
R.B.
fish over mushrooms
miel mayo/mustard
frites
IT WAS DELICIOUS
WE'VE EATEN OUR BEST MEALS AT HOME, WITH INGREDIENTS FROM THE MOUFFETARD!

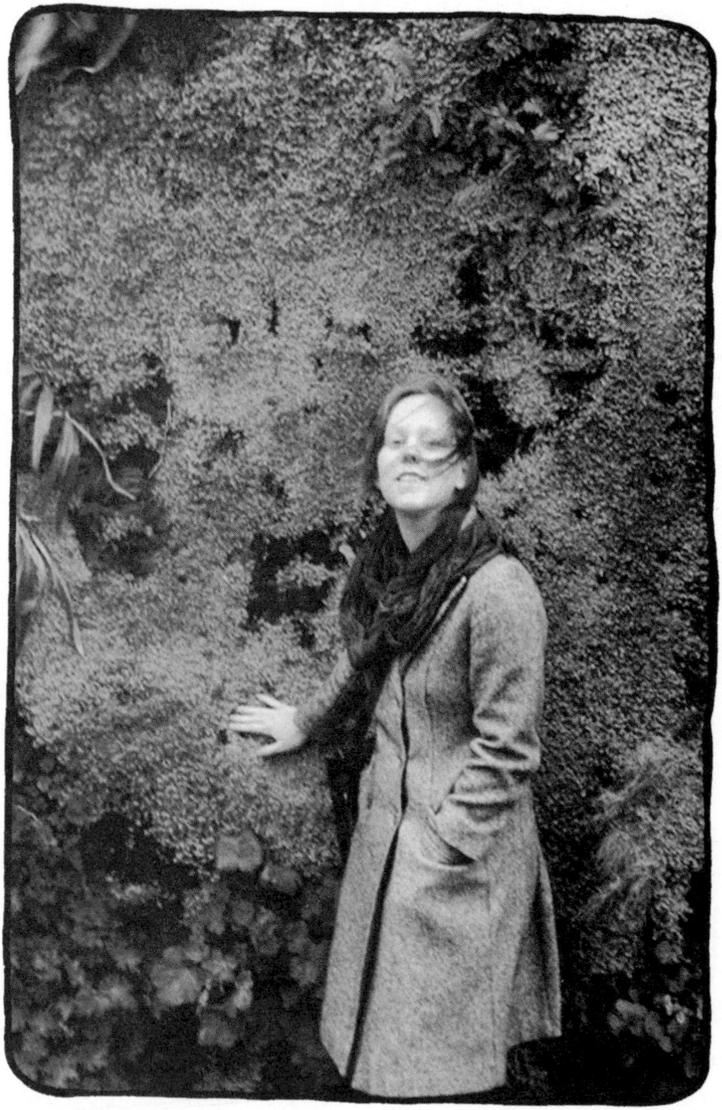

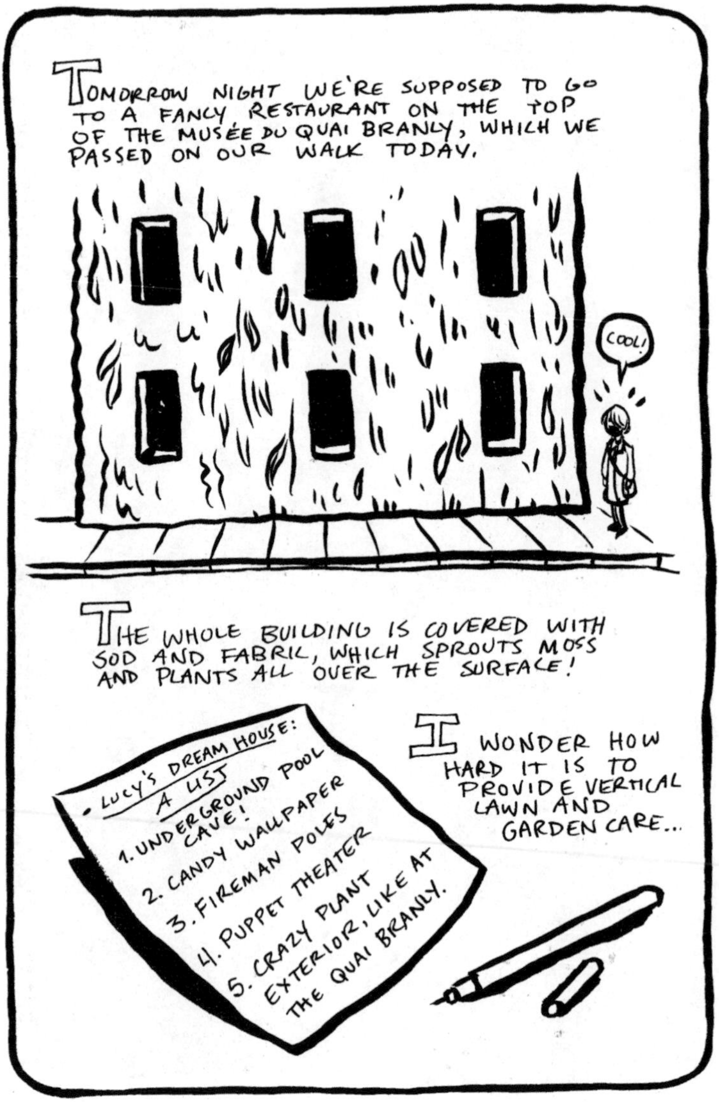

TOMORROW NIGHT WE'RE SUPPOSED TO GO TO A FANCY RESTAURANT ON THE TOP OF THE MUSÉE DU QUAI BRANLY, WHICH WE PASSED ON OUR WALK TODAY.
COOL!
THE WHOLE BUILDING IS COVERED WITH SOD AND FABRIC, WHICH SPROUTS MOSS AND PLANTS ALL OVER THE SURFACE!
LUCY'S DREAM HOUSE: A LIST
1. UNDERGROUND POOL CAVE!
2. CANDY WALLPAPER
3. FIREMAN POLES
4. PUPPET THEATER
5. CRAZY PLANT EXTERIOR, LIKE AT THE QUAI BRANLY.
I WONDER HOW HARD IT IS TO PROVIDE VERTICAL LAWN AND GARDEN CARE...

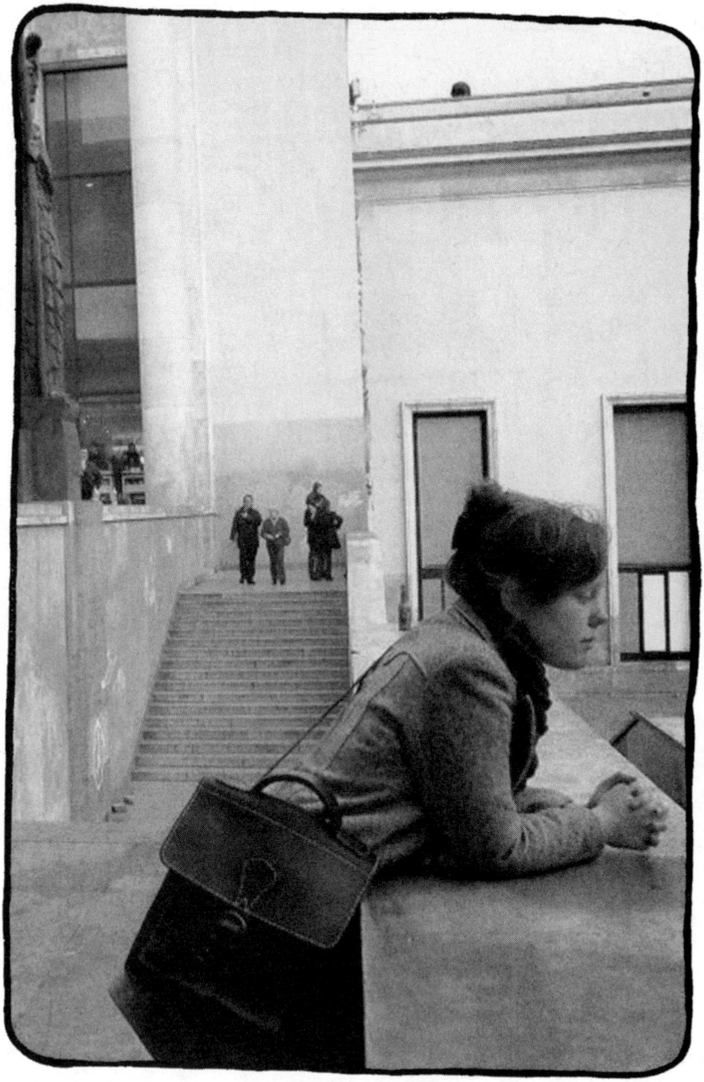

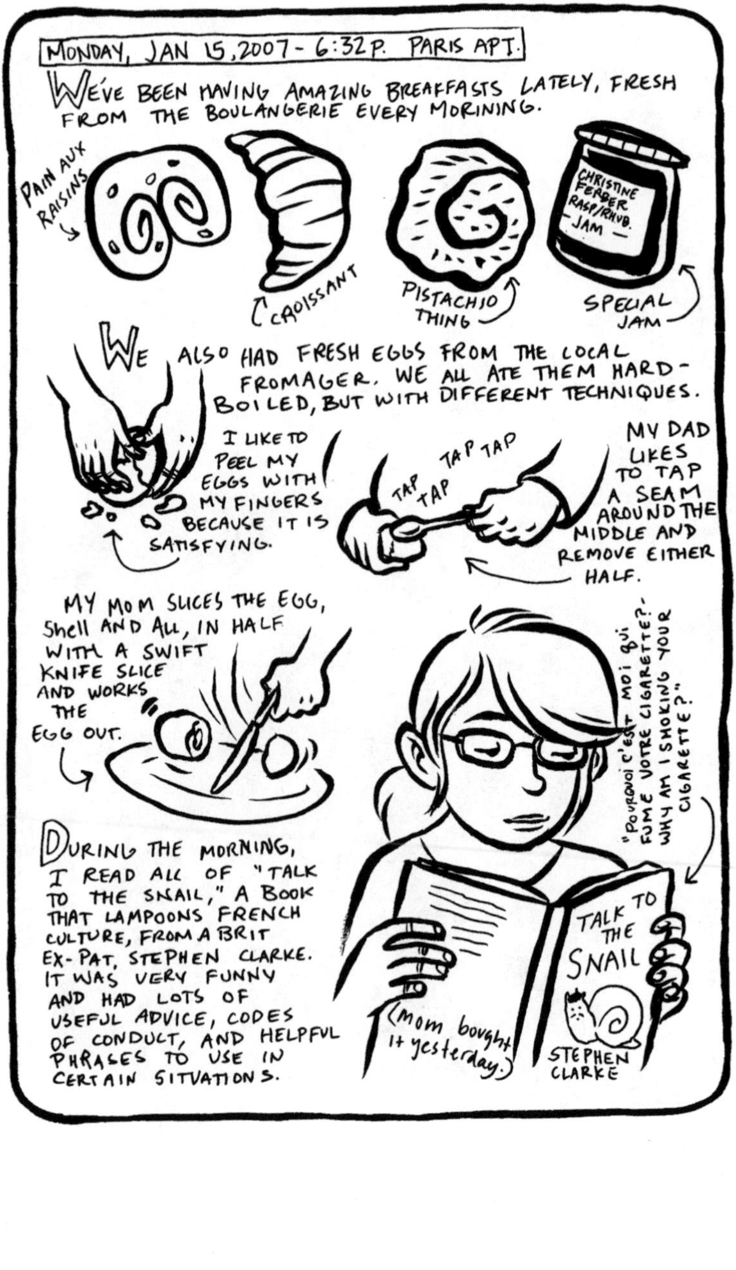
MONDAY, JAN 15, 2007 - 6:32P. PARIS APT.
WE'VE BEEN HAVING AMAZING BREAKFASTS LATELY, FRESH FROM THE BOULANGERIE EVERY MORINING.
PAIN AUX RAISINS
CROISSANT
PISTACHIO THING
CHRISTINE FERBER RASP/RHUB. JAM
SPECIAL JAM
WE ALSO HAD FRESH EGGS FROM THE LOCAL FROMAGER. WE ALL ATE THEM HARD-BOILED, BUT WITH DIFFERENT TECHNIQUES.
I LIKE TO PEEL MY EGGS WITH MY FINGERS BECAUSE IT IS SATISFYING.
TAP TAP TAP TAP
MY DAD LIKES TO TAP A SEAM AROUND THE MIDDLE AND REMOVE EITHER HALF.
MY MOM SLICES THE EGG, Shell AND ALL, IN HALF WITH A SWIFT KNIFE SLICE AND WORKS THE EGG OUT.
"POURQUOI C'EST MOI QUI FUME VOTRE CIGARETTE?" - "WHY AM I SMOKING YOUR CIGARETTE?"
DURING THE MORNING, I READ ALL OF "TALK TO THE SNAIL," A BOOK THAT LAMPOONS FRENCH CULTURE, FROM A BRIT EX-PAT, STEPHEN CLARKE. IT WAS VERY FUNNY AND HAD LOTS OF USEFUL ADVICE, CODES OF CONDUCT, AND HELPFUL PHRASES TO USE IN CERTAIN SITUATIONS.
TALK TO THE SNAIL
STEPHEN CLARKE
(mom bought it yesterday.)

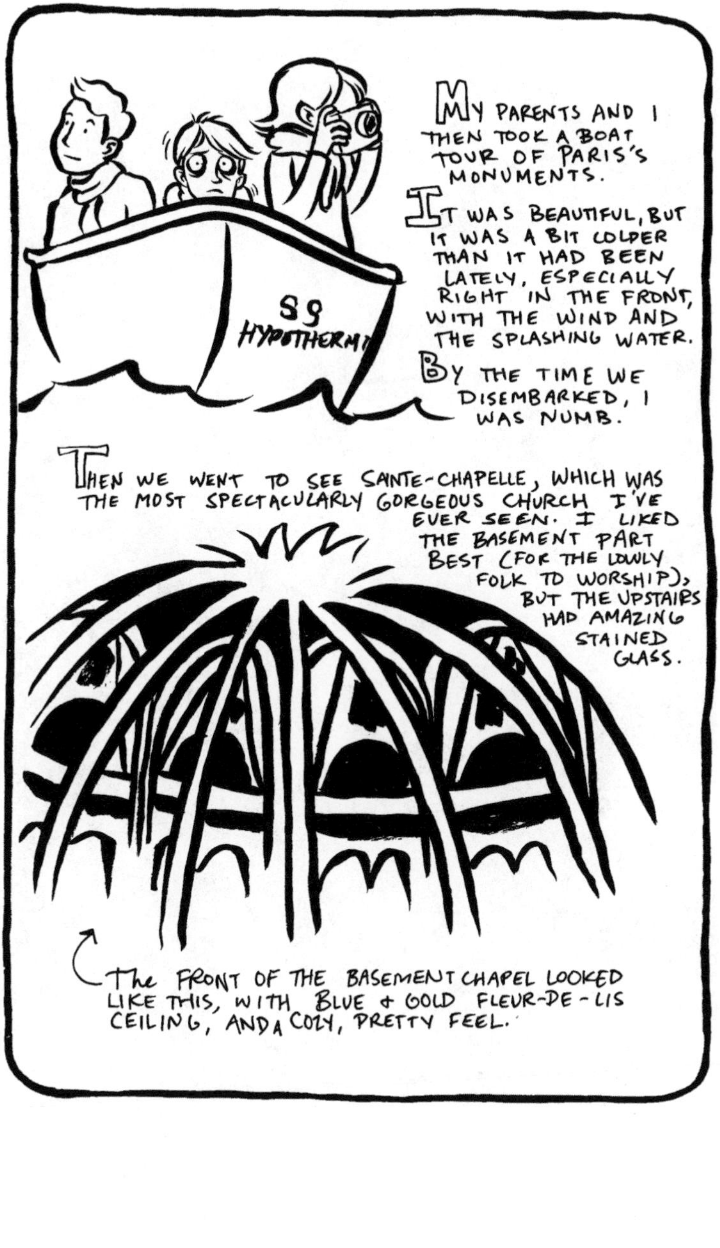
MY PARENTS AND I THEN TOOK A BOAT TOUR OF PARIS'S MONUMENTS.
IT WAS BEAUTIFUL, BUT IT WAS A BIT COLDER THAN IT HAD BEEN LATELY, ESPECIALLY RIGHT IN THE FRONT, WITH THE WIND AND THE SPLASHING WATER.
BY THE TIME WE DISEMBARKED, I WAS NUMB.
SS HYPOTHERMI
THEN WE WENT TO SEE SAINTE-CHAPELLE, WHICH WAS THE MOST SPECTACULARLY GORGEOUS CHURCH I'VE EVER SEEN. I LIKED THE BASEMENT PART BEST (FOR THE LOWLY FOLK TO WORSHIP), BUT THE UPSTAIRS HAD AMAZING STAINED GLASS.
The FRONT OF THE BASEMENT CHAPEL LOOKED LIKE THIS, WITH BLUE & GOLD FLEUR-DE-LIS CEILING, AND A COZY, PRETTY FEEL.

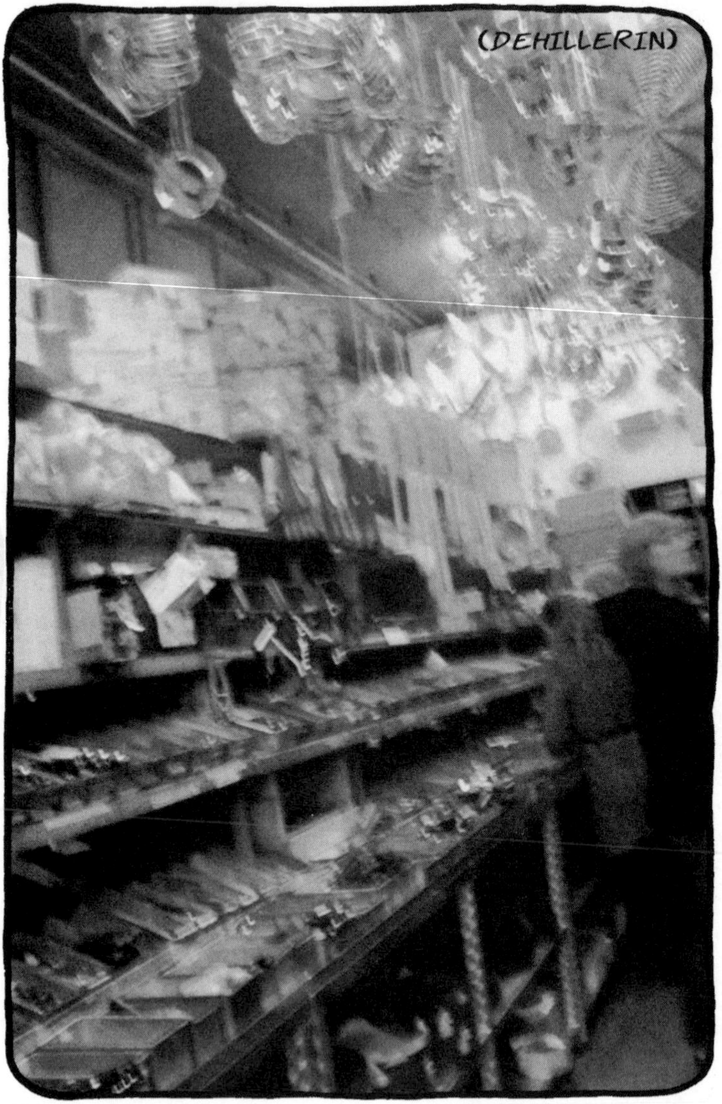
(DEHILLERIN)

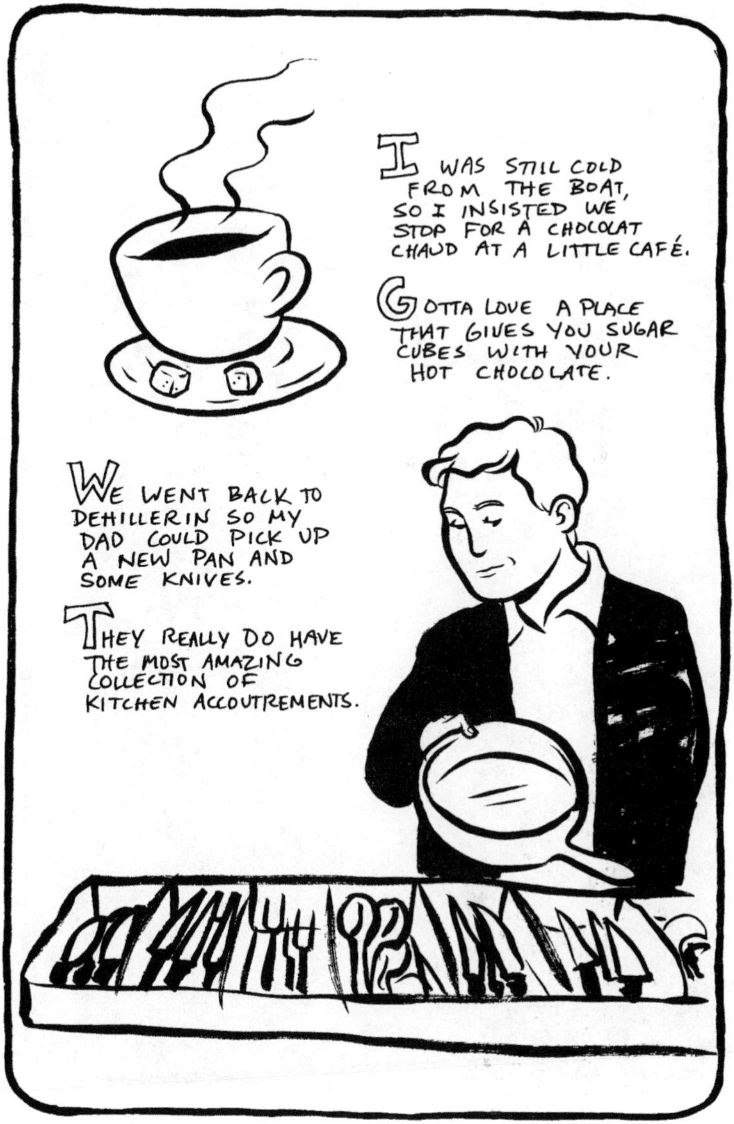
I WAS STIL COLD FROM THE BOAT, SO I INSISTED WE STOP FOR A CHOCOLAT CHAUD AT A LITTLE CAFÉ.
GOTTA LOVE A PLACE THAT GIVES YOU SUGAR CUBES WITH YOUR HOT CHOCOLATE.
WE WENT BACK TO DEHILLERIN SO MY DAD COULD PICK UP A NEW PAN AND SOME KNIVES.
THEY REALLY DO HAVE THE MOST AMAZING COLLECTION OF KITCHEN ACCOUTREMENTS.

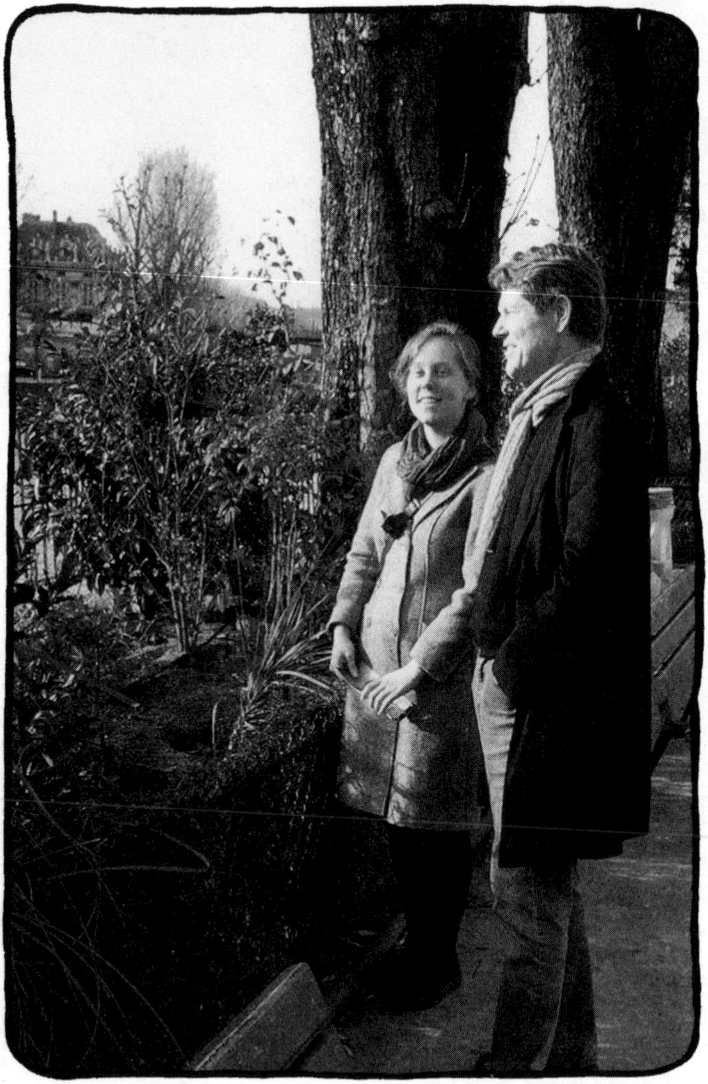

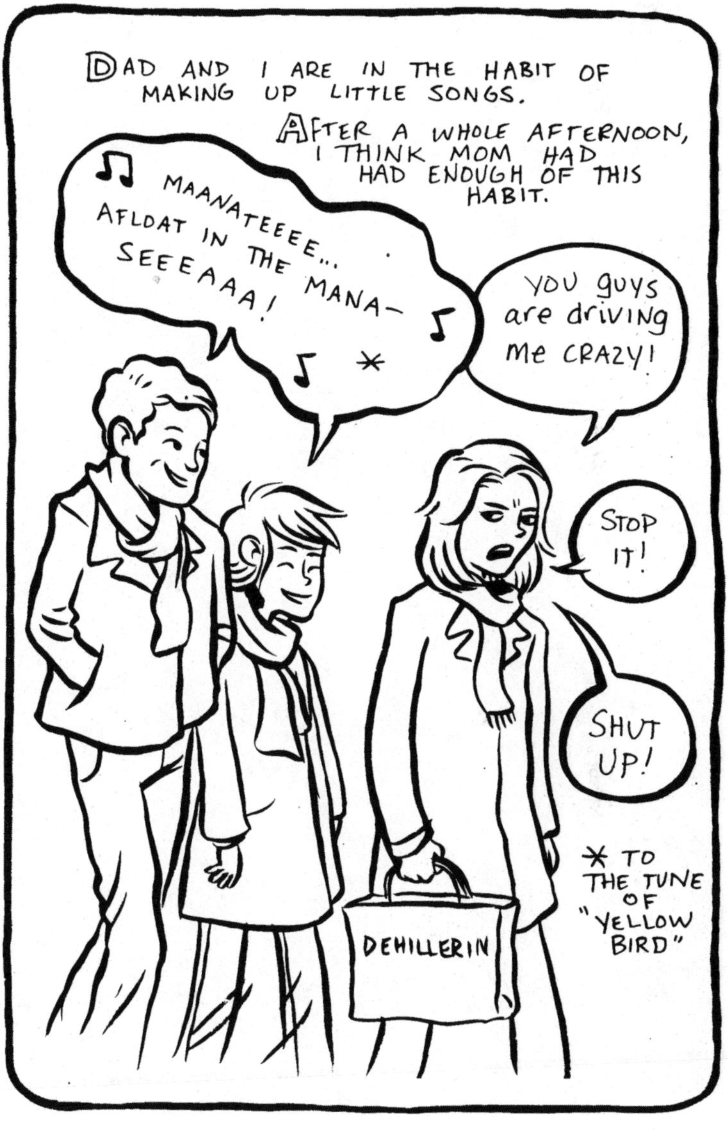
DAD AND I ARE IN THE HABIT OF MAKING UP LITTLE SONGS.
AFTER A WHOLE AFTERNOON, I THINK MOM HAD HAD ENOUGH OF THIS HABIT.
MAANATEEEEE... AFLOAT IN THE MANA- SEEEAAAA! *
YOU GUYS ARE DRIVING ME CRAZY!
STOP IT!
SHUT UP!
DEHILLERIN
* TO THE TUNE OF "YELLOW BIRD"

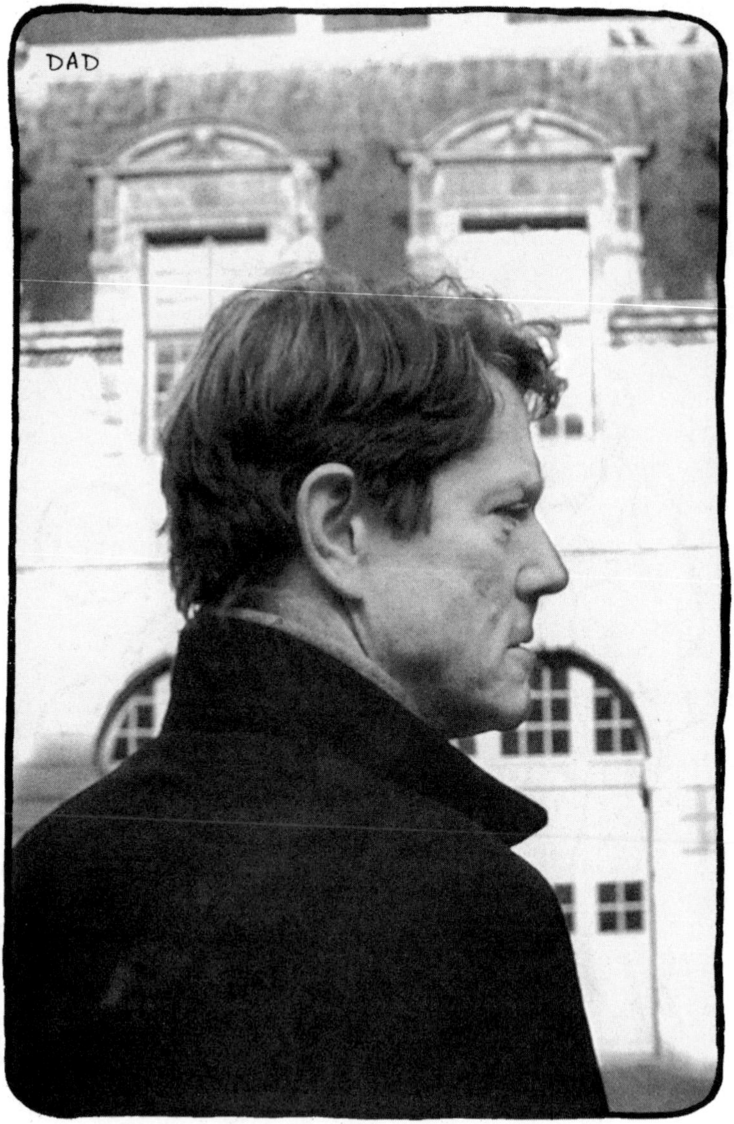
DAD

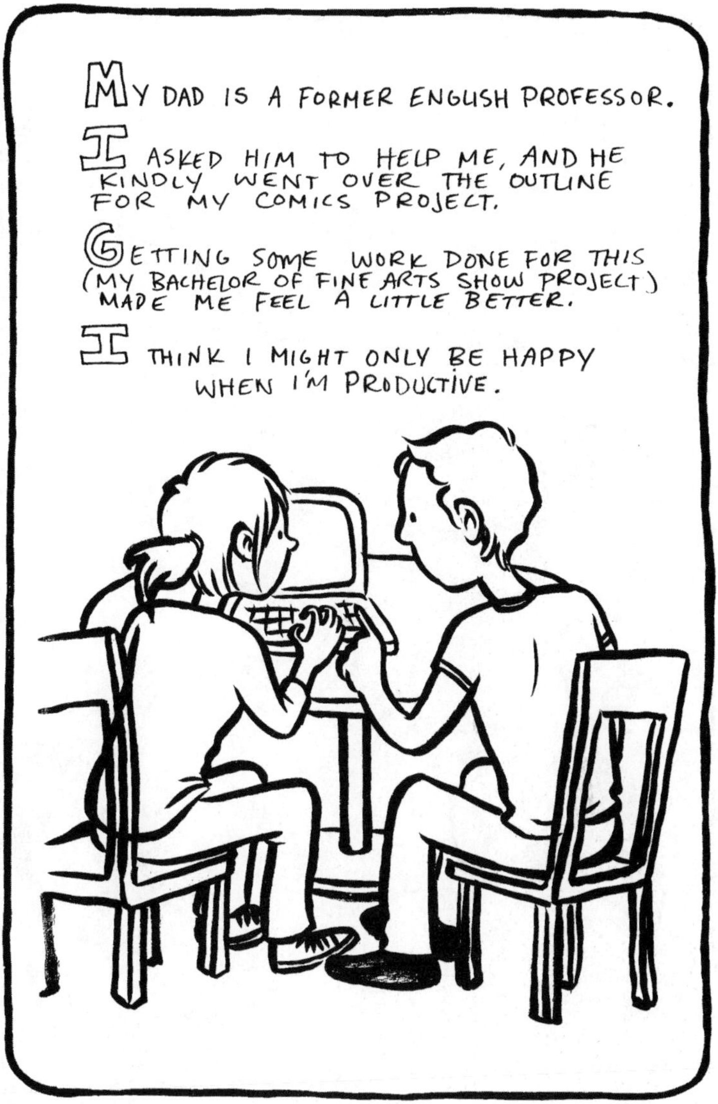
MY DAD IS A FORMER ENGLISH PROFESSOR.
I ASKED HIM TO HELP ME, AND HE KINDLY WENT OVER THE OUTLINE FOR MY COMICS PROJECT.
GETTING SOME WORK DONE FOR THIS (MY BACHELOR OF FINE ARTS SHOW PROJECT) MADE ME FEEL A LITTLE BETTER.
I THINK I MIGHT ONLY BE HAPPY WHEN I'M PRODUCTIVE.

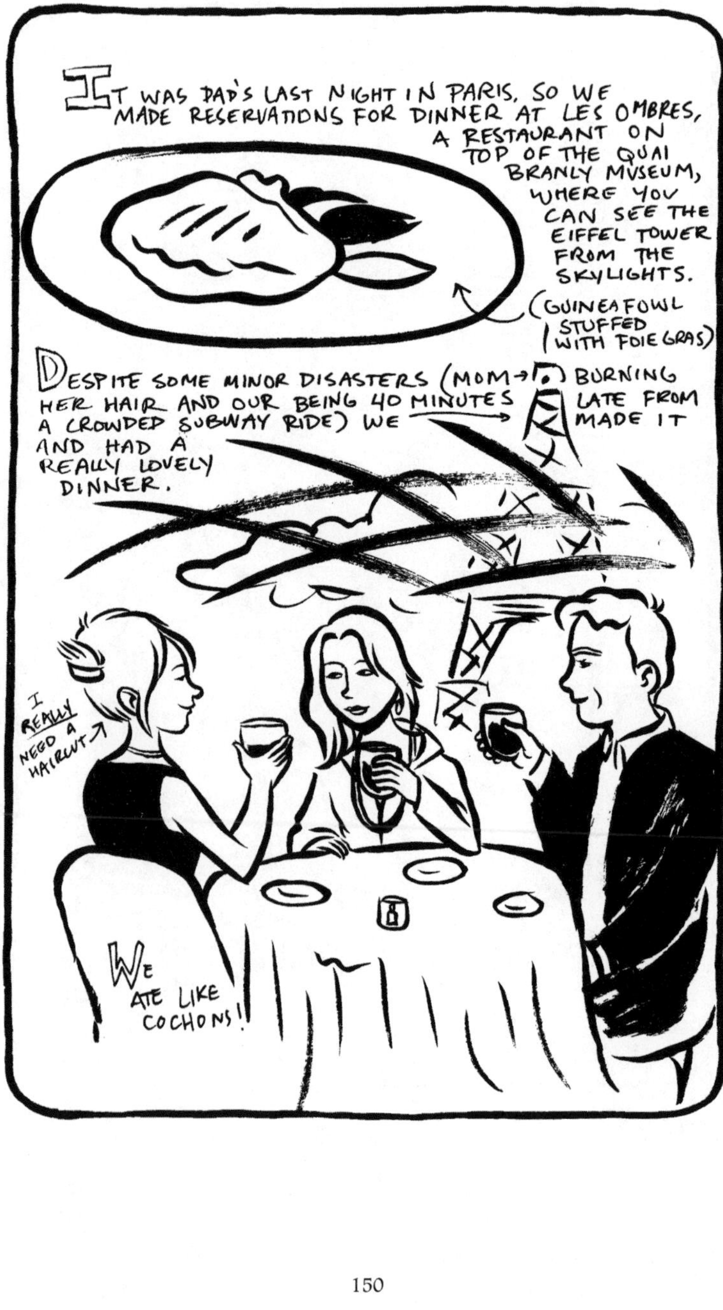
IT WAS DAD'S LAST NIGHT IN PARIS, SO WE MADE RESERVATIONS FOR DINNER AT LES OMBRES, A RESTAURANT ON TOP OF THE QUAI BRANLY MUSEUM, WHERE YOU CAN SEE THE EIFFEL TOWER FROM THE SKYLIGHTS.
(GUINEAFOWL STUFFED WITH FOIE GRAS)
DESPITE SOME MINOR DISASTERS (MOM BURNING HER HAIR AND OUR BEING 40 MINUTES LATE FROM A CROWDED SUBWAY RIDE) WE MADE IT AND HAD A REALLY LOVELY DINNER.
I REALLY NEED A HAIRCUT
WE ATE LIKE COCHONS!

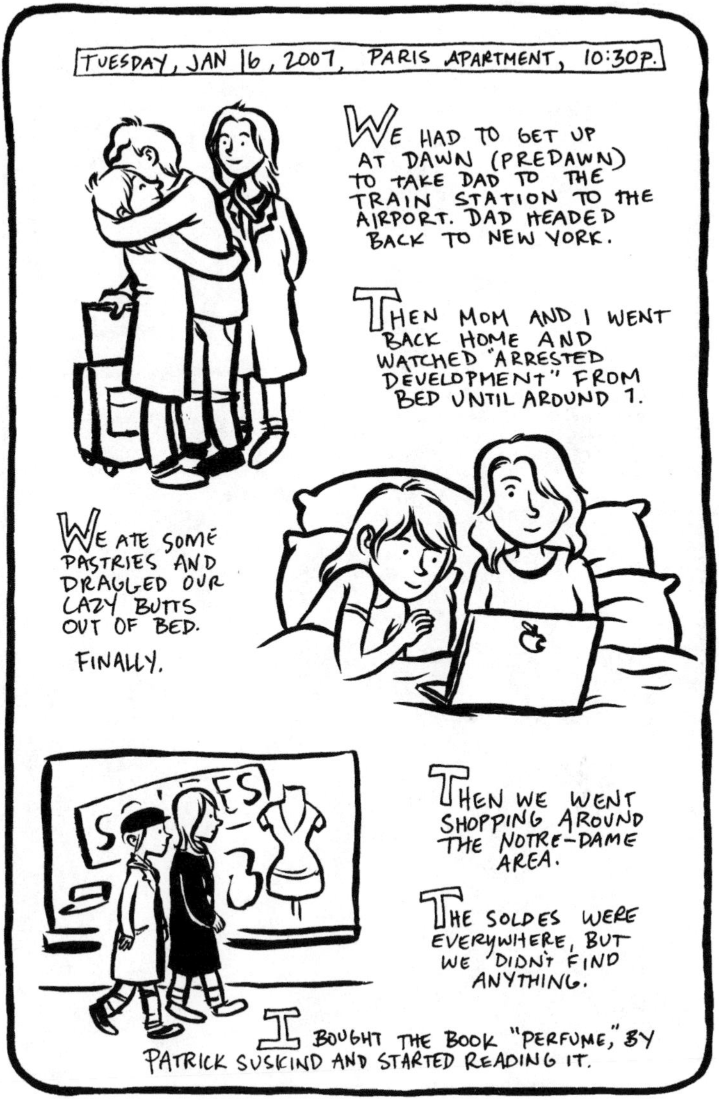
TUESDAY, JAN 16, 2007, PARIS APARTMENT, 10:30P.
WE HAD TO GET UP AT DAWN (PREDAWN) TO TAKE DAD TO THE TRAIN STATION TO THE AIRPORT. DAD HEADED BACK TO NEW YORK.
THEN MOM AND I WENT BACK HOME AND WATCHED "ARRESTED DEVELOPMENT" FROM BED UNTIL AROUND 1.
WE ATE SOME PASTRIES AND DRAGGED OUR LAZY BUTTS OUT OF BED.
FINALLY.
SOLDES
THEN WE WENT SHOPPING AROUND THE NOTRE-DAME AREA.
THE SOLDES WERE EVERYWHERE, BUT WE DIDN'T FIND ANYTHING.
I BOUGHT THE BOOK "PERFUME," BY PATRICK SUSKIND AND STARTED READING IT.

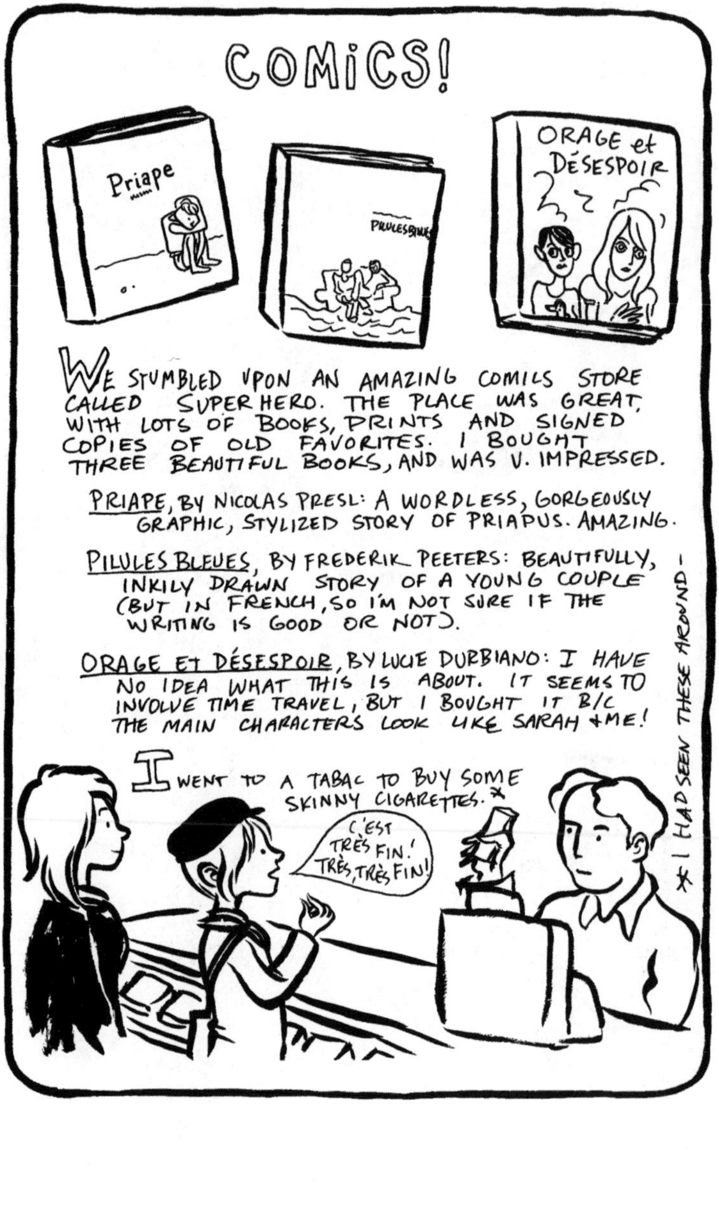
COMICS!
Priape
PILULES BLEUES
ORAGE et DÉSESPOIR
WE STUMBLED UPON AN AMAZING COMICS STORE CALLED SUPERHERO. THE PLACE WAS GREAT, WITH LOTS OF BOOKS, PRINTS AND SIGNED COPIES OF OLD FAVORITES. I BOUGHT THREE BEAUTIFUL BOOKS, AND WAS V. IMPRESSED.
PRIAPE, BY NICOLAS PRESL: A WORDLESS, GORGEOUSLY GRAPHIC, STYLIZED STORY OF PRIAPUS. AMAZING.
PILULES BLEUES, BY FREDERIK PEETERS: BEAUTIFULLY, INKILY DRAWN STORY OF A YOUNG COUPLE (BUT IN FRENCH, SO I'M NOT SURE IF THE WRITING IS GOOD OR NOT).
ORAGE ET DÉSESPOIR, BY LUCIE DURBIANO: I HAVE NO IDEA WHAT THIS IS ABOUT. IT SEEMS TO INVOLVE TIME TRAVEL, BUT I BOUGHT IT B/C THE MAIN CHARACTERS LOOK LIKE SARAH + ME!
I WENT TO A TABAC TO BUY SOME SKINNY CIGARETTES.*
C'EST TRÈS FIN! TRÈS, TRÈS FIN!
*I HAD SEEN THESE AROUND -

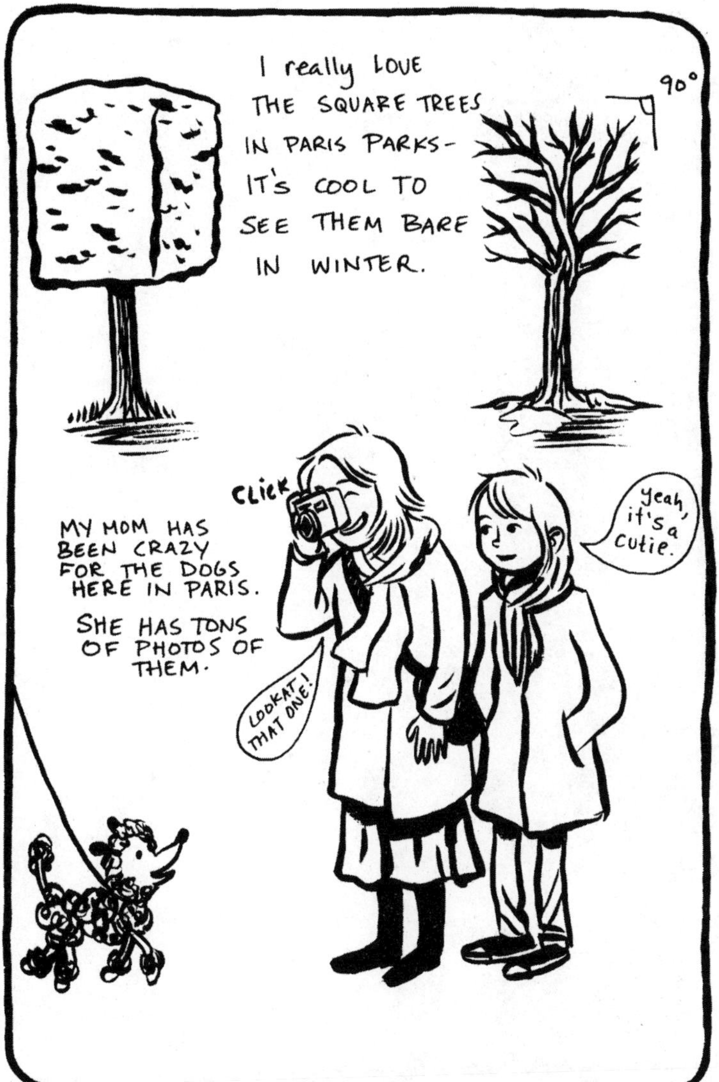
I really LOVE THE SQUARE TREES IN PARIS PARKS- IT'S COOL TO SEE THEM BARE IN WINTER.
90°
MY MOM HAS BEEN CRAZY FOR THE DOGS HERE IN PARIS.
SHE HAS TONS OF PHOTOS OF THEM.
CLICK
LOOKAT THAT ONE!
yeah, it's a cutie.

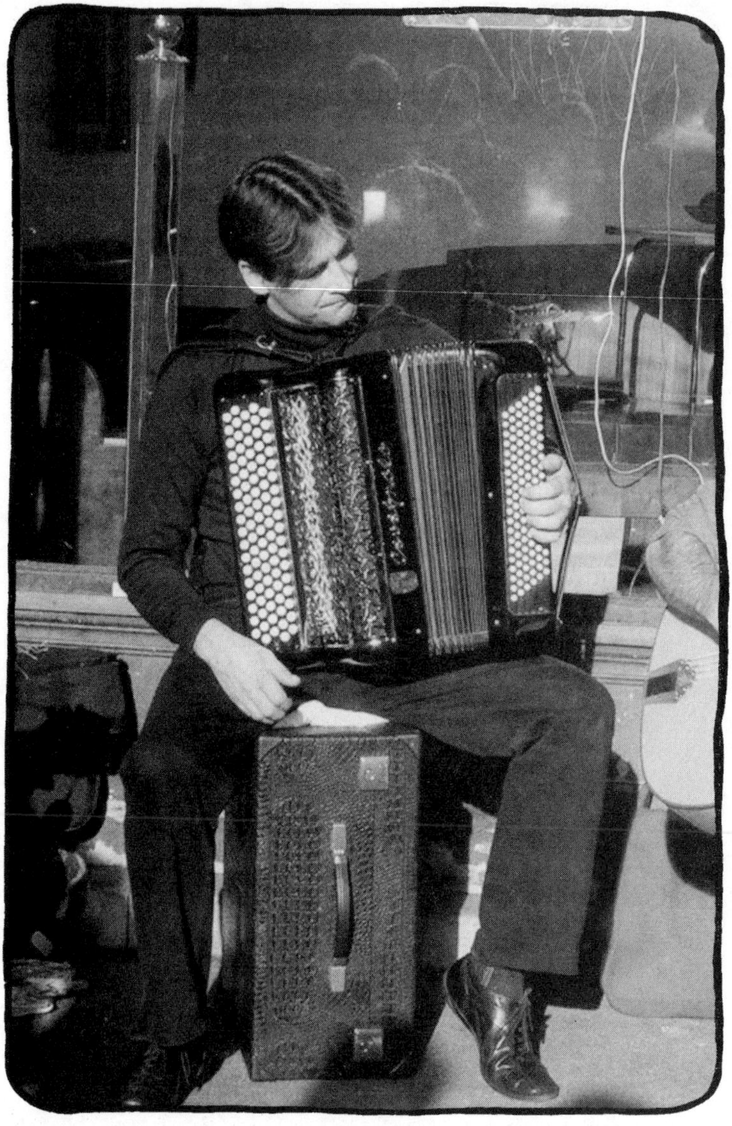

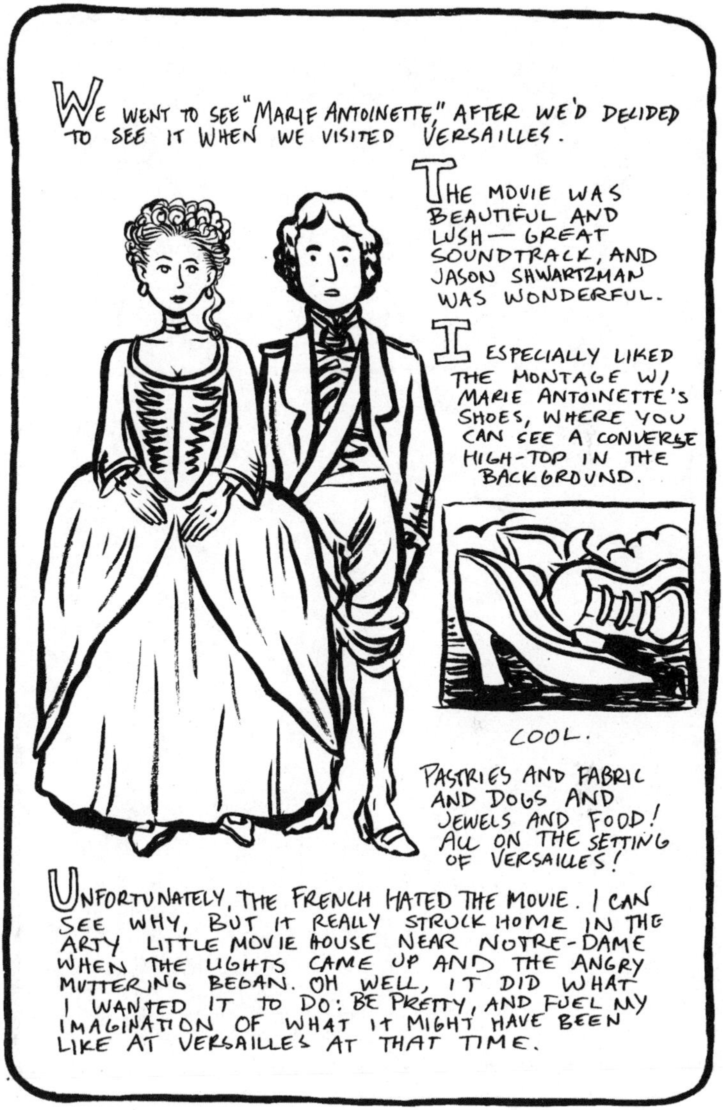
WE WENT TO SEE "MARIE ANTOINETTE," AFTER WE'D DECIDED TO SEE IT WHEN WE VISITED VERSAILLES.
THE MOVIE WAS BEAUTIFUL AND LUSH—GREAT SOUNDTRACK, AND JASON SHWARTZMAN WAS WONDERFUL.
I ESPECIALLY LIKED THE MONTAGE W/ MARIE ANTOINETTE'S SHOES, WHERE YOU CAN SEE A CONVERSE HIGH-TOP IN THE BACKGROUND.
COOL.
PASTRIES AND FABRIC AND DOGS AND JEWELS AND FOOD! ALL ON THE SETTING OF VERSAILLES!
UNFORTUNATELY, THE FRENCH HATED THE MOVIE. I CAN SEE WHY, BUT IT REALLY STRUCK HOME IN THE ARTY LITTLE MOVIE HOUSE NEAR NOTRE-DAME WHEN THE LIGHTS CAME UP AND THE ANGRY MUTTERING BEGAN. OH WELL, IT DID WHAT I WANTED IT TO DO: BE PRETTY, AND FUEL MY IMAGINATION OF WHAT IT MIGHT HAVE BEEN LIKE AT VERSAILLES AT THAT TIME.

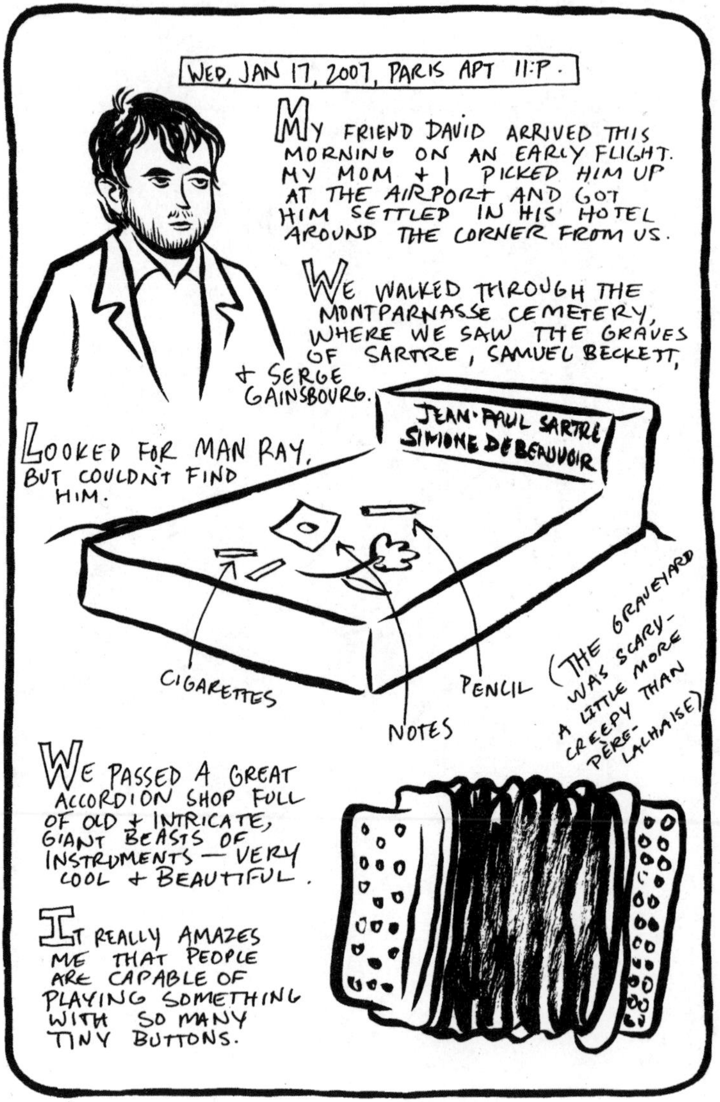
WED, JAN 17, 2007, PARIS APT 11:P.
MY FRIEND DAVID ARRIVED THIS MORNING ON AN EARLY FLIGHT. MY MOM + I PICKED HIM UP AT THE AIRPORT AND GOT HIM SETTLED IN HIS HOTEL AROUND THE CORNER FROM US.
WE WALKED THROUGH THE MONTPARNASSE CEMETERY, WHERE WE SAW THE GRAVES OF SARTRE, SAMUEL BECKETT, + SERGE GAINSBOURG.
JEAN-PAUL SARTRE
SIMONE DE BEAUVOIR
LOOKED FOR MAN RAY, BUT COULDN'T FIND HIM.
CIGARETTES
NOTES
PENCIL
(THE GRAVEYARD WAS SCARY-A LITTLE MORE CREEPY THAN PÈRE-LACHAISE)
WE PASSED A GREAT ACCORDION SHOP FULL OF OLD + INTRICATE, GIANT BEASTS OF INSTRUMENTS — VERY COOL + BEAUTIFUL.
IT REALLY AMAZES ME THAT PEOPLE ARE CAPABLE OF PLAYING SOMETHING WITH SO MANY TINY BUTTONS.

chocolat chaud →

WE HAD LUNCH AT A BRASSERIE (I HAD DUCK CONFIT WITH THIN SPUDS COOKED IN DUCK FAT), AND THEN WANDERED THE MONTPARNASSE AREA FOR A WHILE.

DAVID BOUGHT SOME PENS + MOM BOUGHT SOME NOTEBOOKS + PHOTO ALBUMS FROM A LITTLE BOOKMAKING/STATIONERY STORE, AND I BOUGHT A DRESS AT A CHIC LITTLE DRESS SHOP.

POUR trois, S'IL VOUS PLAÎT

DAVID AND I PICKED UP SOME TAKEOUT FROM A LITTLE PATISSERIE DOWN THE BLOCK, AND WE HAD A NICE, EASY DINNER OF CHICKEN + VEGETABLES BEFORE WE ALL CONKED OUT.

MY SKINNY CIGARETTES TASTE KINDA AWFUL. THEY'RE CALLED "VOGUES."

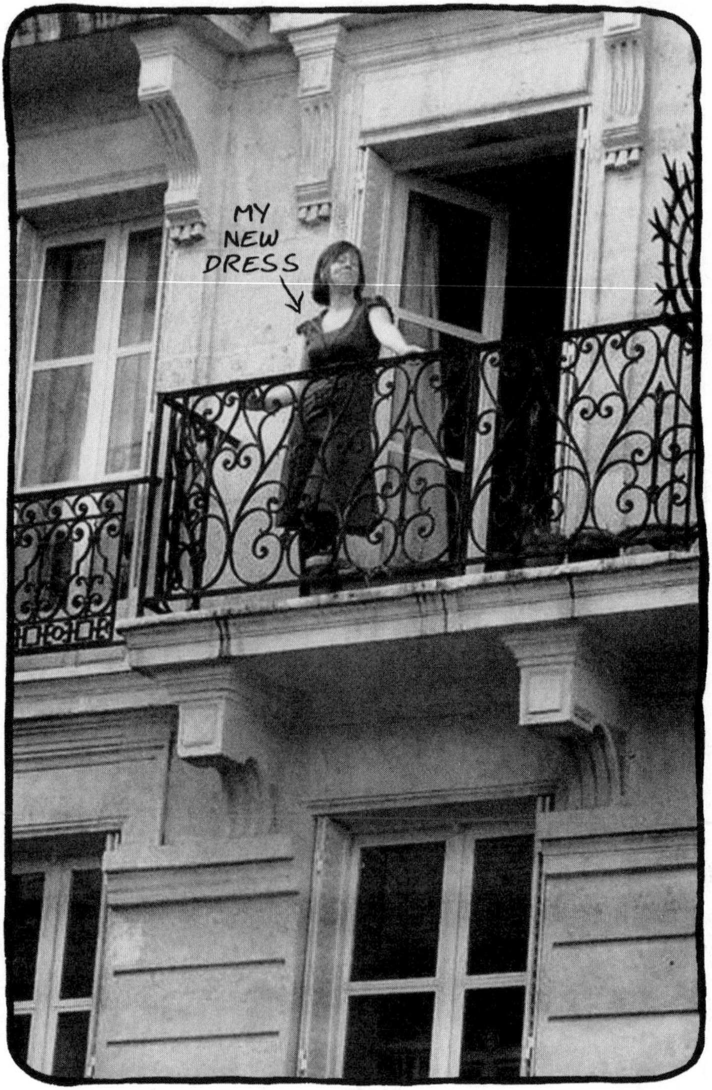
MY
NEW
DRESS

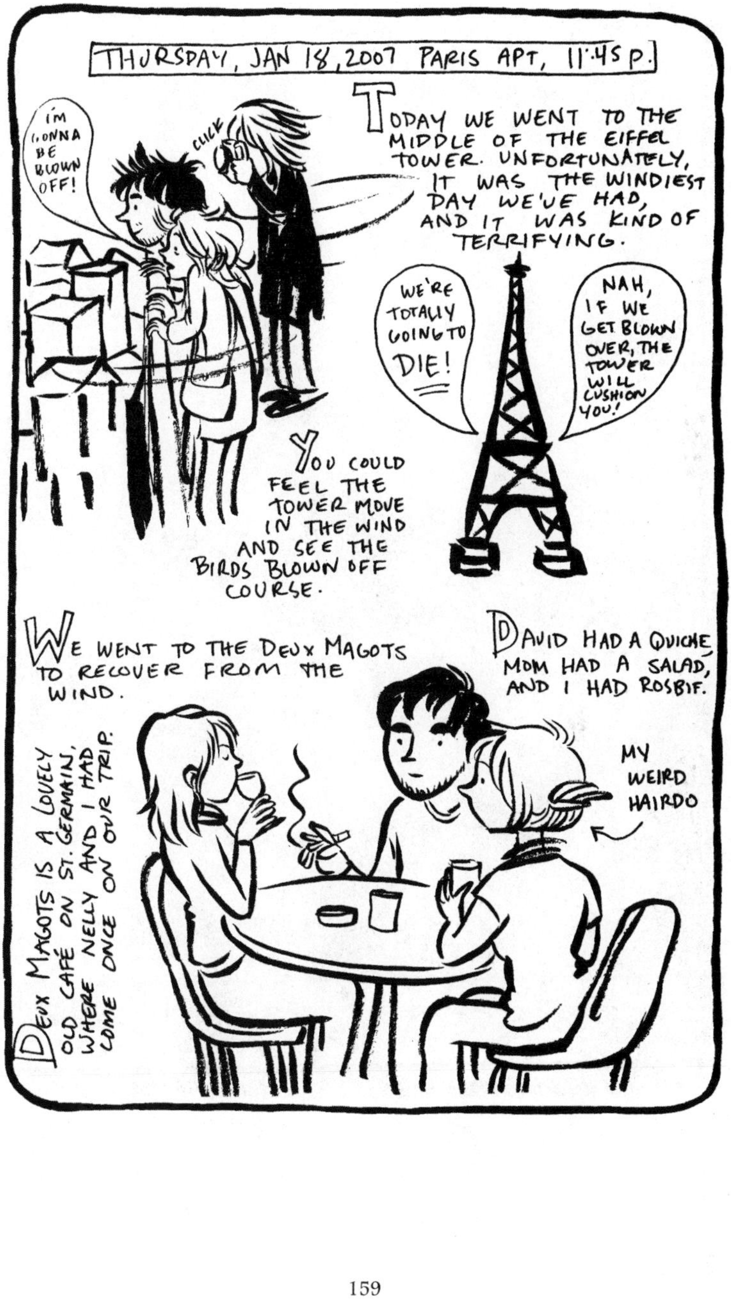

THURSDAY, JAN 18, 2007 PARIS APT, 11:45 p.
TODAY WE WENT TO THE MIDDLE OF THE EIFFEL TOWER. UNFORTUNATELY, IT WAS THE WINDIEST DAY WE'VE HAD, AND IT WAS KIND OF TERRIFYING.
I'M GONNA BE BLOWN OFF!
CLICK
WE'RE TOTALLY GOING TO DIE!
NAH, IF WE GET BLOWN OVER, THE TOWER WILL CUSHION YOU!
YOU COULD FEEL THE TOWER MOVE IN THE WIND AND SEE THE BIRDS BLOWN OFF COURSE.
WE WENT TO THE DEUX MAGOTS TO RECOVER FROM THE WIND.
DAVID HAD A QUICHE, MOM HAD A SALAD, AND I HAD ROSBIF.
DEUX MAGOTS IS A LOVELY OLD CAFÉ ON ST. GERMAIN, WHERE NELLY AND I HAD COME ONCE ON OUR TRIP.
MY WEIRD HAIRDO

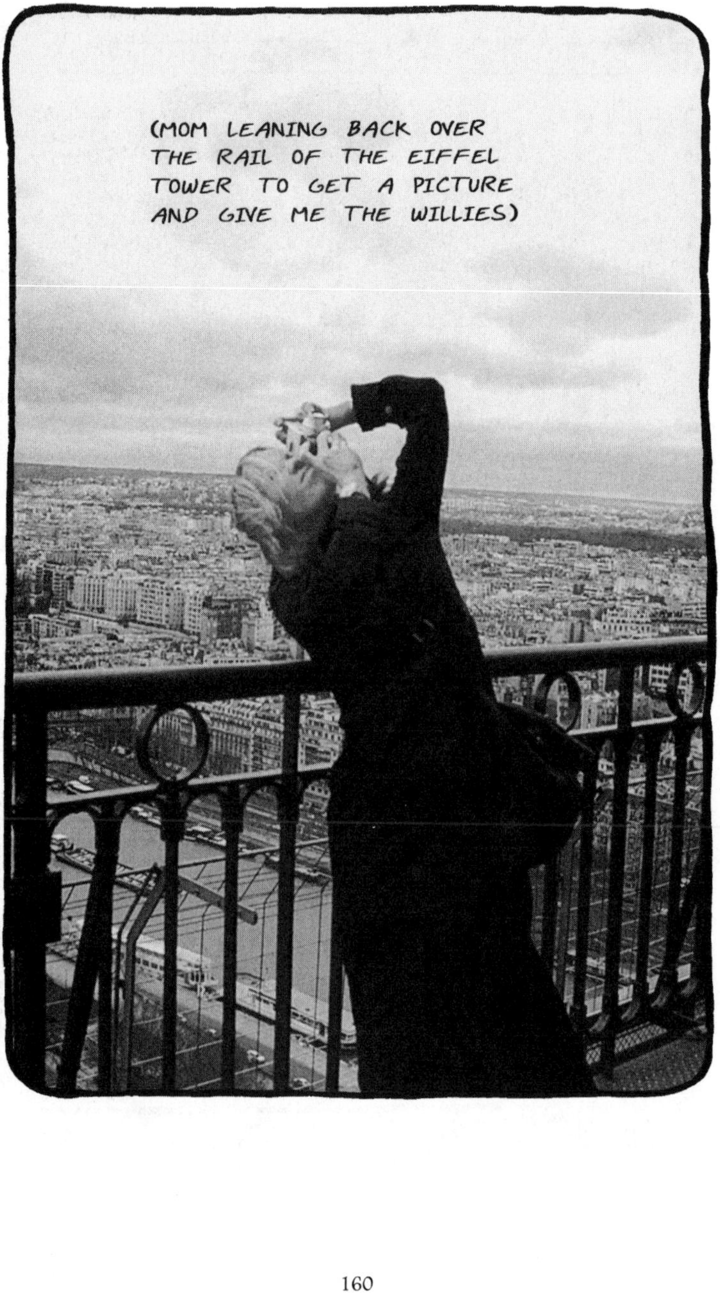
(MOM LEANING BACK OVER THE RAIL OF THE EIFFEL TOWER TO GET A PICTURE AND GIVE ME THE WILLIES)

WE WALKED HOME IN THE RAIN AND I STOPPED TO BUY SOME FRENCH UNDERWEAR & STOCKINGS.

DAMNED IF I'M GOING HOME WITHOUT SOME FRILLY FRENCH UNDER THINGS !!

WE ATE A WONDERFUL DINNER AT HOME.

OYSTERS

FOIE GRAS

MIGNONETTE

TORTELLINI W/ VEGETABLES

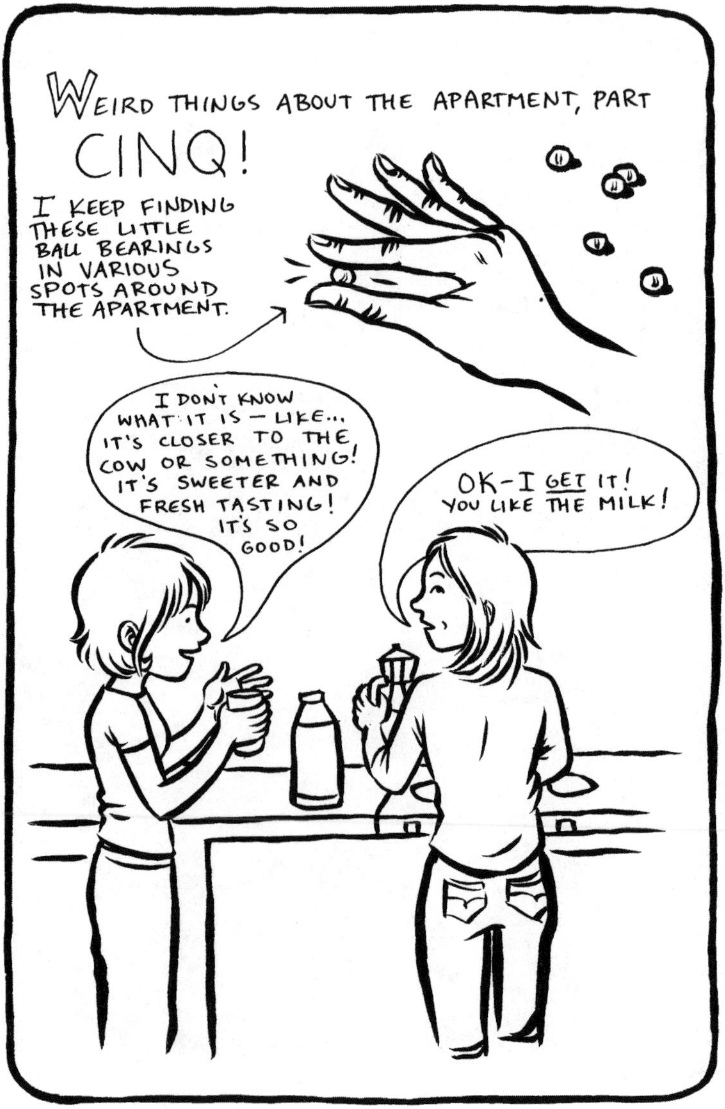
WEIRD THINGS ABOUT THE APARTMENT, PART
CINQ!
I KEEP FINDING THESE LITTLE BALL BEARINGS IN VARIOUS SPOTS AROUND THE APARTMENT.
I DON'T KNOW WHAT IT IS — LIKE... IT'S CLOSER TO THE COW OR SOMETHING! IT'S SWEETER AND FRESH TASTING! IT'S SO GOOD!
OK-I GET IT! YOU LIKE THE MILK!

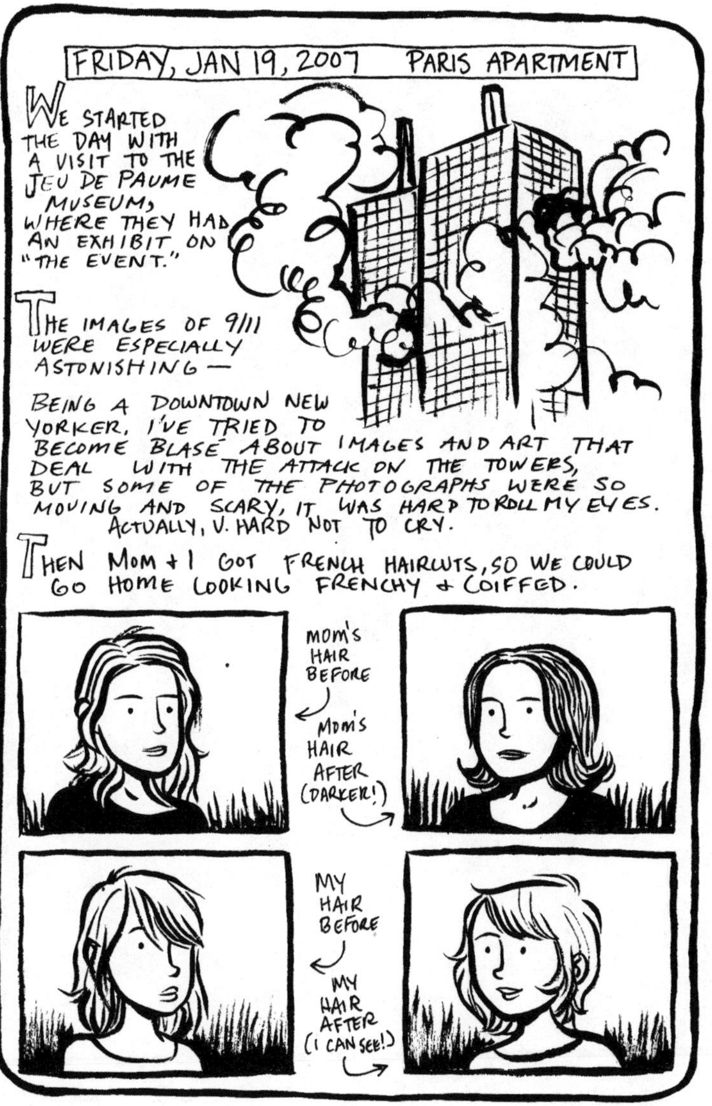
FRIDAY, JAN 19, 2007 PARIS APARTMENT
WE STARTED THE DAY WITH A VISIT TO THE JEU DE PAUME MUSEUM, WHERE THEY HAD AN EXHIBIT ON "THE EVENT."
THE IMAGES OF 9/11 WERE ESPECIALLY ASTONISHING —
BEING A DOWNTOWN NEW YORKER, I'VE TRIED TO BECOME BLASÉ ABOUT IMAGES AND ART THAT DEAL WITH THE ATTACK ON THE TOWERS, BUT SOME OF THE PHOTOGRAPHS WERE SO MOVING AND SCARY, IT WAS HARD TO ROLL MY EYES.
ACTUALLY, V. HARD NOT TO CRY.
THEN MOM + I GOT FRENCH HAIRCUTS, SO WE COULD GO HOME LOOKING FRENCHY + COIFFED.
MOM'S HAIR BEFORE
MOM'S HAIR AFTER (DARKER!)
MY HAIR BEFORE
MY HAIR AFTER (I CAN SEE!)

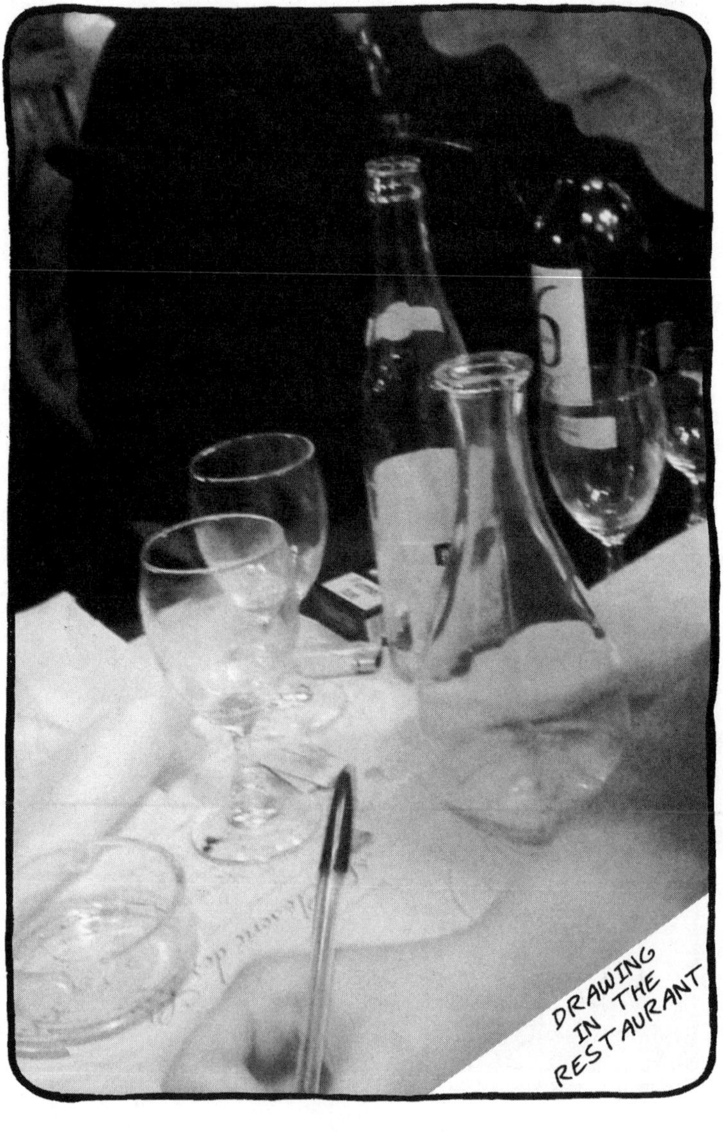
DRAWING
IN THE
RESTAURANT

MOM + I SAT IN A CAFÉ NEAR DAVID'S HOTEL TO CATCH HIM ON THE WAY BACK FROM HIS VISIT TO THE MUSÉE D'ORSAY. THEN WE WENT TO USE THE INTERNET IN DAVID'S HOTEL, WHERE WE FIGURED OUT WHAT TO DO FOR OUR DINNER.

WE WENT TO THE CLOSERIE DES LILAS — A FANCY LITTLE BRASSERIE WHERE ERNEST HEMINGWAY OFTEN CAME. WE DRANK LOTS OF WINE IN HIS HONOR!

MY NEW DRESS

BASS

STEAK

VEAL

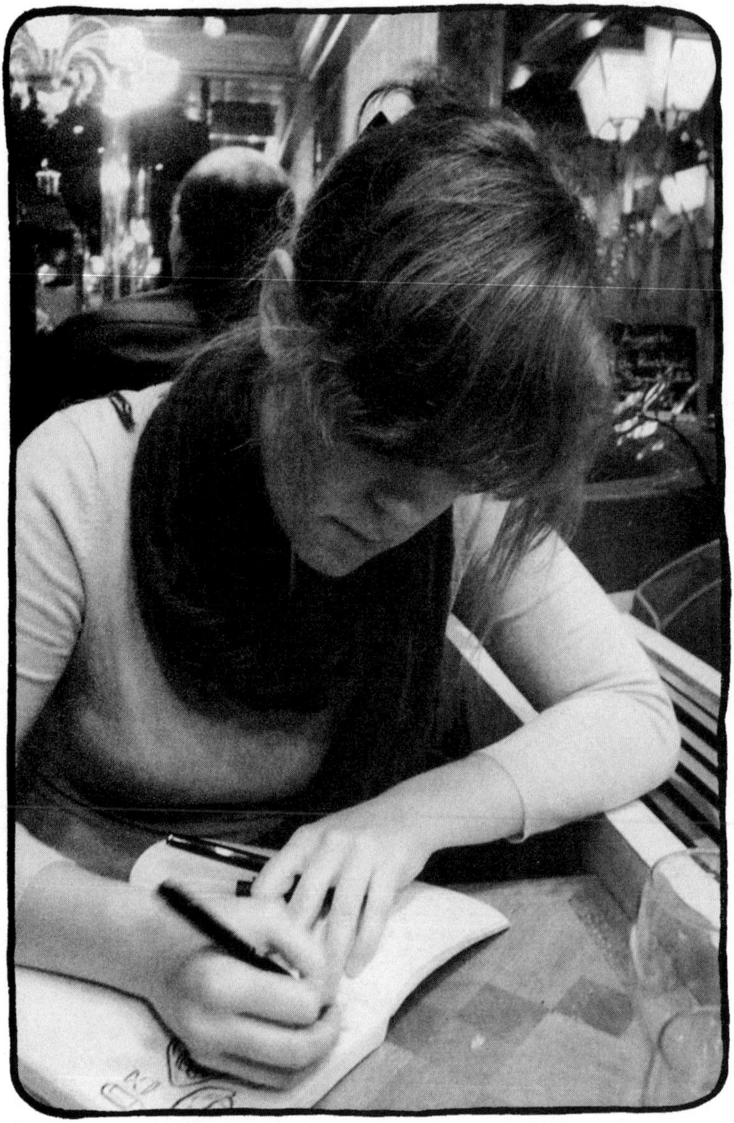

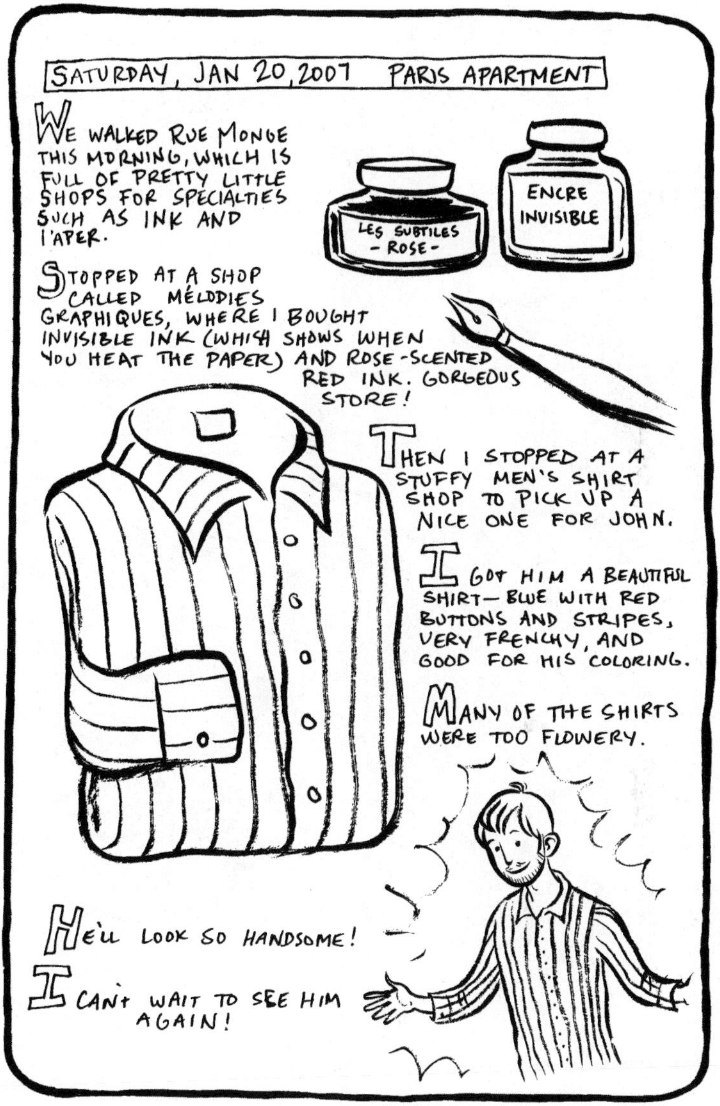
SATURDAY, JAN 20, 2007 PARIS APARTMENT
WE WALKED RUE MONGE THIS MORNING, WHICH IS FULL OF PRETTY LITTLE SHOPS FOR SPECIALTIES SUCH AS INK AND PAPER.
LES SUBTILES - ROSE -
ENCRE INVISIBLE
STOPPED AT A SHOP CALLED MÉLODIES GRAPHIQUES, WHERE I BOUGHT INVISIBLE INK (WHICH SHOWS WHEN YOU HEAT THE PAPER) AND ROSE-SCENTED RED INK. GORGEOUS STORE!
THEN I STOPPED AT A STUFFY MEN'S SHIRT SHOP TO PICK UP A NICE ONE FOR JOHN.
I GOT HIM A BEAUTIFUL SHIRT— BLUE WITH RED BUTTONS AND STRIPES, VERY FRENCHY, AND GOOD FOR HIS COLORING.
MANY OF THE SHIRTS WERE TOO FLOWERY.
HE'LL LOOK SO HANDSOME!
I CAN'T WAIT TO SEE HIM AGAIN!

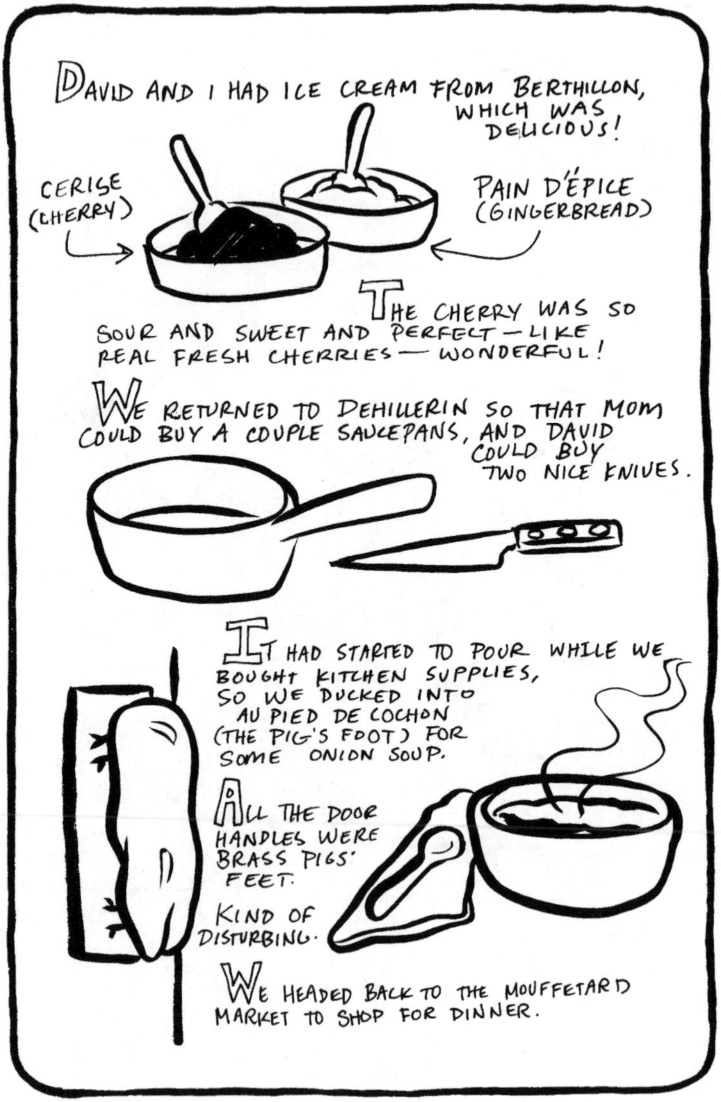
DAVID AND I HAD ICE CREAM FROM BERTHILLON, WHICH WAS DELICIOUS!
CERISE (CHERRY)
PAIN D'ÉPICE (GINGERBREAD)
THE CHERRY WAS SO SOUR AND SWEET AND PERFECT—LIKE REAL FRESH CHERRIES—WONDERFUL!
WE RETURNED TO DEHILLERIN SO THAT MOM COULD BUY A COUPLE SAUCEPANS, AND DAVID COULD BUY TWO NICE KNIVES.
IT HAD STARTED TO POUR WHILE WE BOUGHT KITCHEN SUPPLIES, SO WE DUCKED INTO AU PIED DE COCHON (THE PIG'S FOOT) FOR SOME ONION SOUP.
ALL THE DOOR HANDLES WERE BRASS PIGS' FEET.
KIND OF DISTURBING.
WE HEADED BACK TO THE MOUFFETARD MARKET TO SHOP FOR DINNER.

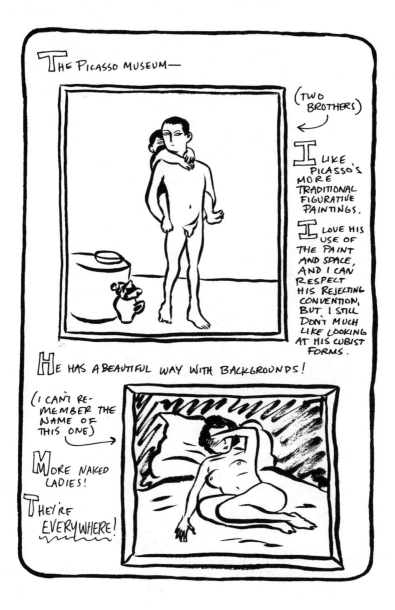

THE PICASSO MUSEUM—

(TWO BROTHERS)

I LIKE PICASSO'S MORE TRADITIONAL FIGURATIVE PAINTINGS.

I LOVE HIS USE OF THE PAINT AND SPACE, AND I CAN RESPECT HIS REJECTING CONVENTION, BUT, I STILL DON'T MUCH LIKE LOOKING AT HIS CUBIST FORMS.

HE HAS A BEAUTIFUL WAY WITH BACKGROUNDS!

(I CAN'T RE-MEMBER THE NAME OF THIS ONE)

MORE NAKED LADIES!

THEY'RE EVERYWHERE!

I FINISHED MY BOOK ("PERFUME") AND THEN WE HAD:

D̲INNER:̲

OYSTER CHOWDER

HARICOTS VERTS + TOMATOES W/ BALSAMIC VINEGAR

CHEESE

BAGUETTE

DUCK + COUNTRY PATÉ + CORNICHONS!

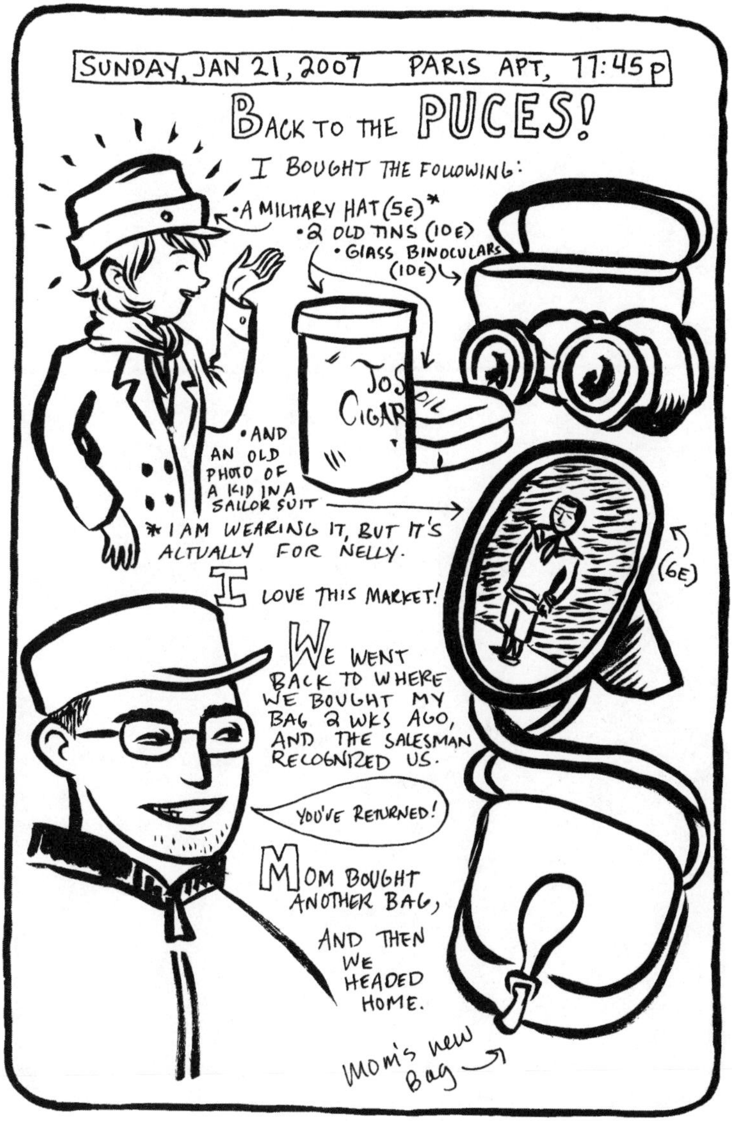
SUNDAY, JAN 21, 2007 PARIS APT, 11:45p
BACK TO THE PUCES!
I BOUGHT THE FOLLOWING:
• A MILITARY HAT (5€)*
• 2 OLD TINS (10€)
• GLASS BINOCULARS (10€)
• AND AN OLD PHOTO OF A KID IN A SAILOR SUIT
(6€)
*I AM WEARING IT, BUT IT'S ACTUALLY FOR NELLY.
I LOVE THIS MARKET!
WE WENT BACK TO WHERE WE BOUGHT MY BAG 2 WKS AGO, AND THE SALESMAN RECOGNIZED US.
YOU'VE RETURNED!
MOM BOUGHT ANOTHER BAG,
AND THEN WE HEADED HOME.
Mom's new Bag

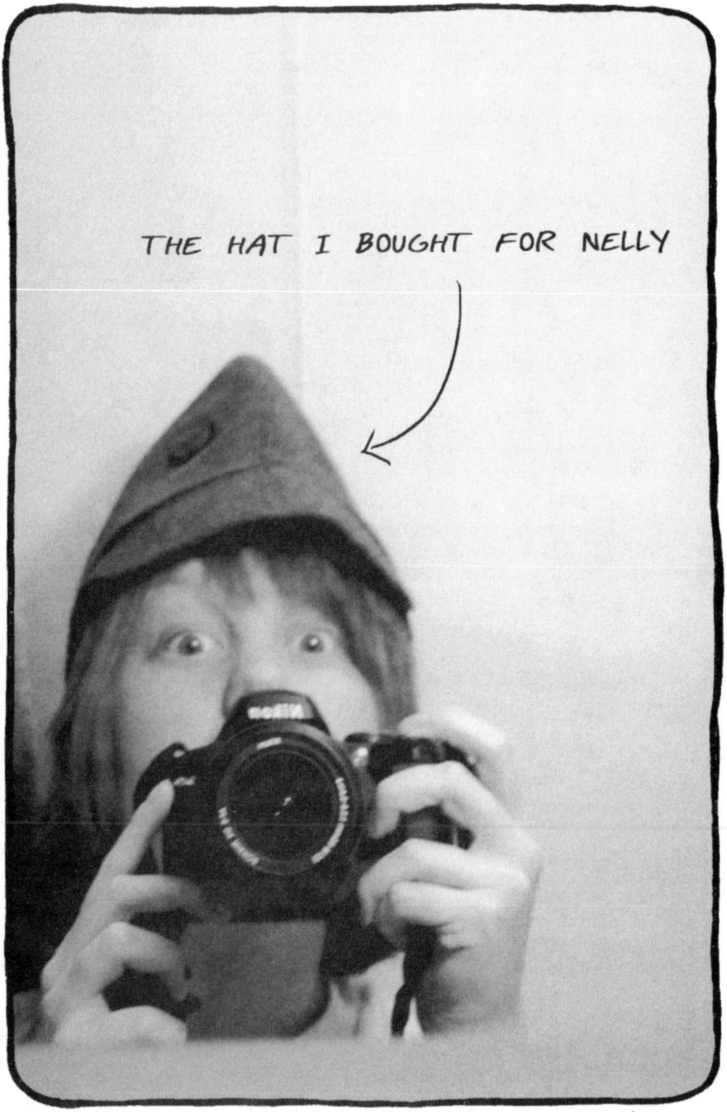
THE HAT I BOUGHT FOR NELLY
Nikon

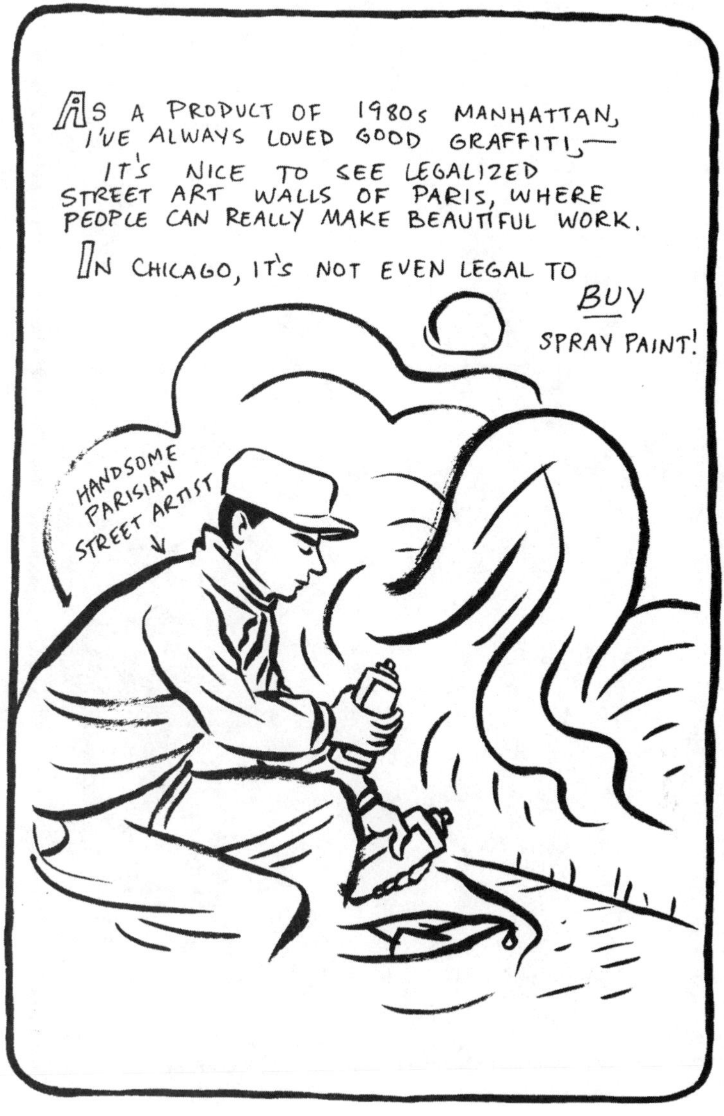
AS A PRODUCT OF 1980s MANHATTAN, I'VE ALWAYS LOVED GOOD GRAFFITI,— IT'S NICE TO SEE LEGALIZED STREET ART WALLS OF PARIS, WHERE PEOPLE CAN REALLY MAKE BEAUTIFUL WORK.
IN CHICAGO, IT'S NOT EVEN LEGAL TO BUY SPRAY PAINT!
HANDSOME PARISIAN STREET ARTIST

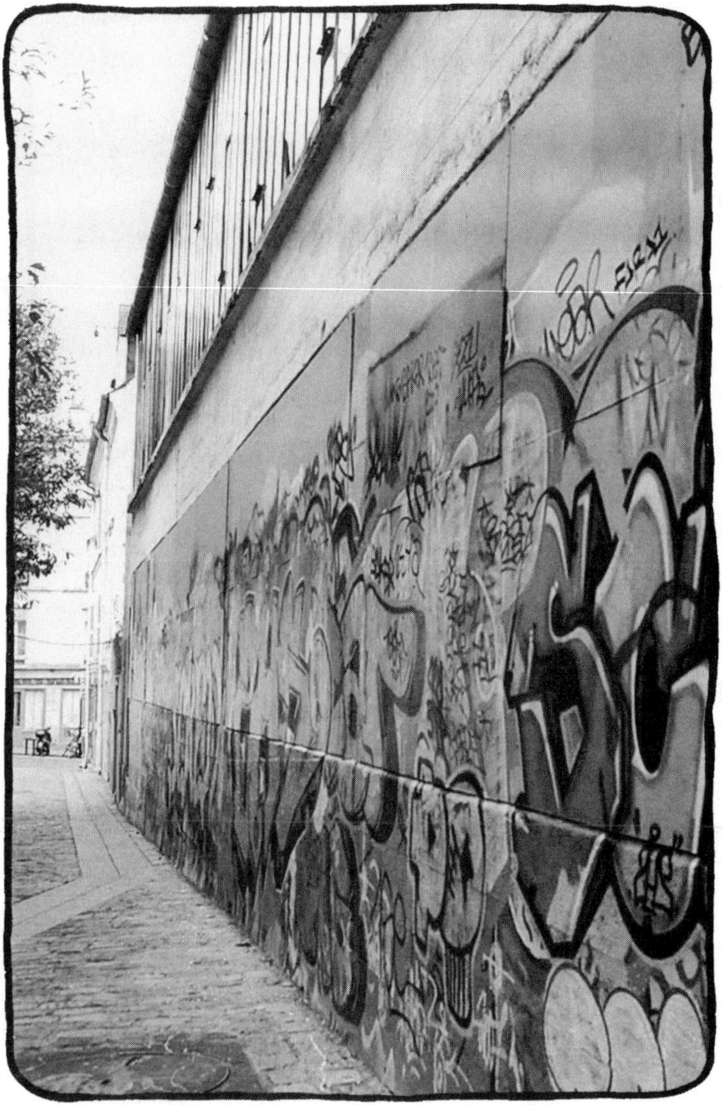

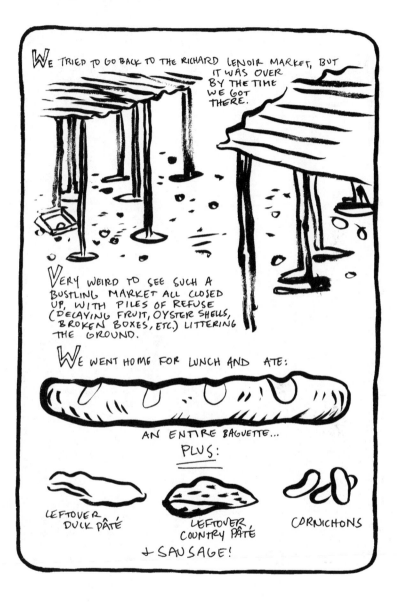

WE TRIED TO GO BACK TO THE RICHARD LENOIR MARKET, BUT IT WAS OVER BY THE TIME WE GOT THERE.

VERY WEIRD TO SEE SUCH A BUSTLING MARKET ALL CLOSED UP, WITH PILES OF REFUSE (DECAYING FRUIT, OYSTER SHELLS, BROKEN BOXES, ETC.) LITTERING THE GROUND.

WE WENT HOME FOR LUNCH AND ATE:

AN ENTIRE BAGUETTE...

PLUS:

LEFTOVER DUCK PÂTÉ

LEFTOVER COUNTRY PÂTÉ

CORNICHONS

+ SAUSAGE!

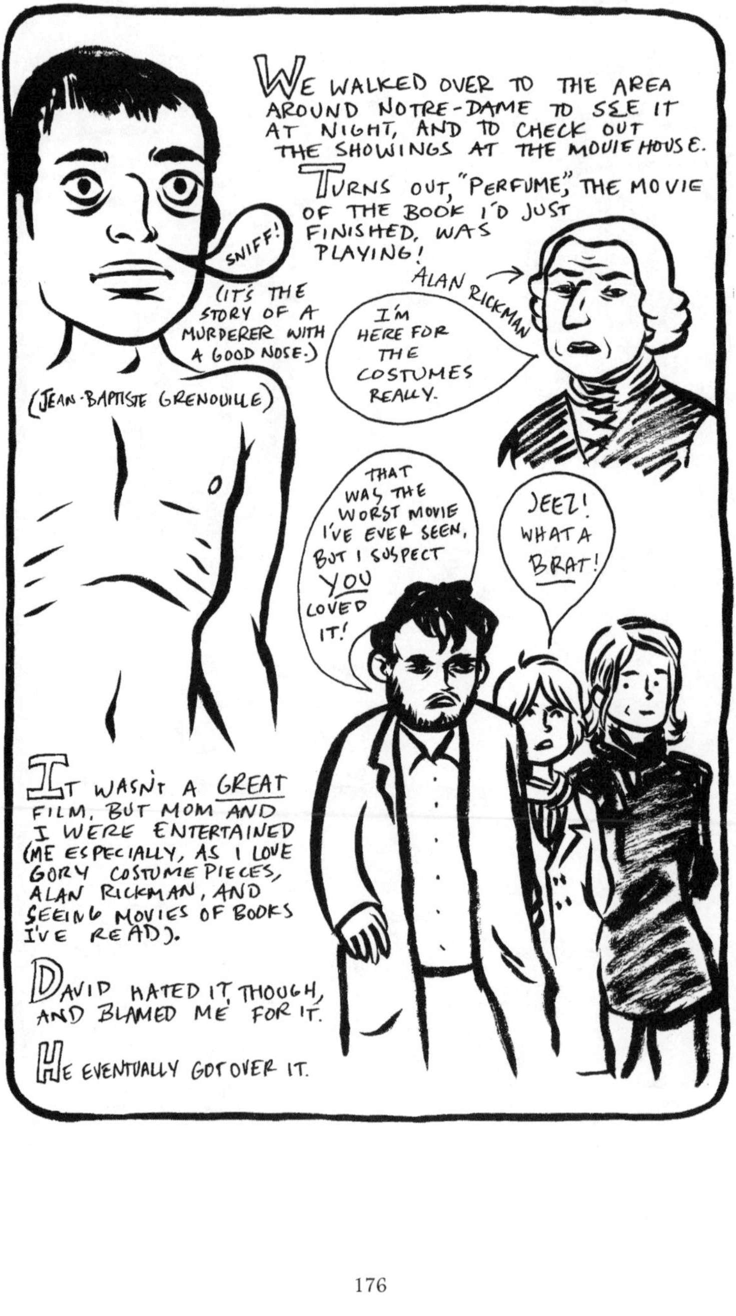
WE WALKED OVER TO THE AREA AROUND NOTRE-DAME TO SEE IT AT NIGHT, AND TO CHECK OUT THE SHOWINGS AT THE MOVIE HOUSE.
TURNS OUT, "PERFUME," THE MOVIE OF THE BOOK I'D JUST FINISHED, WAS PLAYING!
SNIFF!
(IT'S THE STORY OF A MURDERER WITH A GOOD NOSE.)
(JEAN-BAPTISTE GRENOUILLE)
ALAN RICKMAN
I'M HERE FOR THE COSTUMES REALLY.
THAT WAS THE WORST MOVIE I'VE EVER SEEN, BUT I SUSPECT YOU LOVED IT!
JEEZ! WHAT A BRAT!
IT WASN'T A GREAT FILM, BUT MOM AND I WERE ENTERTAINED (ME ESPECIALLY, AS I LOVE GORY COSTUME PIECES, ALAN RICKMAN, AND SEEING MOVIES OF BOOKS I'VE READ).
DAVID HATED IT, THOUGH, AND BLAMED ME FOR IT.
HE EVENTUALLY GOT OVER IT.

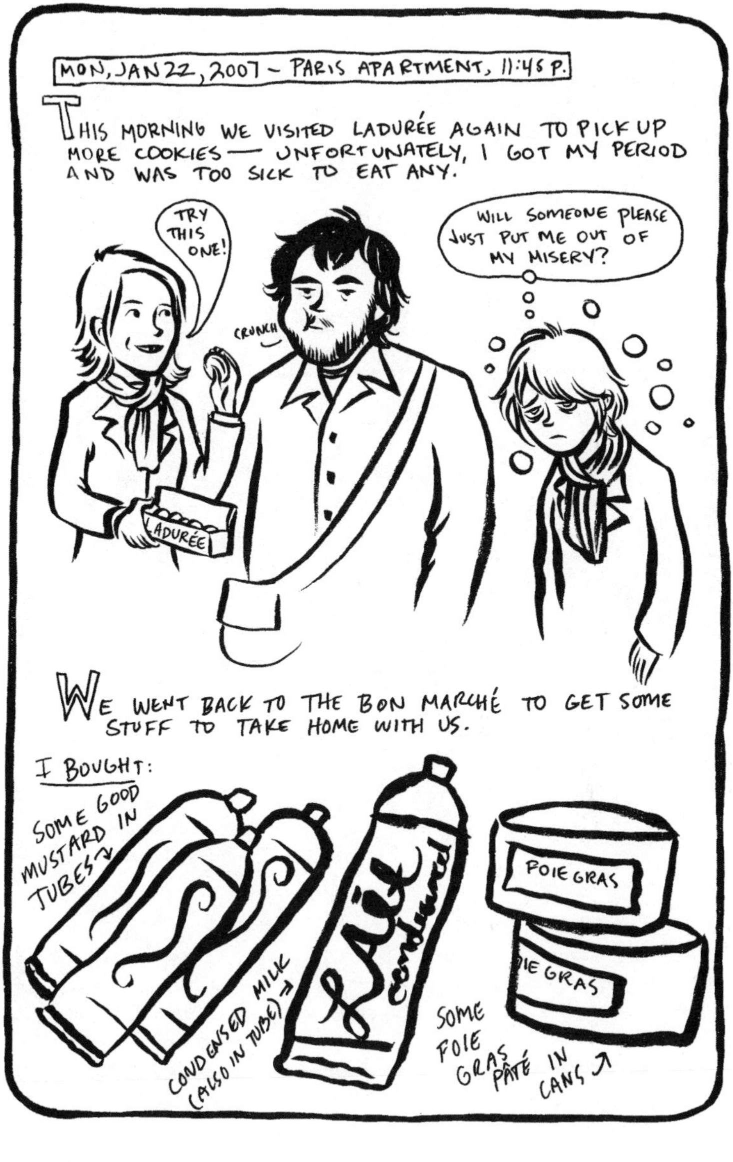
MON, JAN 22, 2007 ~ PARIS APARTMENT, 11:45 P.
THIS MORNING WE VISITED LADURÉE AGAIN TO PICK UP MORE COOKIES — UNFORTUNATELY, I GOT MY PERIOD AND WAS TOO SICK TO EAT ANY.
TRY THIS ONE!
CRUNCH
WILL SOMEONE PLEASE JUST PUT ME OUT OF MY MISERY?
LADURÉE
WE WENT BACK TO THE BON MARCHÉ TO GET SOME STUFF TO TAKE HOME WITH US.
I BOUGHT:
SOME GOOD MUSTARD IN TUBES
CONDENSED MILK (ALSO IN TUBE)
Lait condensé
FOIE GRAS
IE GRAS
SOME FOIE GRAS PÂTÉ IN CANS

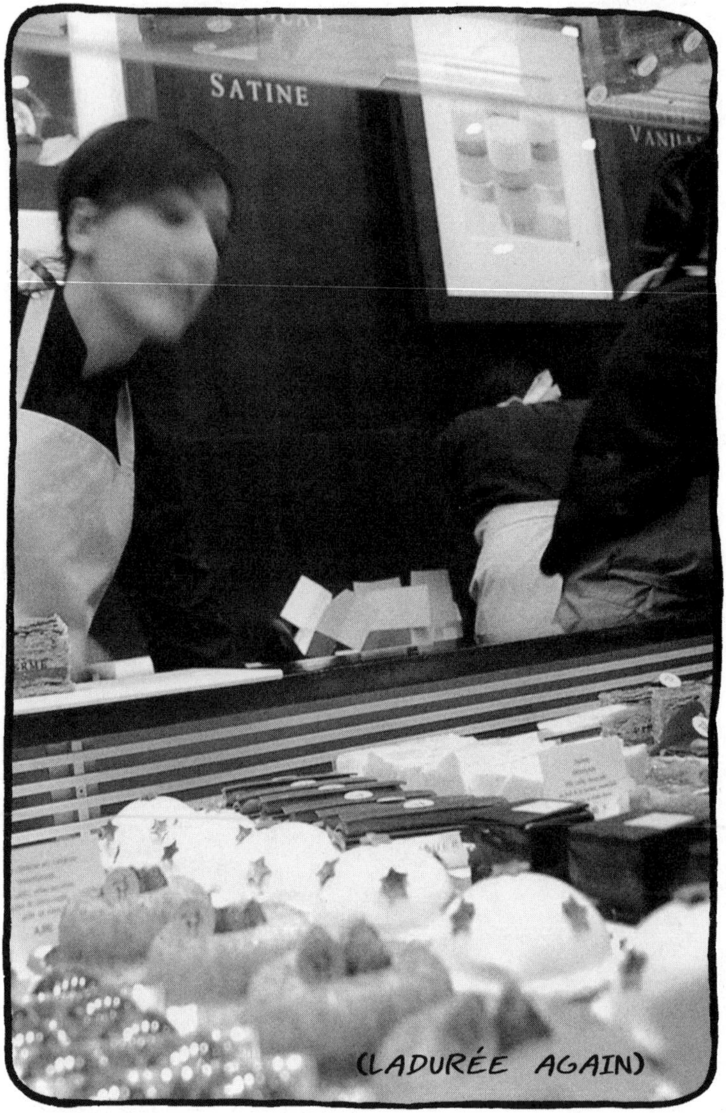
SATINE
(LADURÉE AGAIN)

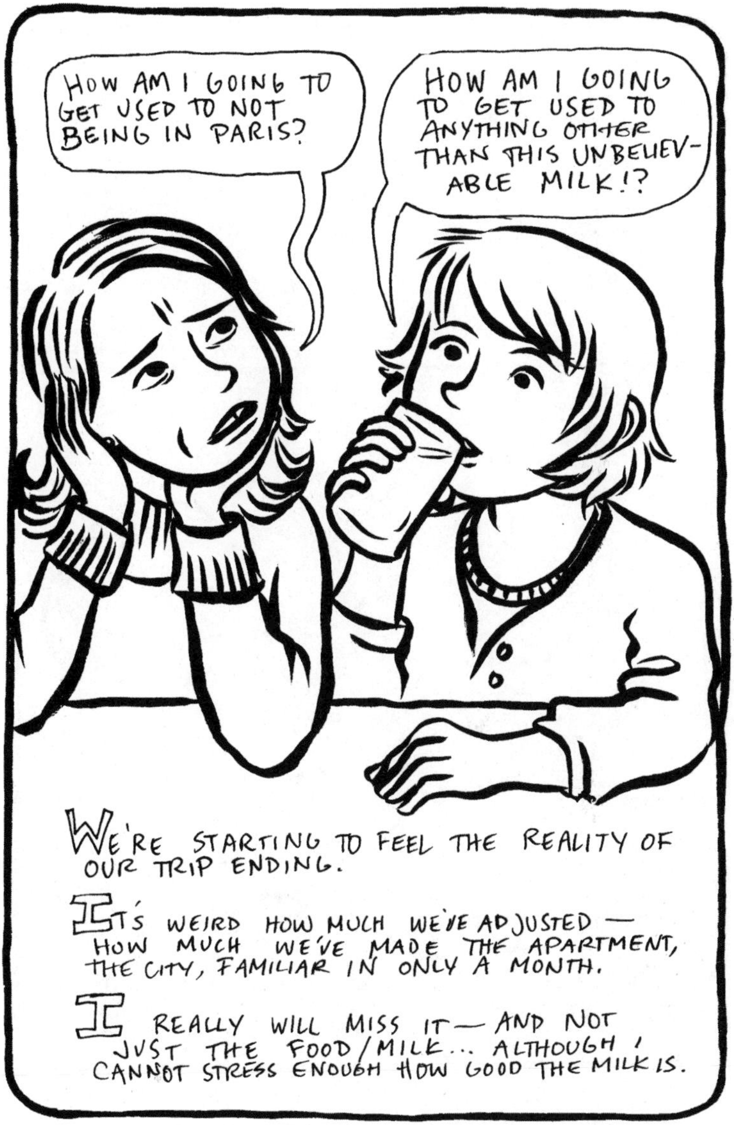
HOW AM I GOING TO GET USED TO NOT BEING IN PARIS?
HOW AM I GOING TO GET USED TO ANYTHING OTHER THAN THIS UNBELIEVABLE MILK!?
WE'RE STARTING TO FEEL THE REALITY OF OUR TRIP ENDING.
IT'S WEIRD HOW MUCH WE'VE ADJUSTED — HOW MUCH WE'VE MADE THE APARTMENT, THE CITY, FAMILIAR IN ONLY A MONTH.
I REALLY WILL MISS IT — AND NOT JUST THE FOOD/MILK... ALTHOUGH I CANNOT STRESS ENOUGH HOW GOOD THE MILK IS.

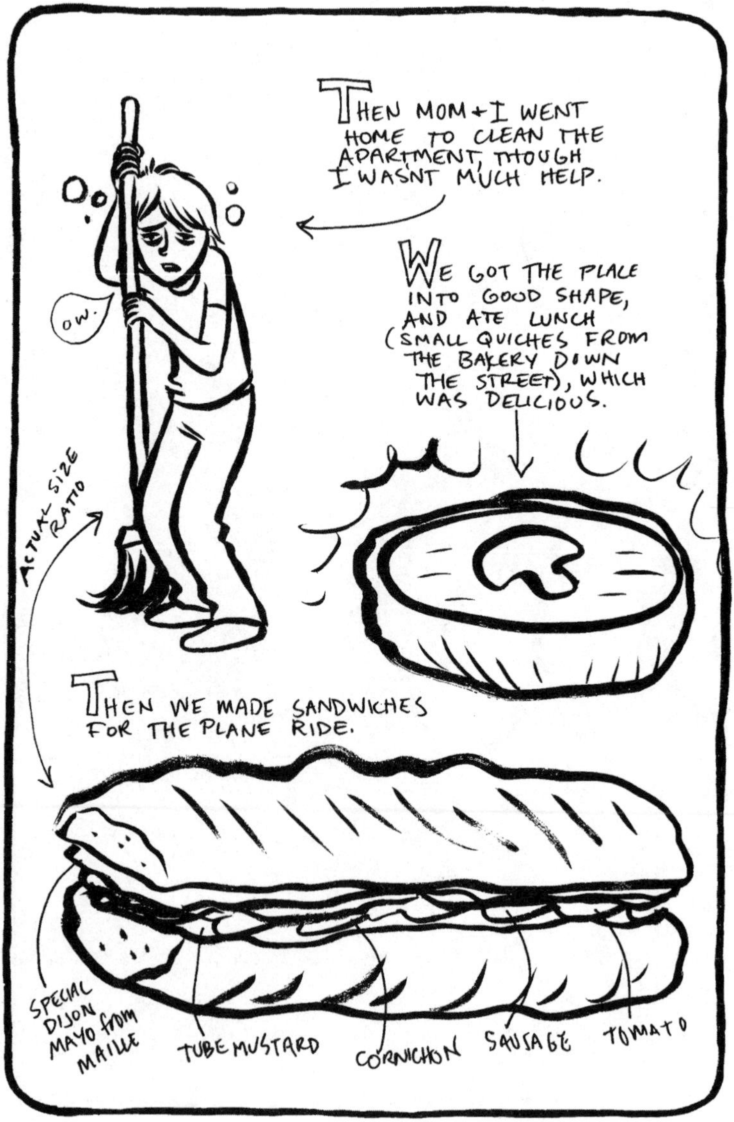
THEN MOM + I WENT HOME TO CLEAN THE APARTMENT, THOUGH I WASN'T MUCH HELP.
OW.
WE GOT THE PLACE INTO GOOD SHAPE, AND ATE LUNCH (SMALL QUICHES FROM THE BAKERY DOWN THE STREET), WHICH WAS DELICIOUS.
ACTUAL SIZE RATIO
THEN WE MADE SANDWICHES FOR THE PLANE RIDE.
SPECIAL DIJON MAYO FROM MAILLE
TUBE MUSTARD
CORNICHON
SAUSAGE
TOMATO

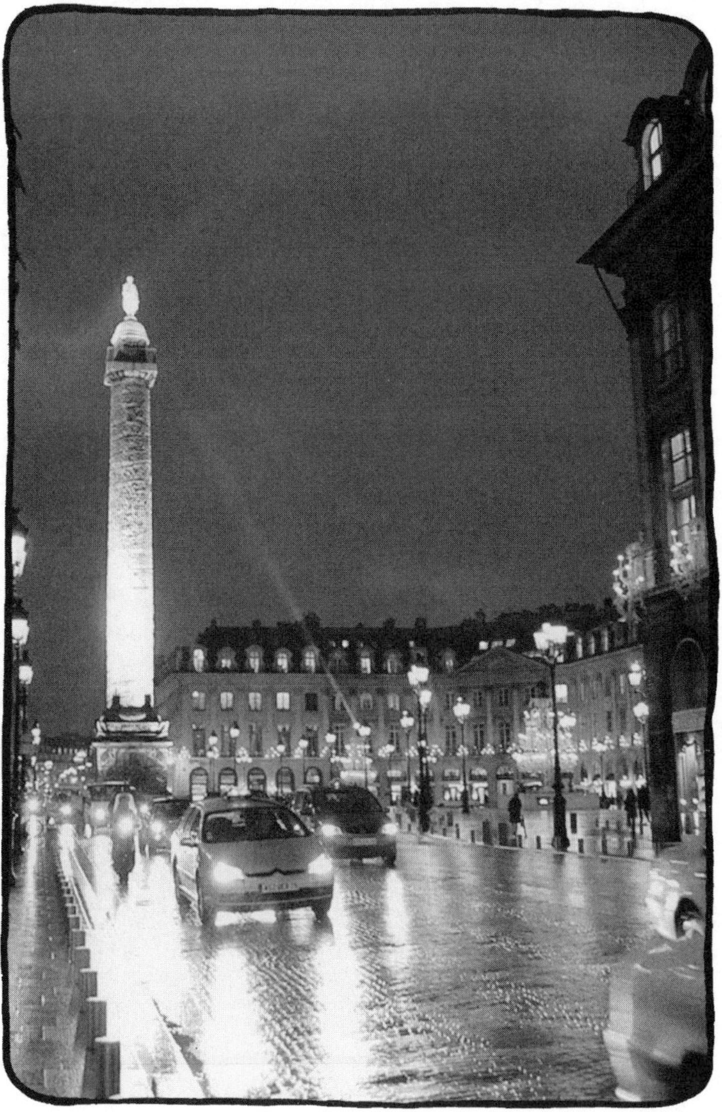

I WAS FEELING A LITTLE BETTER LATER THAT EVENING, SO WE GOT DRESSED UP AND HAD DRINKS & TALKED ABOUT WHAT TO DO FOR OUR LAST DINNER IN PARIS.

WE DRANK A WHOLE BOTTLE OF CHAMPAGNE

MOM WANTED TO GO TO A RESTAURANT ON THE RUE DES ÉCOLES CALLED LE BALZAR, BUT THE MAITRE D' INFORMED US THERE WAS NO ROOM.

HE ACTUALLY HAD THIS MUSTACHE

HMPH!

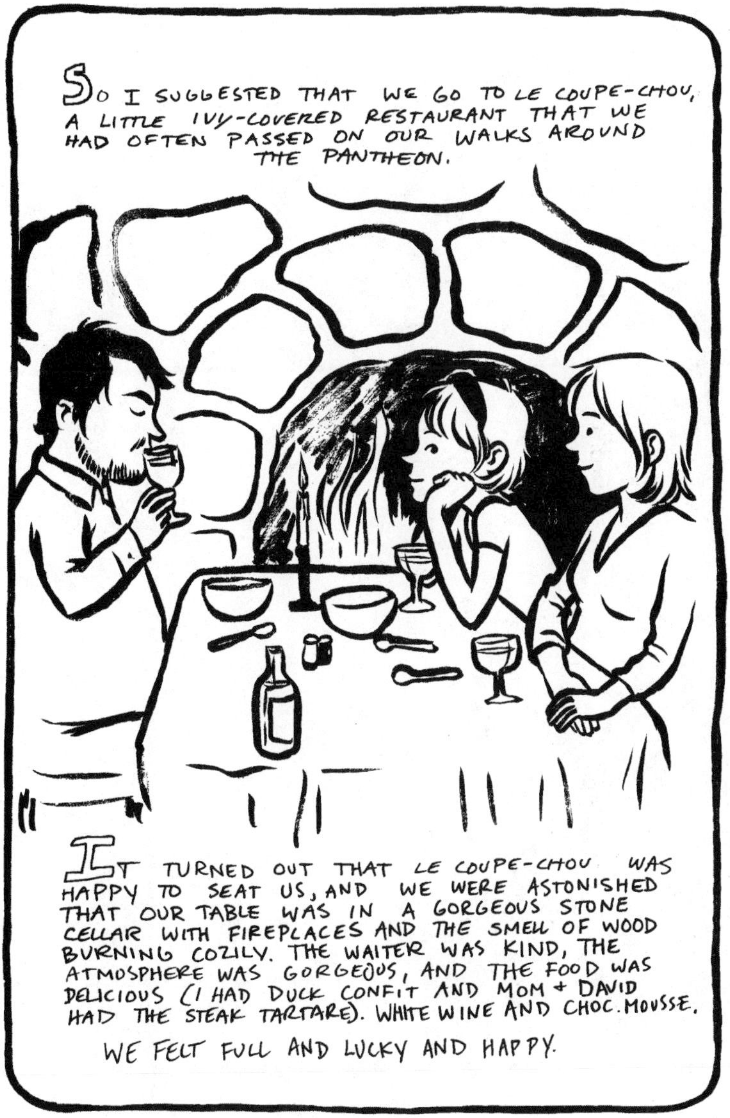
SO I SUGGESTED THAT WE GO TO LE COUPE-CHOU, A LITTLE IVY-COVERED RESTAURANT THAT WE HAD OFTEN PASSED ON OUR WALKS AROUND THE PANTHEON.
IT TURNED OUT THAT LE COUPE-CHOU WAS HAPPY TO SEAT US, AND WE WERE ASTONISHED THAT OUR TABLE WAS IN A GORGEOUS STONE CELLAR WITH FIREPLACES AND THE SMELL OF WOOD BURNING COZILY. THE WAITER WAS KIND, THE ATMOSPHERE WAS GORGEOUS, AND THE FOOD WAS DELICIOUS (I HAD DUCK CONFIT AND MOM + DAVID HAD THE STEAK TARTARE). WHITE WINE AND CHOC. MOUSSE.
WE FELT FULL AND LUCKY AND HAPPY.

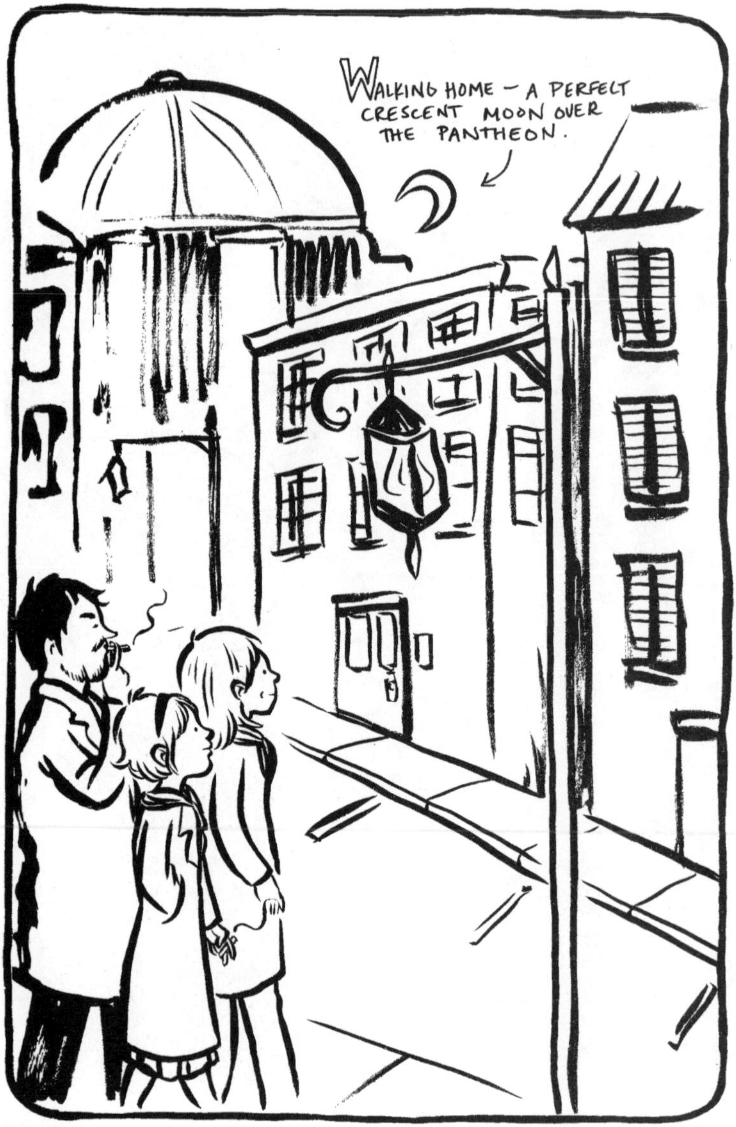
WALKING HOME – A PERFECT CRESCENT MOON OVER THE PANTHEON.

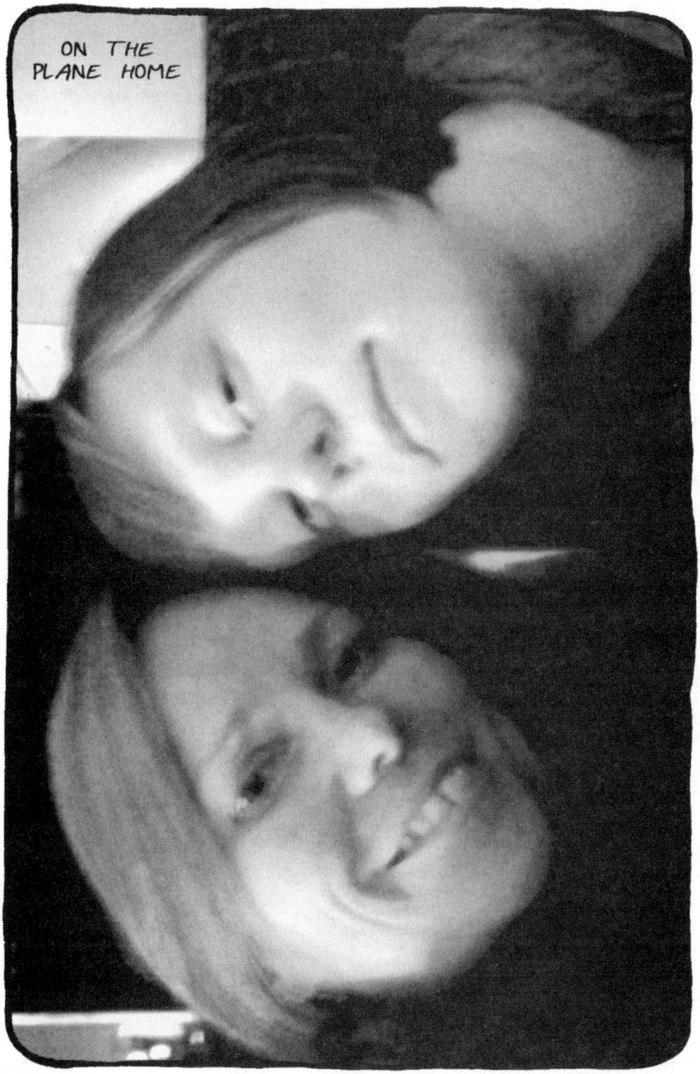
ON THE
PLANE HOME

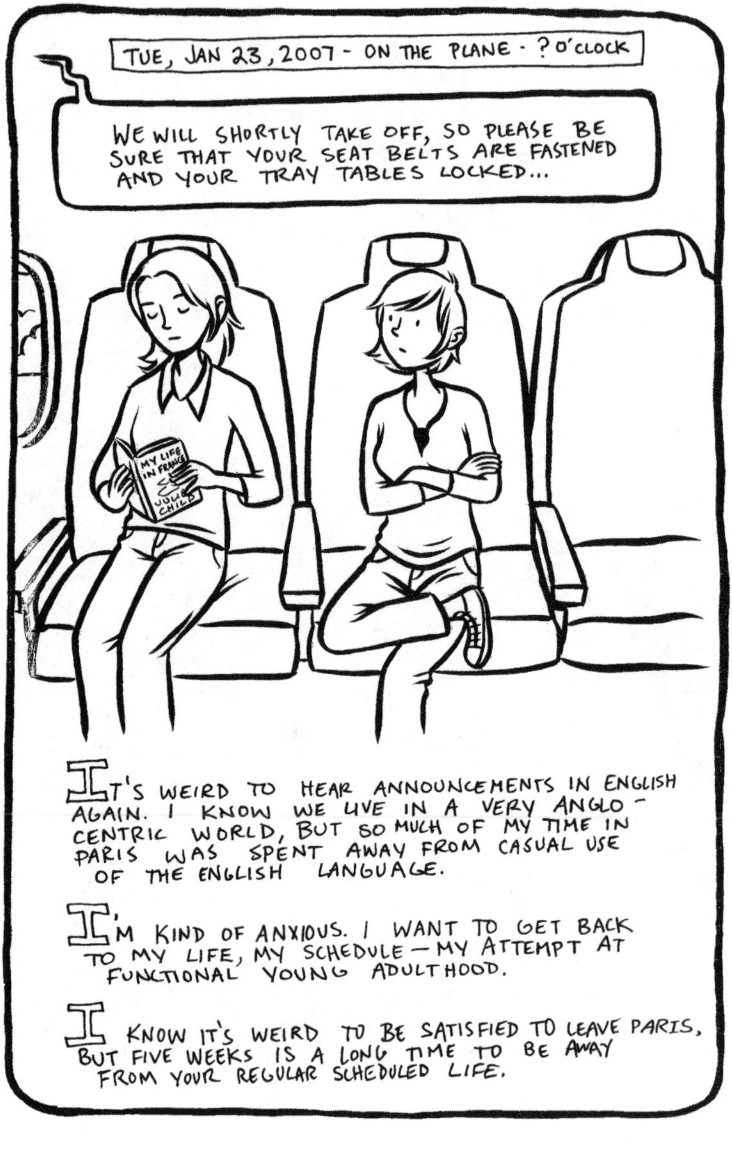

TUE, JAN 23, 2007 - ON THE PLANE - ? O'CLOCK
WE WILL SHORTLY TAKE OFF, SO PLEASE BE SURE THAT YOUR SEAT BELTS ARE FASTENED AND YOUR TRAY TABLES LOCKED...
MY LIFE IN FRANCE
IT'S WEIRD TO HEAR ANNOUNCEMENTS IN ENGLISH AGAIN. I KNOW WE LIVE IN A VERY ANGLO-CENTRIC WORLD, BUT SO MUCH OF MY TIME IN PARIS WAS SPENT AWAY FROM CASUAL USE OF THE ENGLISH LANGUAGE.
I'M KIND OF ANXIOUS. I WANT TO GET BACK TO MY LIFE, MY SCHEDULE—MY ATTEMPT AT FUNCTIONAL YOUNG ADULTHOOD.
I KNOW IT'S WEIRD TO BE SATISFIED TO LEAVE PARIS, BUT FIVE WEEKS IS A LONG TIME TO BE AWAY FROM YOUR REGULAR SCHEDULED LIFE.

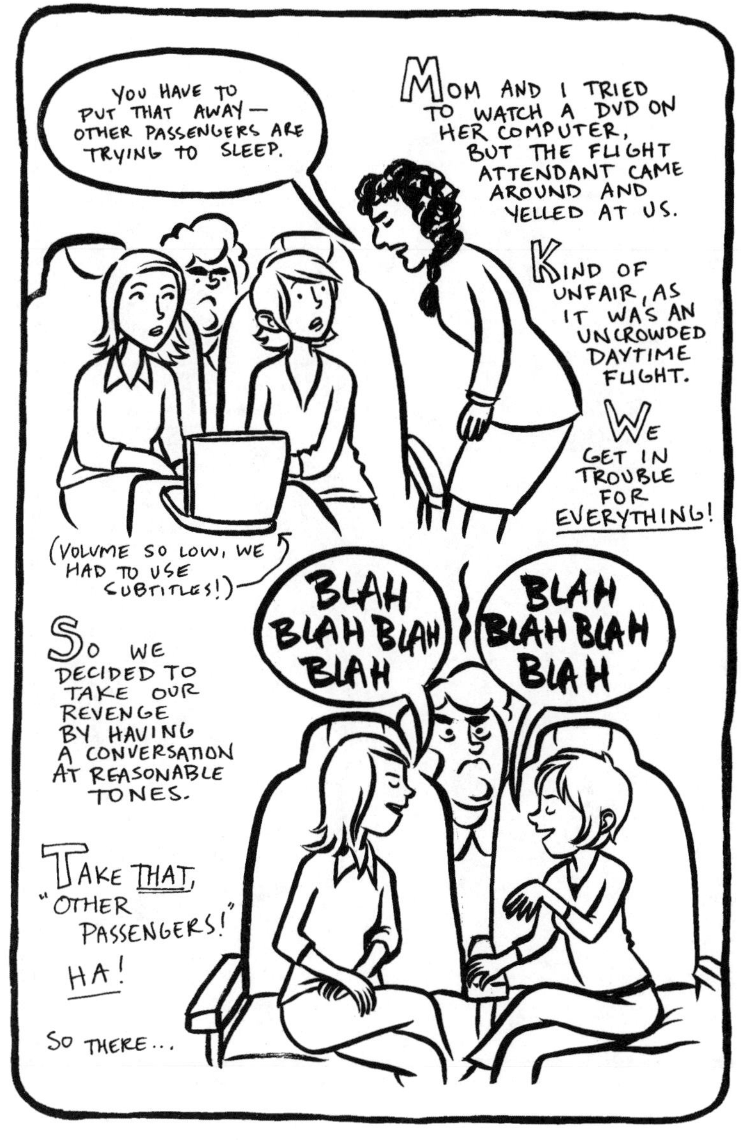
YOU HAVE TO PUT THAT AWAY— OTHER PASSENGERS ARE TRYING TO SLEEP.
MOM AND I TRIED TO WATCH A DVD ON HER COMPUTER, BUT THE FLIGHT ATTENDANT CAME AROUND AND YELLED AT US.
KIND OF UNFAIR, AS IT WAS AN UNCROWDED DAYTIME FLIGHT.
WE GET IN TROUBLE FOR EVERYTHING!
(VOLUME SO LOW, WE HAD TO USE SUBTITLES!)
SO WE DECIDED TO TAKE OUR REVENGE BY HAVING A CONVERSATION AT REASONABLE TONES.
BLAH BLAH BLAH BLAH
BLAH BLAH BLAH BLAH
TAKE THAT, "OTHER PASSENGERS!"
HA!
SO THERE...

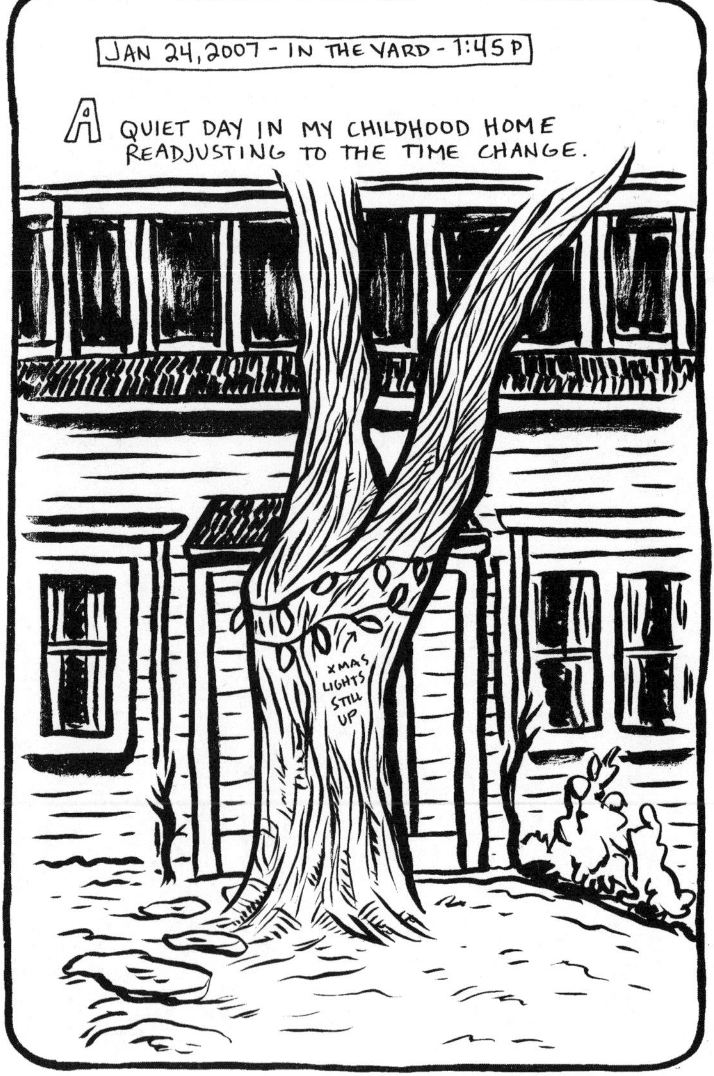
JAN 24, 2007 - IN THE YARD - 1:45 P
A QUIET DAY IN MY CHILDHOOD HOME READJUSTING TO THE TIME CHANGE.
XMAS LIGHTS STILL UP

JAN 25, 2007 - ALBANY → CHICAGO PLANE, 12:00P

AT THE AIRPORT IN ALBANY, I AM SHOCKED BY HOW UGLY AND HUGE AMERICANS CAN BE. THE FASHION + AESTHETIC DIFFERENCES BETWEEN PARIS AND RURAL/SUBURBAN AMERICA ARE VAST.

BUT CHICAGO IS BREATHTAKINGLY, CRISPLY BEAUTIFUL—SNOW-DUSTED AND BLUE-SKYED. IT'S NICE TO SEE THE SUN AGAIN.

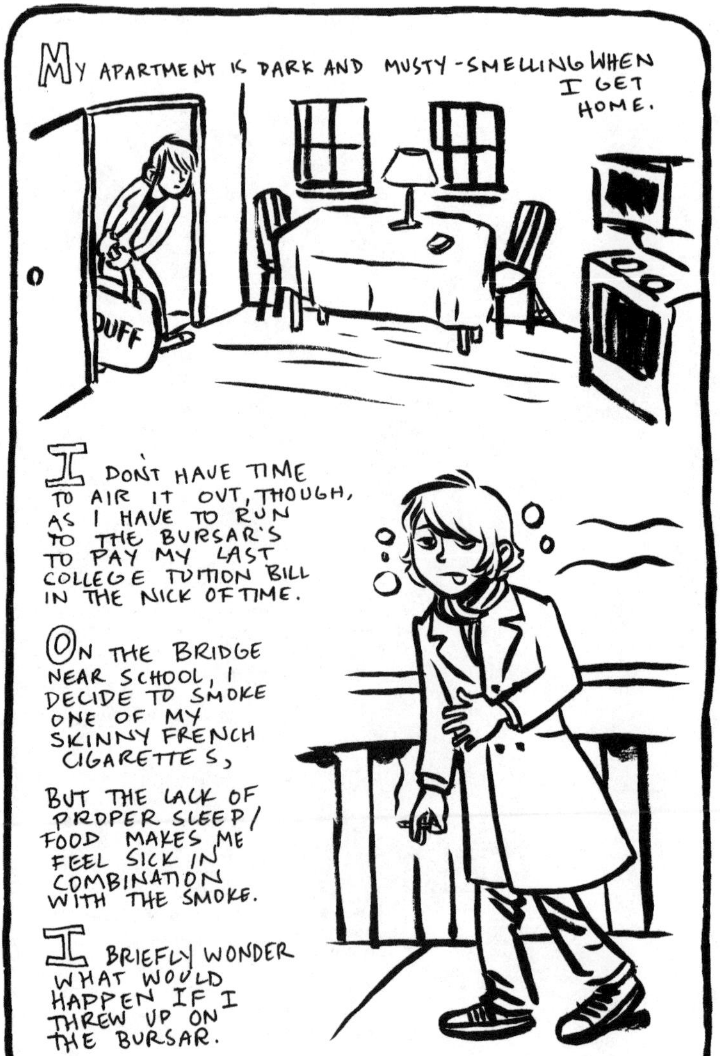
MY APARTMENT IS DARK AND MUSTY-SMELLING WHEN I GET HOME.
DUFF
I DON'T HAVE TIME TO AIR IT OUT, THOUGH, AS I HAVE TO RUN TO THE BURSAR'S TO PAY MY LAST COLLEGE TUITION BILL IN THE NICK OF TIME.
ON THE BRIDGE NEAR SCHOOL, I DECIDE TO SMOKE ONE OF MY SKINNY FRENCH CIGARETTES,
BUT THE LACK OF PROPER SLEEP/FOOD MAKES ME FEEL SICK IN COMBINATION WITH THE SMOKE.
I BRIEFLY WONDER WHAT WOULD HAPPEN IF I THREW UP ON THE BURSAR.

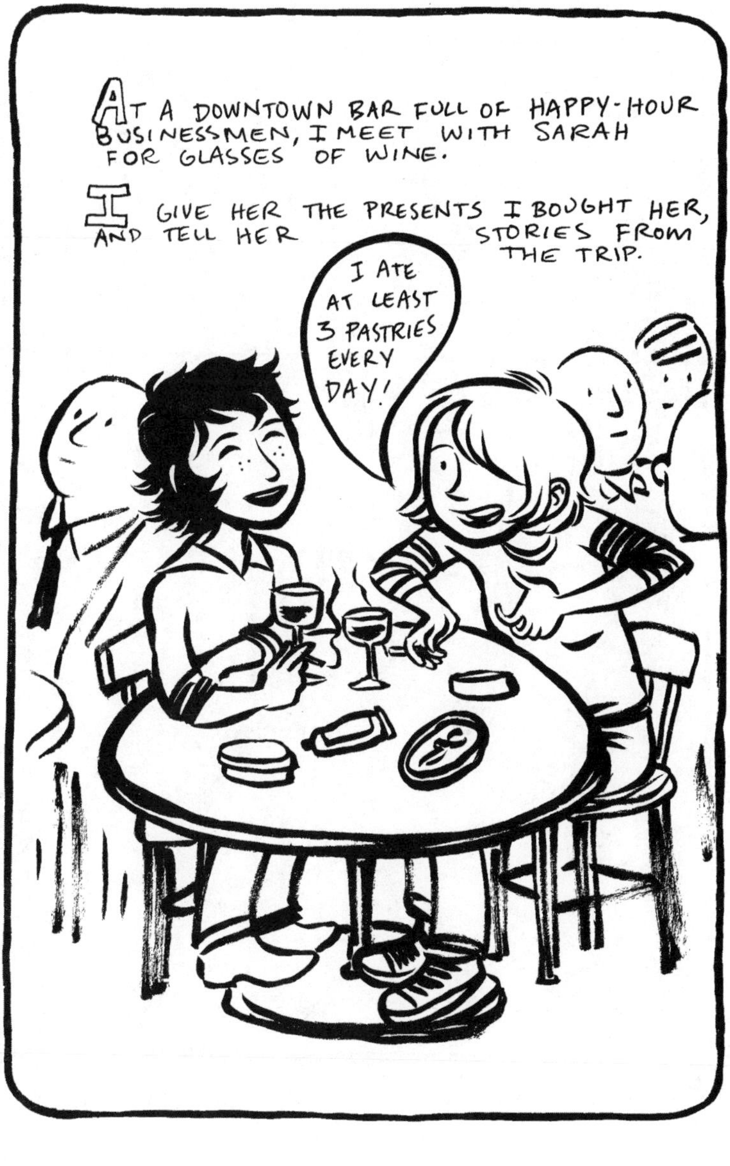
AT A DOWNTOWN BAR FULL OF HAPPY-HOUR BUSINESSMEN, I MEET WITH SARAH FOR GLASSES OF WINE.
I GIVE HER THE PRESENTS I BOUGHT HER, AND TELL HER STORIES FROM THE TRIP.
I ATE AT LEAST 3 PASTRIES EVERY DAY!

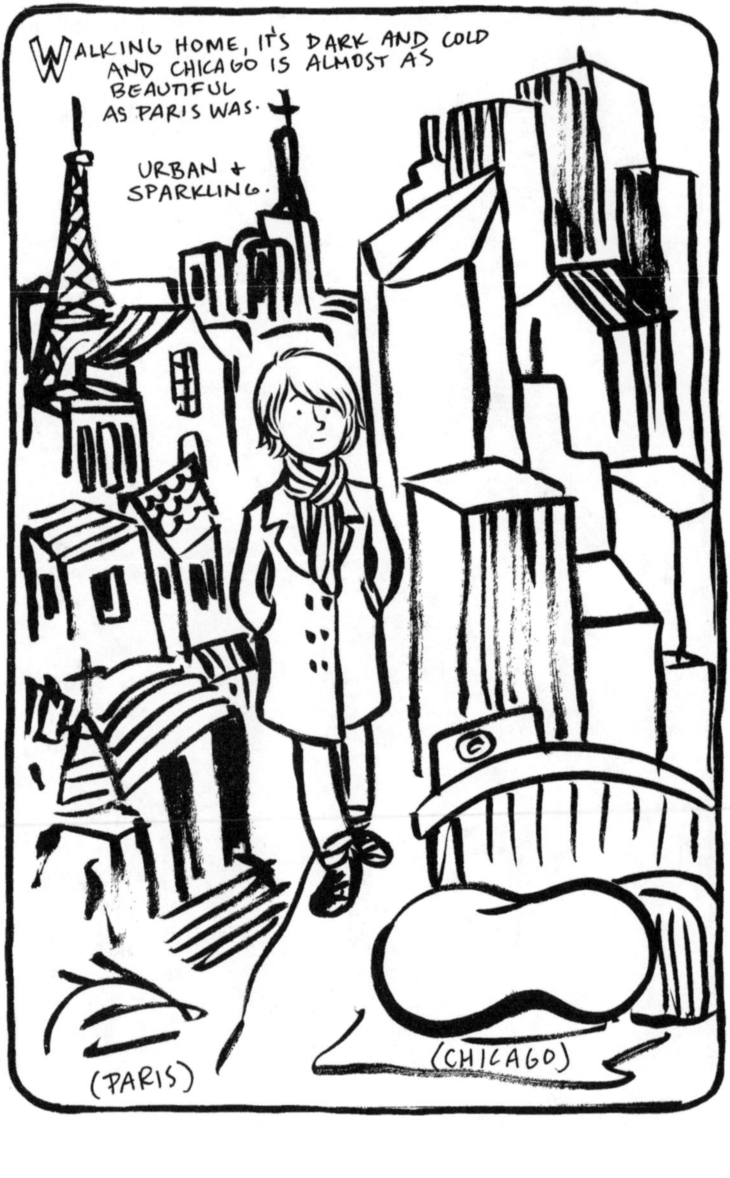
WALKING HOME, IT'S DARK AND COLD AND CHICAGO IS ALMOST AS BEAUTIFUL AS PARIS WAS.
URBAN + SPARKLING.
(PARIS)
(CHICAGO)

JAN 26, 2007, HOME, 5:30A
JOHN ASLEEP AFTER I'VE WOKEN UP DUE TO MY LINGERING JET-LAG.
SZNNZ...

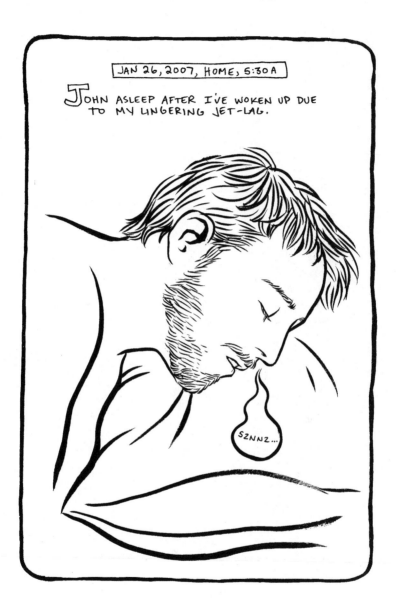

Paris looms large in history—
centuries of importance in human existence.
It's possessed by love and beauty.

And Chicago looms large in my mind, with
personal importance. It has taken me
4 years to find myself at home here.

In Paris, I was part of its ancient
organism for a time — my arguments
with my mom, my fingerprints on
the bridge railings, my breath — added
to the human history of Paris.

And now I'm home, and my everyday life
is gradually returning to normal,
building the memories that will age
Chicago as Paris has aged.

I miss the food, the language, the
buildings, the art — even the
cloudy mornings in Paris.

In the end, it was easy to give in
to loving Paris...

To give in to the culture, traditions
and cuisine...

To give in to my changing relationship
with my mother...

To give in to the reality of being
in love while accepting the
possibility of heartbreak...

To slowly, slowly give in to the
inevitability of adulthood, in
the hopes that I will age as
gracefully as Paris has.

The milk here is nowhere
near as good as French milk.

But Chicago is sweeter
for the differences, and from the
long absence.

Despite the inferior dairy.

Acknowledgments

My thanks to my publishers and editors at
Touchstone, particularly the marvelous Amanda Patten.
I'm very grateful to Holly Bemiss for her much needed
help and expertise. Thank you to my dad, for being such
a supportive presence in the development of this book,
and to 192 Books, where they were so kind to me and
to French Milk. Much gratitude to Louisa Ermelino at
Publishers Weekly, for interviewing this unknown. Steve
Bissette at The Center for Cartoon Studies, for his
advice and encouragement, thank you. To my little
town of Rhinebeck, and all the people there who spread
my book around, I'm so grateful. I owe a great deal to
Hope Larson for her friendship and guidance, and to
Bryan Lee O'Malley for letting me hang around their
convention tables and home. My comic book God and
Goddess, Scott McCloud and Lynda Barry, thank you
eternally for the inspiration and the permission to keep
my pen moving. With thanks to SAIC, and my wonderful
teachers. Thank you to everyone who bought the first
edition of this book, straight from my hands. Thank
you and love to Zan, Nelly, Sarah, MC, David, Grant,
Bernie, Jeremy, Beck, Sara, Jess, Matthew, Joel, Dean,
Becca, Renee, Leathem, Mark, Alec, Aaron, Laura and
the other wonderfully talented artists I am lucky
enough to call my friends. Thank you to John, for
missing me while I was away.

Mostly, I would like to thank my mom, Georgia, who's
contributions to the making of this book are too
numerous to list, and mean so much to me. Without her
help and perpetual calm and love, both my life and my
art would be even messier, and not nearly any good.

ABOUT THE AUTHOR

David Demaree

Lucy Knisley is a graduate of The School
of the Art Institute of Chicago.
She currently attends the Center
for Cartoon Studies.
She lives and works in Chicago,
and is 23 years old.

During the month she spent in Paris, she is
estimated to have eaten approximately
60 croissants, over 400 cornichons,
and a metric ton of chocolate mousse.

41